OPENNESS OF COMICS

Openness of Comics
Generating Meaning within Flexible Structures

Maaheen Ahmed

University Press of Mississippi   Jackson

www.upress.state.ms.us

The University Press of Mississippi is a member of the Association of American University Presses.

Copyright © 2016 by University Press of Mississippi
All rights reserved

First printing 2016
∞
Library of Congress Cataloging-in-Publication Data

Names: Ahmed, Maaheen, author.
Title: Openness of comics : generating meaning within flexible structures / Maaheen Ahmed.
Description: Jackson : University Press of Mississippi, [2016] | Includes bibliographical references and index.
Identifiers: LCCN 2015042219 | ISBN 9781496805935 (hardcover : alk. paper)
Subjects: LCSH: Comic books, strips, etc.—History and criticism. | Graphic novels—History and criticism.
Classification: LCC PN6710 .A45 2016 | DDC 741.5/9—dc23 LC record available at http://lccn.loc.gov/2015042219

British Library Cataloging-in-Publication Data available

For Naveen and Ajaz Ahmed

"Non tener pur ad un loco la mente"
Dante, *Purgatorio,* 10.46

CONTENTS

Acknowledgments viii

Introduction: Instrumentalizing Openness 3

1. Fictionalized Memories and Biographies 23

2. Adventure and Superheroes 54

3. Noir, Black Comedy, and Crime 75

4. Fantasy and Science Fiction 93

5. Comparisons between Forms of Visual Narration 123

Conclusion: Generating Openness in Comics 150

Notes 169

Bibliography 208

Index 218

ACKNOWLEDGMENTS

As with any similar undertaking, a large group of people (and organizations) supported the writing of this book and deserve being warmly acknowledged.

Thanks is due, first and foremost, to Immacolata Amodeo for all her support, keen interest, and advice during the early days of the project. I am likewise thankful to both Ursula Frohne and K. Ludwig Pfeiffer for their comments, with an extra thank you to Ludwig Pfeiffer for taking the time to read yet another version of the manuscript as it was trying to mutate into a book. Another careful reader, to whom gallons of thanks is due, is Martin Lund. This book would not have been half as readable or cohesive had he not agreed to jump in over one winter. I would also like to thank the peer reviewers, as well as Chris Murray and Julia Round for their helpful comments on earlier versions of the book. In addition, my gratitude goes to Vijay Shah for believing in the book project, being prompt, friendly, encouraging, and patient—I could not have asked for more in an editor. I would also like to thank the staff at the University Press of Mississippi, in particular Anne Stascavage, Valerie Jones, and John Langston, for all their help. I am especially grateful to Peter Tonguette for his careful and thorough copyediting, Ed M. Fontanilla for his index, and Cedric Van Dijck for being brave enough to proofread. For the paperback edition, I would like to warmly thank Pedro Moura for his sharp corrections and for being such a keen, thought-provoking reader.

A warm thank you to my parents and friends, especially Miriam and Pier, who witnessed the turbulent years of the manuscript's inception and progression, providing unfailing emotional support whenever needed. I am also grateful for the intellectual stimulation and encouragement offered by the wonderful colleagues I have encountered over the years. Furthermore, I would like to thank the many artists who kindly gave me permission to use their work here.

Lastly, this book and the research that went into it would not have been possible without the financial support provided by Jacobs University Bremen, the Finnish Centre for International Mobility, the Académie Universitaire Louvain, the Marie Curie Actions, as well as the Flemish Research Council.

I hope it proves worthy of at least some of the support provided to me.

OPENNESS OF COMICS

INTRODUCTION

Instrumentalizing Openness

This book examines a representative but often overlooked selection of American and European comics from the last five decades with the aim of showing how they often work as open texts. Writing on the open work of art and later the open text,[1] the philosopher Umberto Eco describes openness as a feature by which the reader—or listener or viewer, as the case may be—is offered several possibilities of interpretation that are ensconced in a cohesive narrative and aesthetic structure.[2] In taking up Eco's concept of openness here, the visual-, literary-, and comics-specific features used by the analyzed comics to form open rather than closed texts are described. This analytical approach seeks to shed more light on how comics generate (or limit) meaning, increase and structure the scope of reading into a work, and thus contradict the stereotype of simplicity attached to the medium. While such a reader-dependent notion inevitably limits the analyses, the analytical guideline used aims at bringing in an objective dimension to the readings.

The book unfolds as follows:

1. The first part begins with explaining Umberto Eco's concept of the *opera aperta* or open work of art. Aspects from Anglophone and Francophone theories on comics, emphasizing the role of the reader and the workings of comics, are used to highlight the ways through which openness can function in comics. The literary and visual characteristics and comics devices contributing to openness in comics are then described.
2. The book's second and largest part is devoted to descriptive analyses of selected works in English, French, German, and Finnish.[3] Discussed chronologically within each section, the comics have been categorized under four groups of genres corresponding to the genres that they are closest to. The chronological arrangement provides a historical contextualization of the ways in which openness is generated. The last chapter contains comparisons with other forms of visual narratives and books—illustrated novels, artists' books—in order to bring out comics' interaction with, and

appropriation of, techniques from other media for increasing and structuring interpretational possibilities.
3. The final part summarizes the specific ways in which the features mentioned in Part One are manipulated to increase the openness of the analyzed comics. It ends by discussing the relationship between the contemporary multimedia environment and two of the ways in which comics create openness—namely, references to other media and the use of indirect connections within and beyond the panel.

OPENNESS AS AN ANALYTICAL TOOL

Comics depend on visual and verbal elements involved in varying degrees of symbiosis. Each panel, with its combination of words and images, is embedded in a network of relationships with other panels and media within and beyond the comic book.[4] The uniqueness and the subversiveness of the medium stems from the free combination of conventions of other media which, though related by virtue of using similar verbal and/or visual channels of communication, are active on vastly different planes. Such media include the extensive range of printed words and pictures, such as newspapers, posters, and literary publications, while also encompassing films and the multidimensional realm of more exclusive artistic works, such as paintings, sculptures, and installations. The mixed nature of comics, besides providing possible visual pleasure,[5] also contains the potential for greater reader participation in construing and reconstruing the narrative.

The main point of departure for openness is the conceptualization of interpretation "as an interactive process between reader and text."[6] This process is literalized[7] in comics due to the reader's involvement in the creation of a comics story through cognitively piecing the panels together, thus echoing the process of interpretation described by Eco:

> The aesthetic dialectics between openness and closedness of texts depends on the basic structure of the process of text interpretation [...] This structure is made possible by the nature of the system of codes and subcodes constituting the world [...] The reader finds his freedom (i) in deciding how to activate one or another of the textual levels and (ii) in choosing which codes to apply.[8]

Even though Eco used modern works of literature (notably Joyce's *Finnegans Wake*) to exemplify the concept of openness, he began his book on the open work by mentioning the malleable serial and electronic compositions of Karlheinz Stockhausen and Luciano Berio, as well as artworks like *art informel* paintings and Alexander Calder's *Mobiles*. Such modern works exemplify the notion of a "work in movement," a particular kind of openness, which thrives on the movement generated by the work's "unplanned or physically incomplete structural units."[9] Such movement is discernible in some of the more experimental comics analyzed here, such as Olivier Deprez's *Le Château* and Jens Balzer and Martin tom Dieck's *Salut, Deleuze!*: openness is ensconced in the structure of each comic which "moves" due to its incompleteness in *Le Château* and due to its repetitiveness in *Salut, Deleuze!* For Eco, such openness in the second degree distinguishes itself from earlier manifestations of openness by incorporating plurivocality or multiple modes of interpretation and appreciation in the very form of the work, whereby "the ambiguity of the signs cannot be separated from their aesthetic organization [...] the two are mutually supportive and motivating."[10]

However, even when a work is incomplete, like Mallarmé's *Livre*, or is driven by seemingly aleatory elements, as in the plots of stream-of-consciousness novels, certain cohesive elements persist which hold the fragments of the work together, circumscribing the movement often without seeming to do so, as in *Finnegans Wake*. Eco goes further to point out that the haphazard or incomplete structure reflects a particular notion of the world as "a web of possibilities."[11] The work in movement is therefore an essentially modern product reflecting changed conceptions of the world including, for instance, the emergence of relativity and the uncertainty principle in the realm of science.[12] Einstein's relativities in particular are significant because they, like the concept of openness, highlight the variability of forces and their effects, all of which change depending on the viewer's position and that of the object:

> As in the Einsteinian universe, in the "work in movement" we may well deny that there is a single prescribed point of view. But this does not mean complete chaos in its internal relations. What it does imply is an organizing rule which governs these relations. Therefore [...] we can say that the "work in movement" is the possibility of numerous different personal interventions, but it is not an amorphous invitation to indiscriminate participation. The invitation offers the performer the opportunity for an oriented insertion into something which always remains the world intended by the author.[13]

Hence, limits channeling the possible interpretations in a specific direction are essential to an open work. Eco is careful to point out "the dialectic between form and openness," implying that a structure persists which interweaves the several points of view offered by the work.[14] In other words, openness is not to be confused with a complete freedom of interpretation but implies the presence of multiple, interlinked interpretations that remain unique to the work:

> A work of art [...] is [...a] *closed* form in its uniqueness as a balanced organic whole, while at the same time constituting an *open* product on account of its susceptibility to countless different interpretations which do not impinge on its unadulterable specificity.[15]

In his later work (partially collected in English in *The Role of the Reader*), Eco elaborates on the model readers foreseen by closed and open texts. Authors of closed texts "have in mind an average addressee referred to a given social context" and "obsessively aim at arousing a precise response on the part of more or less empirical readers."[16] Eco places Superman comics and Ian Fleming's novels in this category, saying that such texts are so inflexibly constructed with the aim of speaking to everyone that they are "in fact open to any possible 'aberrant' decoding," varying according to each reader's frame of reference.[17] Writes Eco: "why not read Superman stories only as a new form of romance that is free from any pedagogical intention. Doing so would not betray the nature of the saga. Superman comic strips are also this. And much more. They can be read in various ways, each way being independent of the other."[18] I would like to argue, however, that certain comics can go beyond such closedness and call for multiple interpretations that do not diverge from each other, but rather converge to add further dimensions to the story.

Open texts on the other hand envisage readers who are "able to master different codes and eager to deal with the text as a maze of many issues [...] You cannot use the text as you want, but only as the text wants you to use it. An open text, however 'open' it be, cannot afford whatever interpretation [...] An open text outlines a 'closed' project of its Model Reader as a component of its structural strategy."[19] Thus, for the closed text, any kind of interpretation is possible and although a fixed interpretation is not proposed for the open text, levels of semiosis are established which cannot be allowed to break from each other and which unfold at the mobile node where the context and the reader's interaction with it meet. Consequently, if Franz Kafka's *The Trial*, for instance, is read as "a trivial criminal novel," the text "collapses—it has been burned out, just as a 'joint' is burned out to produce a private euphoric state."[20]

While the structural movement described above, where ambiguity is inseparable from the "aesthetic organization" of the work,[21] is in some ways a newer means of generating openness, the more traditional means include the use of ambiguous signs and references to generate a univocal message, in contrast to the plurivocal message of the work in movement. Eco explains this through contrasting Dante's *Divina Commedia* with Joyce's *Finnegans Wake*.[22] Most comics incorporate openness on the level of verbal and visual language rather than extrapolating it to the structure as well. That said, some movement and plurivocality is potentially present in the medium itself thanks to its combination of visual and verbal signs.[23] The openness discernible in all of the comics discussed here (including those "in movement") unfolds primarily through the ambiguity generated by words and images, individually and through their interactions. Eco describes two main, not mutually exclusive, ways by which a work is infused with ambiguity: suggestiveness and unconventionality.

For Eco, "*suggestiveness* is a deliberate move to 'open' the work to the free response of the addressee. An artistic work that suggests is also one that can be performed with the full emotional and imaginative resources of the interpreter."[24] Hence, the kind of suggestion that generates openness is not merely a reference (with or without several possible connotations) but it also evokes emotive and imaginative responses. Writes Eco: "This way of enhancing both the vagueness of the reference and its mnemonic appeal [...] is characteristic of a particular mode of communication that I shall define as 'aesthetic', in the broadest sense of the term."[25]

The second means of creating ambiguity is through breaking conventions.[26] Such ambiguity is the product of entropy for "all deviation from the most banal linguistic order entails a new kind of organization, *which can be considered as disorder in relation to the previous organization, and as order in relation to the parameters of the new discourse.*"[27] The disorder created by the rejection of established rules of interpretation results in several possibilities of interpretation.

In comics, ambiguity through suggestiveness is often generated via figuration, including the use of tropes, the allusive rendition of stories and characters, as well as self-reflexive elements. Ambiguity through subversion of conventions often manifests itself in comics through indirect word-image relationships and transitions. When brought together in a collaborative structure, these features can create openness and will be elaborated upon after discussing certain medium-specific aspects contributing to openness that have already been brought up in comics theory.

OPENNESS AND COMICS THEORY

Elements contributing to openness in comics can be situated in comics scholar Thierry Groensteen's stages in the creation of fiction.[28] Groensteen's stages include the invention of the story, its organization into a structure, and its expression or production through a medium. In undergoing transsemiotization or transposition to another medium, the *sujet* or the story's structure is adapted to overcome the constraints of the new medium.[29] The coexistence of words and images in comics entails the complementary division of the narration between visual and verbal elements, both of which come with a distinctive, rich heritage of possibilities for expression, such as the novel and painting. Comics tap into this heritage and even comment upon it, depending on the nature of the reference, as with Yslaire's *XXe Ciel* series where the panels often mimic computer screens and the flow of the story itself is more hypertextual than linear. Such a transposition involves determining the role of the reader, envisaging a model reader for either closed comics or open ones. For this, the manipulation of the reading process by some of the basic constituents of comics needs to be looked at more closely.

Although sequentiality is characteristic of the comic strip that sets it apart from painting—since it is "le sens général né d'une succession qui determine à chaque instant la valeur d'une image" (the general meaning engendered by a sequence that determines the value of an image at each moment)[30]—it is rarely rigidly upheld in experimental comics on the panel-to-panel level, where sequentiality is not directly generated by the content. Certain panels can thus remain meaningful on their own through, for instance, offering an additional sphere of references and limiting their dependence on the other panels. Beyond fandom and comics scholarship, however, clarity and oversimplification, allowing for quick easy readings, continue to be regarded as the basic traits of comics which, although valid for many comics, do not hold for an increasing number of them.

While sequentiality also forms the core of comics artist and theoretician Scott McCloud's definition of comics as "[j]uxtaposed pictorial and other images in deliberate sequence, intended to convey information and/or produce an aesthetic response in the viewer," the importance of words and consequently the multi-modal facet of comics is excluded.[31] McCloud also inflates the range of possible comics to include Max Ernst's *Une Semaine de Bonté*, as well as the Bayeux Tapestry.

In contrast, the comics scholar Pierre Fresnault-Deruelle calls the basic unit of the *bande dessinée* a *syntagme complèxe*, since verbal elements function along two axes, vertically collaborating with the picture in the same frame and horizontally forging a linguistic message across the frames.[32] Yet, as will be shown in the course of the analyses, such linear verbal and visual connections are frequently subverted in open comics to create greater ambiguity and interpretational scope. Complex word-image relationships, such as indirect connections between panels, require a reader capable of making the right connections for fleshing out the story.

Given this openly reader-dependent nature of comics, analyses of their sequentiality have also taken a cognitive turn, with scholars like Neil Cohn emphasizing the complexity of the mental processes involved in reading comics, including the nonlinear functioning of sequences and their effect on the temporality of the story being told.[33] Offering an alternative to Cohn's focus on the technical aspects of comics, Karin Kukkonen works with the "clues and gaps" that guide readers in their interpretations and range from intertextual references to the representation of characters' mindsets.[34] Indicative of the move away from semiotic analyses of comics, these cognitive approaches highlight the potential intricacy of the process through which a comics narrative unfolds in the reader's mind. While analyses in this book are based on a similar premise, they are anchored in the possibilities of openness offered by the medium, using specific visual and verbal features as a point of departure and focusing on their interweaving and effects on the scope of interpretation.

The notion of the open work can be linked to the very form of comics, with the gutters providing room for the reader's input, and the panels structuring the interpretations. Comparable to Fresnault-Deruelle's complex syntagm, which lies at the core of comics, the open text "is a paramount instance of a syntactic-semantico-pragmatic device" where, in addition, the "foreseen interpretation is a part of its generative process."[35] Comics panels likewise punctuate the story's flow, guide and even flavor interpretations according to their content, shape, and relationships with the other panels.

According to Fresnault-Deruelle, "le discontinu fonde l'univers de la bande dessinée" (discontinuity is the basis of the comics universe) whereby partial, intrinsic discontinuity exists because each individual image is a frozen moment and total, extrinsic discontinuity persists through the gaps between each frame.[36] This aspect of frozen time also echoes Joseph Hillis Miller's interpretation of illustrations, which highlights the distinctive, nonverbal impact of images.[37] At the reader's end, the act of *lecture-vision* is based upon the poles of narration (*le dire*, which is communicated by images) and fiction (*le dit* incorporating *le fait*, communicated by words). The reader fills in the gaps between these poles to form a coherent narrative. This is comparable to literary scholar Wolfgang Iser's theory of how readers construe meaning when interacting with a text, a construal that is filtered through the collective imaginary and their own imagination, both of which are, to a considerable extent, also formed by texts.[38] According to Julia Round, "[c]omics literalize

Iser's mode of literary experience" through mapping out the story in a spatio-temporal network concretized by the panels.[39] Although interpretation is also filtered through images in comics, the interplay between the work, the reader's own imagination, and the collective imaginary in bringing the story to life persists.

Correspondingly, the reader's role in construing comics is often underscored in comics theories, as with McCloud's use of closure, to describe the construction of wholes from parts by readers/viewers.[40] In exacerbating the original discontinuity of comics, the element of incompleteness also contributes to openness, depending on the degree of movement in the panels and between them. The possibilities of closing the gaps between the panels are crucial for gauging openness: interconnecting the possible interpretational possibilities instead of exposing the comic to numerous unlinked interpretations would make it an open rather than a closed text. By calling for deeper readings and rereadings, open comics contradict Fresnault-Deruelle's claim that Tzvetan Todorov's emphasis on the need to read and reread fantastic literature is not applicable to comics since "la B.D. n'est pas qu'un canevas en images; l'énigme resolue avec la première lecture" (comics are nothing but a canvas of images; the mystery is resolved in the first reading).[41]

Comics scholar Jan Baetens describes the graphic novel as a complex, ungraspable and eventually an open genre.[42] For him, "the graphic novel reveals deep transformations in the connections between novel and medium, the latter being no longer naturally seen as the word or the book, but hinting now toward the notion of what literary scholar Marjorie Perloff calls the 'differential text,'"[43] which "exist[s] in different material forms, with no single version being the definitive one."[44] The notion of the graphic novel as blurring boundaries and being *per se* an ungraspable medium can be extended to comics themselves. This book will not, to take up Baeten's words once again, "distinguish the subfield of the graphic novel from the broader field of comics" owing to the former's terminological inconsistency.[45] Instead, the high art and literary intonations of graphic novels will be taken as an incentive for exploring the ways in which intermedial interactions can generate openness in comics.

The analytical foci described below consist of aesthetic and poetic or structural features that generate openness in comics through words and images and their interaction. Although these foci are conceptualized along the dimensions of content and form, or the story and the techniques used for its telling, the inseparability of the two on certain levels is also borne in mind. Formal devices include visual and literary figuration, as well as references to other media and texts. In open comics, these aspects are often imbued with a self-reflexive relevance (for both the story and the medium) since "authors of 'open' works [. . .] innovate at the level of artistic form, which is always their ultimate content."[46] An open work embeds such features in a narrative offering flexible interpretations within a cohesive structure that filters out irrelevant interpretations.

SITUATING OPENNESS
Self-reflexive themes[47]

The analysis of the stories overlaps with accounting for their functions since "we always produce vision" through stories,[48] through mediating realities and imaginaries. Self-reflexive and critical elements create openness by offering additional perspectives from which to view the work. As comics scholar Richard Reynolds points out, it is the media-awareness and self-criticism incorporated in *Watchmen* that distinguishes it from other comics.[49] This self-criticism often unfolds through the subversion of conventions and stereotypes, as is the case with the flailing heroes in *Watchmen*. Such subversion was however, to a certain extent, part of comics since the beginning, and persisted in superhero adventures.[50] Frequently hailed as an exemplary graphic novel, *Watchmen* includes another element linked to its self-criticism and complexity, which has become increasingly prominent in alternative comics and the mainstream: psychological realism, which in the *Watchmen* is situated in a dystopic reality remaining uncomfortably close to the recent past. In this book, the critical distortions and metafictional distance in dystopias, such as the worlds portrayed in Yslaire's *XXe Ciel* and Enki Bilal's *La Trilogie Nikopol*, likewise work in a revisionist manner to subvert notions of normative histories.

Another element that can contribute towards the openness of a text through its self-reflexive nature is autofiction.[51] Stemming from contemporary literary theory, autofiction has been regarded as a literary reality television alternative, or less critically as an extension of the confessional-retributional function of autobiographies. Serge Doubrovsky, the writer and literary scholar who gave the term currency, drew the following analogy between a book and life: "Un livre, comme une vie, se brise" (A book, like a life, breaks).[53] Comprising of ruptures, it is fitting that this "fiction événements et de faits strictement réels" (fiction of strictly real events and facts) is recurrent in many autobiographical comics, based as they are on connections and rifts between panels, words, and images.[54] The recurrence of autofiction in comics can be traced to the double significance inherent in visual elements which allows for "appearance to be seen as both mirror and metaphor."[55]

Analyses of the characters will focus on their nonconformity to stereotypes, and their psychological complexity. Referring to media scholar Marshall McLuhan, McCloud highlights the immediate identification potential of images.[56] Yet this function is also fulfilled textually through the transposition of certain archetypical characters—such as the Everyman, the Fool, or Oedipus—whereby the types are transformed and imbued with additional, more specific features that are revealing for their milieu, as is the case with the fragmentation and confusion of identities in characters like Batman and Nikopol. One of the classic examples of the migration and metamorphosis of a folk culture figure to a popular culture icon is the appropriation of the circus strongman's costume by superhero comics,[57] and the superhero's acquisition of increasing psychological complexity and ambiguity in alternative comics such as *Arkham Asylum* and *Sandman*. As will be shown in this book's second part, the splicing of identities—occurring, for instance, through the identity confusion between Nikopol and his son or the similarities underscored by Grant Morrison between the Joker and the Fool—complement the very form of comics. The successful transmission of identity concerns and psychological mindsets through comics also highlights the medium's ability to render the disjunction in its technique relevant for its stories.

Literary scholar Brian McHale points out that characters can also function as "disturbers of the ontological hierarchy of levels through their awareness of the recursive structures in which they find themselves."[58] Such instances where the characters' worlds collide with the reader's, where the characters transcend the limits of the story and make direct contact with the reader, also contain metafictional commentary. Literary scholar Linda Hutcheon's words below show how closely metafiction is related to the openness of the text through its generation of self-awareness in the reader:

> [W]hile being made aware of the linguistic and fictive nature of what is being read, and thereby distanced from any unself-conscious identification on the level of character or plot, readers of metafiction are at the same time made mindful of their active role in reading, in participating in making the text mean.[59]

Metafiction, or the manifestation of fiction theorizing itself, is particularly relevant for highlighting the potential of exploiting the literary and visual traditions related to comics, reworking them in complex configurations and thus offering multiple levels of interpretation.

In comics, two kinds of reader involvement are distinguishable. One encourages vicarious participation where the reader gets involved in the story and its characters, possibly identifying with a main character; the other forces an awareness of the mechanisms of the material being read and entails interpretational input from a more distanced, critical level. In more open comics, the awareness of the workings of the medium—especially its sequentiality and the disjunction of words and images—is another factor encouraging the reader's involvement in the construal of not only worlds and characters but also the various levels within the story. Yet another kind of involvement lies in the aesthetic pleasure which can be offered by comics through both images and words (such as the poetry of Alan Moore's and Neil Gaiman's stories, or the visual lyricism of Edmond Baudoin's drawings). The presence of these different levels of reader engagement and, above all, the possibility of interpretations on multiple levels can also be seen as contributing towards the making of the open "work in movement" discussed above.[60]

Self-reflexive references and figuration

Media scholar Paul Atkinson explains Benoît Peeters's concept of *double temporalité* as emerging from "the two aspects of viewing the panel—as a 'tableau' [picture, painting] and as a 'récit' [story, narrative]."[61] Hence, besides narrating a story, comics images also retain the reader's attention on the aesthetic plane. While, as Atkinson adds, this kind of contemplation is unlikely to be the same as that in a gallery, more detailed, obscure, or unconventional images are likely to hold the reader's attention for a longer period of time for aesthetic appreciation and for continuing the comics narrative. Thus, images in comics, through their dialectic of autonomy and dependence in a sequence of panels, can render the story more open through captivating the reader by their visual detail, through using more ambiguous or suggestive techniques and styles, such as the degree of abstraction, or through unusual or indirect relationships with the words—both of which offer multiple possibilities of interpretation. In this respect, it is worth noting that even when the image serves a narrative purpose, it functions on a level beyond words, which J. Hillis Miller grounds in the difference between the absence of what words refer to and the powerful visual presence of images.[62]

Amongst the formal features, the use of figurative language or images is significant for openness. Metaphors, for instance, by widening the range of meaning encompassed by a particular sign, also subvert conventions.[63] Tropes in general enrich the intricacy of a work by engendering worlds "*hesitating* between the literal and the metaphorical."[64] Similarly highlighting the figurative scope of symbols, Eco mentions how the symbol is commonly seen "as a communicative channel for the indefinite, open to constantly shifting responses and interpretative stances."[65]

References to other media can likewise work suggestively. Literary and other intermedial allusions, while highlighting the medium's hybridity, also demonstrate its ability to employ a variety of visual and verbal devices to increase its scope of signification. This referencing of other media is, as literary scholar Werner Wolf points out, "a common form of self-reference" which, like intertextual references, interlinks worlds beyond the main story.[66] These variations of self-referencing recur in the postmodern traits for *bande dessinée* listed by Ann Miller: "metafiction; play on narrative levels through transgression of the boundaries of the diegesis (metalepsis) or through parallelism between first- and second-level narratives (*mise en abyme*); intertextuality; and the display of the codes of the medium."[67]

As Philippe Marion and André Gaudreault emphasize, interaction between media can occur on both formal and conceptual planes.[68] On the formal level, intermedial references include the adoption or imitation of techniques from another medium.[69] On the level of content, intermedial references manifest themselves through the thematization of other media or their figuration in the story.

Within the sphere of word-image narration, iconical words (those that emphasize their visual appearance) are the most materially obvious intermedial phenomena. Providing two examples of word-image unification, calligraphy and calligram (or visual poetry), literary scholar A. Kibédi Varga points out that "[t]he more intensely a word and image are united, the more complicated it becomes to perceive or read them," entailing greater interpretation and innovation from the reader.[70] Montage, the sixth and last possibility in McCloud's list of word-image combinations, also deserves mention in this context since it is described as the instance when "words are treated as integral parts of the picture."[71] Similarly, Varga sees collages as one of the rare means of bypassing the usually inevitable hierarchy superimposing words over images.[72] As will be shown through the analyses, montages or collages can serve as figuratively loaded intermedial elements that also serve to undermine the conventional hierarchy of words over images.[73]

On the other hand, comics have always made use of the physical appearance of words or word iconicity, foremost for sound effects. Hence, precedents for playing with the word as both a carrier of meaning and as an image (as in the case of words embedded in the woodcut panels of Olivier Deprez's *Le Château* or Dave McKean's collages in *Arkham Asylum*) were already present in the medium. Encouragement from the side of the market and publishers for unusual comics with different formats and subject matter was all that was needed to provide an incentive for further experimentation with the medium's basic features and tools.

In addition, the intermedial interaction between comics and films cannot be ignored.⁷⁴ Shots and cuts, being the equivalents of panels and transitions respectively, allow for the transposition of cinematic vocabulary to describe the basic visual content of the panels, especially those signifying cuts, as well as perspective and distance (such as close-ups, point-of-view and long shots, flashbacks), accompanied by their connotations. Moreover, cinematic techniques like rotoscoping and stop-motion also have parallels in comics (in the use of photorealistic drawing styles and moment-to-moment and action-to-action transitions, for instance).⁷⁵ Unsurprisingly, the philosopher Henri Van Lier links the inception of the comic strip to both the contemporaneous emergence of the cinema, as well as the earlier invention of photography. The construal of a narrative through a sequence of images has ties with the cinema, particularly silent films where images alternated with words on the screen.⁷⁶ Photography, on the other hand, contributed the distinctive attribute of framing individual photographs that were indexical instead of semiotic.⁷⁷ The references to photography in comics usually harbor additional connotations playing on photography's realist and documentary claims (albeit superficial) and its formal contrast with drawing, as in *Mariko Parade*.⁷⁸

The very applicability of theories from different fields for analyzing comics underscores the medium's bimodal nature and its consequent potential for openness. For instance, Deleuze's ideas on the human relevance of cinematic pictures can be extrapolated to comics along with his emphasis on the simultaneity of pictures, their interactive nature and transience.⁷⁹ His distinction between European and American cinema also applies to comics as "[l]e vrai truc du cinéma américain [. . .], ça a été le cinéma d'action. Ils ne croient pas aux mondes originaires. L'idée de mondes originaires c'est une idée tellement européenne" (the speciality of American cinema [. . .] was action cinema. They do not believe in originary worlds. The idea of originary worlds is essentially European).⁸⁰ Correspondingly, the majority of the American comics belong to the action-packed superhero genre, whereas many Franco-Belgian comics reveal stronger world-building tendencies (as in Benoît Peeters and François Schuiten's *Cités Obscures* series or Moebius's *Arzach* with its merging of archetypal fantasy spaces).

Other prominent interactions with media in comics include references to digital technology, especially computer games and the Internet, as in Yslaire's *XXᵉ Ciel* books. Not only do computer games often form part of popular comics franchises but, more relevantly, the malleable diegeses of computer games are also emulated by comics narratives.⁸¹ Therefore, media scholar Miriam Rivett regards the nonlinear structure and interactivity of comics as a manifestation of their hypertextuality.⁸² One of the factors distinguishing comics from films and bringing them closer to computer games is the capacity to incorporate an array of media while providing the option of rereading and reconstruing the effects of the different interwoven media and their contexts.

The referencing of media is tied to the slightly older concept of intertextuality that embeds the (literary) work in a large framework made up of textual networks. References to other texts are the most manifest form of intertextuality.[83] Like Gérard Genette, Julia Kristeva also emphasizes the role of subjectivity or reader involvement provoked by intertextuality.[84]

Such references are linked to the functioning of the symbol itself which, in being "a *textual modality*, a way of producing and of interpreting aspects of a text," is frequently "suggested by the co-text and by the intertextual tradition."[85] Consequently, references to other texts and media are a means of expanding the scope of a story, contributing towards openness by connecting the story to a specific network of other texts. Possibly "comics were always striving to be something else, always intertextual, attempting to fill in gaps, to satisfy the reader's growing desire for spectacle and excitement in the burgeoning media culture of the mid-twentieth century."[86] Moreover, the original Greek version of the word symbol, *sumbolon*, which was a sign of recognition formed by an object broken in two and therefore a carrier of meaning through its incompleteness, corresponds to comics' interplay of disjunction and continuity and the subsequent room to read meaning into them. This aspect of disjointedness—exacerbated in works such as Deprez's *Le Château* and Alan Moore and Eddie Campbell's *From Hell*—which calls on the reader to fill in the unusually large gaps, is created not only through intertextual references but also through the frequently complicated formal aspects mentioned above (stylistic variations, metaphors, indirect transitions), as well as the features depending on the nature of the story (its interaction with the reader's reality or metalepsis and the other ways in which it involves the reader through the pertinence of its themes and characters).

Suggestiveness of technique

Besides capturing the reader's attention to varying degrees, the visual technique or style can also carry multiple connotations both within and beyond the story being told. The use of *couleur directe* or direct color is one such technique, which has provoked mixed reactions due to its subversion of the mass-produced nature of comics and its proximity to the fine arts. As explained by Baetens, the shift from "techniques de fabrication conventionnelle [...] avec leur stricte division du travail (croquis, dessin à l'encre, coloriage, lettrage) à la *couleur directe* (qui fusionne en quelque sorte les quatre étapes précédemment séparées) avait déjà considérablement augmenté le degré de présence de la main du dessinateur" (conventional manufacturing techniques [...] with their strict division of labor [drawing, inking, coloring, lettering] to *direct color* [which to a certain extent merges the four previously separated stages] has already considerably increased the degree of presence of the artist's hand).[87] On the other hand, Philippe Marion has emphasized the individuality of drawings in all comics, treating them as *traces* of psychoanalytic relevance.[88] According to Groensteen, this increased prominence of the individual artist has unsettled the situation of comics in the hierarchical categorization of cultural products.[89] Thus, while incrementing the possibility of creating aesthetic appeal in comics, direct color also generates awareness of comics' potential for variation and experimentation, as well as their strong intermedial links with other arts and literature.

The effects of the kind of verisimilitude or abstraction, involved in both words and pictures, can also contribute towards the openness of comics, notably through creating ambiguity or through references to reality, which become self-reflexive when the medium's role in filtering reality is made evident. The degree of verisimilitude can be gauged on an axis positing abstraction on one end and realism on the other.[90] Verisimilitude or the "neutralisation gommant l'hiatus réalité/fiction se renforce donc si l'œuvre débute sous l'aspect de la quotidienneté" (neutralisation erasing the reality/fiction gap is reinforced when the work begins by adopting the perspective of the everyday).[91] It serves to place the reader in the protagonist's shoes because of which "nous sommes en presence non pas d'une *histoire* qui débute mais de la *vie* qui continue" (we are not in the presence of a *story* which is beginning but a *life* which is continuing).[92] This could be one of the reasons behind the appeal of the comics medium and its increasing experimentation, encouraging comics in the exploration of ordinary life and attracting readers beyond the traditional fandom.

Reality and its filtering through media can be seen as a theme that is automatically triggered by representations of reality and the everyday through, for instance, the use of a realistic visual style or the presence of cinematic allusions, as in *Mariko Parade*. The manipulation of reality by media, the insertion of layers of mediation in comics, and other intermedial references are revealing for both the medium and its milieu since "[s]elf-reference is a central issue in modernist aesthetics and its various postmodern revisions."[93] Fragmented representations and the problematization of the real/unreal divide is self-referential for visual media because they allude to the mechanical, limited means of human perception and the resulting habit of constructing wholes, including realities, from parts, which is a cognitive act termed closure by Gestalt psychologists and which also plays a role in reading comics or watching films.[94]

Since an elaborate structure breaks away from the simplicity conventionally attributed to comics, complexity of form serves as another feature calling for greater reader participation and reflecting the potential for openness. In gauging the ways in which authors vary and manipulate their styles and techniques (or the material aspects of the style), key elements of word-image narration, such as layout[95] (including framing and arrangement), along with word-image relationships and panel transitions, are additional, form-related foci of the analyses.

One of the most accessible categorization of page layouts is Benoît Peeters's description of layouts as conventional, decorative, rhetorical, or productive, which he plots out on the axes of narrative and compositional autonomy:[96]

	Narrative-Composition Autonomy	Narrative-Composition Interdependence
Narrative Dominant	Conventional Use	Rhetorical Use
Composition Dominant	Decorative Use	Productive Use

Source: Peeters, "Four Conceptions of the Page," *ImageText* 3 (3), Figure 1.

Since the tension between narrative and composition is one which comics deliberately plays with, the attempt to limit it to the page layout is problematic, since the majority of the layouts would simply fall under rhetorical.[97] Nevertheless, Peeters's table serves as an indicator of major formal variations and ultimately "it is a question of examining the way in which a work benefits from the apparatus that it sets up."[98]

The analyses conducted here rely on a modification of Peeters's system whereby the four kinds of layouts are emancipated from the tabular form and are construed as opposites on two parallel scales in order to remedy some of the problems already pointed out by Cohn and Groensteen.[99] Where words are dominant, the two ends of independence and dependence between words and images can be visualized as follows:

Conventional ◄─────────────► Rhetorical

Similarly, in cases of image dominance, the independent and dependant poles can be represented in the following way[100]:

Decorative ◄─────────────► Productive

While Peeters's categories are used in the modified version described above, the division of word-image relationships in terms of word-dominance, image-dominance, and word-image interdependence (where it is impossible to distinguish which of the two elements plays a greater role due to the extent of their interaction) is another useful feature for determining the degree of reader interaction. Openness is generated through indirect relationships where words and images function metaphorically instead of supporting each other unambiguously.

The element with the greater storytelling burden (i.e., the word or the image) bestows more freedom upon the other one to act beyond narrative constraints.[101] Thus, direct images generally accord words with greater importance, whereas complex images attract the greatest degree of attention. This attention, for both words and images, can be devoted to their interpretation and appreciation. The extent to which relationships are varied throughout a comic and the degree of indirectness of the relationships themselves brings out a comic's inclination towards openness.

The narrative role of word-image interactions is one of the distinguishing features of comics. As literary scholar Kai Mikkonen points out, in the case of limited narrative comments in classic twentieth-century stories using images, it is the interaction with visual information that transmits clues regarding the characters' psyche and additional nuances of the story.[102] This narrative role is not only determined by the stylistic elements of the words and images and their relationships within individual panels but also by the relationships between the panels or panel transitions.

Elaborating on one of the few systematizations of panel transitions in comics theory, McCloud sees action-to-action, subject-to-subject, and scene-to-scene transitions as being the most recurrent, from which the latter two require greater reader input and cover less than one-third of the transitions in Western comics.[103] In contrast, moment-to-moment and aspect-to-aspect transitions are largely absent, particularly in mainstream productions.[104] Many European works reveal a similar use of transitions, albeit with a greater degree of individual variation.[105] In contrast, manga often use transitions that directly play with time, such as moment-to-moment and aspect-to-aspect transitions; while moment-to-moment transitions reduce time to very small gaps between the scenes, aspect-to-aspect switches tend to freeze or ignore time and "let the eye wander."[106] Different panel transitions therefore contribute to different kinds of reading experiences and also varying degrees of freedom for the reader.

The analyses in Part Two unfold as close readings in order to show how openness is generated in comics through the features mentioned above. While a rigid set of characteristics would be something of an anomaly for the tongue-in-cheek medium of comics, configurations of the above aspects serve as indicators of the comic's openness.

OVERVIEW OF THE SELECTED WORKS

Two principal concerns steered the selection of the main body of cases. Firstly, that it should be representative of the last four decades of developments in comics production and reception (of which the spread of the "graphic novel" term is seen as being partially indicative) by encompassing key works that are usually overlooked by comics scholarship.[107] Not only are these works by well-known comics artists and writers but they also exemplify features that contribute towards openness in comics. Nonetheless, although well-known in the milieus of their origin, the analyzed comics are often from the margins of the mainstream. A second concern was that the list should incorporate a roughly equal number of temporally congruent comics from different cultures and the following four genre categories, which combine popular comics genres: fictionalized memories and biographies; adventure and superheroes; noir, black comedy, and crime; fantasy and science fiction. These four groups of genres provide a comparative framework for discerning the ways in which different degrees of openness is generated in comics that share similar genre codes, especially themes and characterization.[108] While the latter three genre categories are recurrent in popular fiction, biographical fiction and memoirs often edge closer to the more "literary" genres. The bias towards popular genres is hardly surprising given that the origins of comic books have affiliations with pulp fiction, the realm in which genres such as science fiction and crime flourished.[109] However, as education and comics scholar Paul Thomas points out, marginalized popular genres can cross over to the literary realm,[110] a movement that is discernible in many of the comics discussed here and is also emblematic of the legitimization of comics.

Every classification system has its limits, and the two most glaring shortcomings of the one used here are as follows: firstly, the classification under the four groups of genres is somewhat arbitrary. This, however, is inevitable due to the "cannibalism" that Christopher Murray notes in the superhero genre's combination of, among others, adventure, crime, romance, and horror,[111] which can be extended to most comics. As Saige Walton points out, such absorption of genres reflects baroque qualities that are also applicable to popular media in general.[112] That said, the four genre groupings used here nonetheless cover the most popular genres for comics currently produced on both sides of the Atlantic. Moreover, owing to the hybridity of genres discernible in many of the comics, features of other popular genres, such as romance (*Mariko Parade*) or Western (*Arzach*), can also be discerned in the comics analyzed in Part Two. Secondly, there is a dearth of female comics artists. Although comics still remains a male-dominated world, female artists have started playing a prominent role in recent decades, especially in the domains of more experimental and personal comics, as exemplified in this book's corpus by Kan Takahama and Frédéric Boilet's *Mariko Parade*. Corresponding to the increasing visibility of female comics artists, significant scholarly attention has already been devoted to them, most notably in Hillary Chute's *Graphic Women: Life Narratives and Contemporary Comics*, which focuses on American artists involved in underground comics and the widely acclaimed French-Iranian artist, Marjane Satrapi.

Since, on both sides of the Atlantic, the origins of the graphic novel are popularly—albeit misleadingly—traced to Will Eisner,[113] who used the term in 1978 for his book *A Contract with God* to describe its mélange of comic strip and literature, this comic along with its sequels (*Life Force*, from 1988, and to a lesser extent *Dropsie Avenue*, from 1995) opens the section grouping fictionalized memories and biographies. The next book, *C'était la Guerre des Tranchées* (1993), is based on Jacques Tardi's "very first comic strip story," from 1970, which fictionalized his grandfather's experiences in the First World War.[114] Biographies of literary and philosophical figures, including Deleuze, Lovecraft, and Saint-Exupéry, follow, and the section concludes with the autofictional *Mariko Parade* (2003), which brings in a transcultural facet to both form and content by merging *bande dessinée* and manga. As a whole, the section highlights the tendency to incorporate biography through freely interweaving fact and fiction, engendering a narrative that adult readers can relate to and read into.

Somewhat earlier than Eisner, the multilingual Hugo Pratt had played on the proximity of comic strips to literature by drawing one of the earliest, longest comic strip narratives. This first Corto Maltese volume, *La Ballade de la Mer Salée* (*Una Ballata Del Mare Salato*, from 1967), opens the section on adventure and superheroes. Other books in the section include two comics playing with the psychological complexity of the superhero genre: Grant Morrison and Dave McKean's *Arkham Asylum* (1989) and Neil Gaiman's collaboration with several illustrators for the first *Sandman* volume (1991). The section ends with the surreal fusion of internal and external worlds in Edmond Baudoin's *Le Voyage* (1997).

The section on noir, black comedy, and crime traces the changes in Tardi's series, *Les Aventures Extraordinaires d'Adèle Blanc-Sec*, which began in 1976 and has continued irregularly to date. A contrast to this series is provided by the complex rendition of the Ripper case in Alan Moore and Eddie Campbell's *From Hell*, originally published as a limited series in the early 1990s and collected in a 572-page volume in 1999. The next two comics, Marko Turunen and Annemari Hietanen's *Kuolema Kulkee Kintereillä* (2004) and Jyrki Heikkinnen's *Tohtori Futuro* (2007), tell stories with undertones of dark humor of superheroes reduced to ordinariness.

Maintaining chronological order within the groups of genres, the section on fantasy and science fiction begins with *L'Album Mythique* (2006), a collection of Moebius's *Arzach* episodes. Moebius's comics, particularly the *Arzach* episodes going back to the 1970s and the fantastic autobiographical experiences recorded in "La Déviation" (1973) have been included because of the artist's far-reaching influence. This collection is followed by Enki Bilal's *La Trilogie Nikopol*, beginning with *La Foire aux Immortels*, from 1980, which was the first book to be both written and drawn by Bilal. Volumes from Yslaire's XXe *Ciel* series (1997–2004), as well as the latest book by Jarmo Mäkilä, *Taxi van Goghin Korvaan* (2008), are then explored.

The last section contrasts comics with other books such as mute novels, illustrated novels, and artists' books in order to show how comics interact with, but also distinguish themselves from, other forms of visual narration. It begins by looking at two recent comics adaptations of short novels: David Mazzucchelli and Paul Karasik's *City of Glass: The Graphic Novel* (1994) and Lorenzo Mattotti and Jerry Kramsky's *Dr. Jekyll & Mr. Hyde* (2002). Going back in time to cover the rise of the woodcut novel in the early decades of the twentieth century, works like Frans Masereel's 1926 *Mon Livre d'Heures*, as well as Deprez's *Le Château* (a 2003 adaptation of Franz Kafka's *The Castle*), are also explored. *Le Château* in turn is contrasted with the visualizations of Kafka's works in Dave Mairowitz and Robert Crumb's *Introducing Kafka* (1993). After describing the relationship between comics and picture books, the section concludes with a discussion of the variety of artists' books, concentrating on features that contribute towards the openness of experimental comics, such as the interaction with the materiality of the book form and the use of unusual or even nonexistent word-image relationships.

Having explained the features that can contribute towards the openness of comics and having briefly introduced the corpus, it is now time to turn to one of the most prominent genres in contemporary alternative comics and graphic novels: fictionalized memories and biography.

CHAPTER ONE

Fictionalized Memories and Biographies

All the books discussed in this section contain biographical subject matter that is fictionalized to varying degrees, with three of the six books directly incorporating material from the artists' lives. Although biographical and autobiographical literature has existed since time immemorial, the presence of the creative authorial voice in both autobiographical and autofictional works acquired particular prominence during Romanticism. It was in the same era that word-image combinations acquired a more hybrid, experimental dimension, most notably with William Blake's "illuminated" poems. This connection between the construction of an authorial self and the indexical nature of art remains relevant for comics.[1] Unsurprisingly, the medium manifests an "overrepresentation of the autobiographical regime."[2] Underscoring the link between alternative works and biographies, as well as the recent eagerness of publishers and the market for such endeavors on a global scale, a pioneering *gekiga* (alternative manga) artist, Yoshihiro Tatsumi, published *A Drifting Life* in 2009, a manga of over 800 pages based on his life.

Thanks to their experimentation with the medium's techniques and conventions, alternative comics—which appeared in the wake of the more rebellious, experimental underground comix of the 1970s and which are often absorbed by the mainstream[3]—are useful for highlighting the means through which openness is created. Relevant aspects include narratives that are contained in one-shots or limited series instead of indefinite ones, as well as the incorporation of figuration and unusual visual styles. Often going beyond the human interest element of personal stories, the lives narrated through words and images in this section encourage—if only to a limited extent in the earlier two comics—reader involvement in the interpretation and piecing together of the stories.

Chronologically arranged, the section begins with *The Contract with God Trilogy* and *C'était la Guerre des Tranchées* (*It Was the War of the Trenches*), both of which are based on experiences the artists were intimate with.

The next subsection contains four comics portraying the lives and ideas of popular literary and philosophical figures: *Saint-Exupéry*, *Lovecraft*, and *Salut, Deleuze!* The last book, *Mariko Parade*, manifests cultural interaction in both form and theme by narrating the pseudo-autobiographical experiences of a French artist and his Japanese love and model.

A comparative analysis reveals certain characteristics that contribute towards forming a more open comic. These include a non-serial, often relatively long narrative, which is already present in *C'était la Guerre* but absent in the episodic stories from *The Contract with God Trilogy*, although the latter's book form, seeking to contain the narrative, is noteworthy. These works indicate the move towards more contained, longer narratives which provide room for developing and limiting the story's structure. Such structures in turn function as frameworks within which openness can unfold. Another element is the self-reflexive interaction with the genre and the medium, which calls for model readers capable of decoding such features. These self-reflexive features include the narratively pertinent techniques of collages and watercolors in *Lovecraft*, which represent, respectively, confusion and reassembled memories, and which are superimposed by metafictional concerns regarding the making of the comic, the telling of stories, and the interweaving of the writer, artist, and subjects' contexts. In addition, intermedial and intertextual references increase the interpretational scope of the more open comics here, namely, *C'était la Guerre*, *Salut, Deleuze!*, *Lovecraft*, *Saint-Exupéry*, and *Mariko Parade*, while also commenting on the medium's embedding of diverse references in different ways. Subject matter like the philosophical discourse in *Salut, Deleuze!* brings in openness through the broad range of its allusions, which require the reader to be familiar with the ideas of several philosophers as well as their interconnections. The diverse ways in which the features from Part One manifest themselves will be elaborated by starting with the oldest works which, apart from their subject matter and format, is more conventional and relatively closed compared to the other works discussed in this section.

TRACES OF PERSONAL MEMORIES: *THE CONTRACT WITH GOD TRILOGY*

Will Eisner's (1917–2005) debut in the magazine *Wow!* was followed by moderately successful comics series, among which *The Spirit* is the longest and most well-known. Begun in 1940, it was interrupted by Eisner's compulsory military service in 1942, only to acquire greater popularity after the war, sustaining interest until the early 1950s. Eisner kept away from mainstream comics for around sixteen years before coming out with *A Contract with God*, his graphic novel in the vein of the woodcut artists he had been inspired by—Otto Nückel, Frans Masereel, and Lynd Ward—all of whom had "published serious novels told in art without text" in the 1930s.[4] Often credited with bringing the graphic novel term into currency with *Contract*, Eisner has also called it "literary comics."[5]

Each of the three books making up *The Contract with God Trilogy* have the length of a short novel: *A Contract with God* (1978) covers 180 pages, *A Life Force* (1988) takes up 140 pages, and *Dropsie Avenue* (1995) amounts to 173 pages. Most of them are short stories inspired by Eisner's experiences, which, especially in *Contract with God* and *Life Force*, sometimes overlap with autobiographical moments.[6]

Besides the use of the book form, references to traditional literary formats are also made via the inclusion of prologues and epilogues. In the trilogy's first book, the epilogue has the form of an episode bringing in another character, who never appears again but who is also a resident on the same Dropsie Avenue where the stories unfold.[7] Since this character, a little boy, finds the protagonist Frimme's stone contract, a certain link is established between the otherwise disparate four tenement tales making up *Contract with God*. Such epilogues are used by several comics, emphasizing their book form while maintaining the possibility of continuations, as in the *Sandman* volume analyzed later.

All of the trilogy's stories loosely connect several lives instead of concentrating on only one, thus reflecting the episodic rhythm of serial publication. *A Contract with God* juxtaposes the stories of vastly different characters, beginning with the middle-aged Frimme Hersh losing faith after the burial of his adopted daughter, and continuing with the itinerant street singer Eddie's brief affair with a failed soprano, the suicide of a tenement supervisor, and the brief summer vacation of various city dwellers at a "cookalein," a low-priced, shared vacation house in the countryside.

Although *A Contract with God* and *Dropsie Avenue* were issued as one-shots, *Life Force* was originally serialized. One of the main binding features in the three books is the place of residence, primarily the tenements and the Bronx street, Dropsie Avenue. Though *Life Force* tries to maintain a more unified structure by returning to characters introduced before, especially its protagonist, the middle-aged Jewish American Jacob, the story, echoing its serialized, episodically improvised production, remains disjointed without offering possibilities for bridging the gaps or offering different perspectives for viewing it.

Being graphite sketches, the frontispieces preceding the four short stories making up *Contract with God* suggest greater affinity to the traditional arts than to comics. Exemplifying the increasingly blatant interaction of comics with the other arts, these pieces were created recently for a special edition of the trilogy.[8] In the stories themselves, the comics conventions of caricaturized features, exaggerated gestures, and an overall reductive visual style persist, containing, as with most artists' work, characters resembling those from other comics drawn by the same hand. Other visual repetitions serve as motifs due to their link with the content of the narrative, such as the signs of urban impoverishment reinforcing the atmosphere of the economic depression of the 1930s.[9]

While typification also prevails in the layout and transitions, some diversity is discernible. Due to the general dominance of the word, the layout, to use Peeters's categories, is often conventional but tilts towards the rhetorical end when the panels' size and arrangement is adjusted to complement the flow of the story, as when Frimme throws the stone contract outside the window.[10] A productive layout is used at the beginning of the deranged Aaron's brief appearance in *Life Force* when he is holding his imaginary conversations: although the narrator's words retain their dominance, their arrangement as thought waves mold the story's flow while visualizing the mad confusion in the character's mind.[11] For Peeters, such "virtual frames" are one of the hallmarks of Eisner's skill, since even in the absence of frames, the pictures adhere to an internal order.[12] Another instance with a dynamic layout that engulfs panel divisions, transforming the page into a coherent unit of expression, occurs during the building superintendent's fantasies, where a swirl of images taking up half of the page show him looking at pornographic images with the fantasies later playing out in the hollows of his eyes.[13] This loaded set of images is an instance of openness: besides revealing a central aspect of the protagonist's character, the images bring in an element of self-reference by attesting to the power of visuals and their ability to generate psychosomatic effects. Moreover, the hollows in the man's eyes function figuratively by foreshadowing the suicide that is to a great extent an outcome of his guilty lustfulness.

Characteristic for pictorial narratives in general, the often excessive theatricality of the stories is marked by the incorporation of conventions similar to those of the cinema, particularly the cuts in cinematic choreography, with individual panels representing different film shots and encompassing varying angles and perspectives, ranging from close-ups to the more theatrical spotlights on the main figure dramatizing the happenings. Changing narrative tempos,[14] along with rarer techniques such as dissolving and superimposing panels, are likewise present in some particularly expressionistic panels, including the two instances of productive layouts described above.[15] While these are also intermedial references, they do not work to create suggestions or self-reflexivity but only dramatize the events.

As indicated above, the same setting (the Bronx, primarily its tenements during the economic upheaval of the 1930s) and theme (the average—often Jewish—man's will to survive in the face of bleak circumstances) serve as the chief connectors between the stories. This was Eisner's own context, and the autofictional element is evident in his declaration that "I have an ancient mariner's need to share my accumulation of experience and observations. Call me, if you will, a graphic witness reporting on life, death."[16] Correspondingly, each of the brief introductions to the stories in his preface describes the personal experience that led to them. According to Eisner, Jacob voices his personal dilemmas and the "Cookalein" episode in *A Contract with God* is "an honest account" of his adolescence.[17] Hence, memory and fiction, like facts and their narration, have been blended, although these connections are not explored in the stories themselves. Similarly, even though the tenements serve as *lieux de mémoire* concretizing collective memory,[18] they remain situational features, restricted to the background.

When it comes to the word-image relationships involved, the entire trilogy hovers between resembling illustrated novels, with their dependence on words, and the word-image interaction common to comics. This is particularly evident in each episode's introduction, where the picture simply corroborates the text. *Life Force*, in contrast to Frimme's story that opens *Contract with God*, unfolds more independently of the omniscient narrator, by using newspaper cuttings to clarify the context. The relationship between the words and images is therefore generally a straightforward case of word-dominance. While the device of newspaper clippings to describe the situation is an innovative variation and is supplemented by poorly printed newspaper-like images of the officials, this too is overused in the latter half of the book, as in the case of weather report clippings covering the entire page.[19]

Other than the interweaving of biographical elements, the trilogy's main novelty lies in the use of the book form for the three books, as well as the telling of stories that are unconventional for comics. Replacing fascicules with the trade paperback format is indicative of the aspiration to acquire a higher status comparable to that of literature, which was, and still is, seen as deserving more critical, sustained attention. It is noteworthy that in trying to adopt a more literary form, Eisner, especially in his first book, *A Contract with God*, relied on word-image connections similar to those of typical illustrated books, with the narration occurring almost exclusively through the words, and the images serving as mere illustrations. It is during the use of more balanced word-image relationships or certain situations of image-dominance that greater experimentation with the technique and narration of the stories is discernible. Nonetheless, this experimentation does not have particular relevance for more than fleeting moments of the story, as in Aaron's case. Moreover, since the story is spelled out rather than suggested, there is little that calls for further interlinked interpretations. In Eco's terms, the information is there, but the "poetic meaning," including its "quotient of imagination" or the "full resonance of the poetic word" is absent.[20]

Correspondingly, there is a dearth of figurative devices or relevant references to other media that could introduce additional levels in the story.[21] By spelling out the messages in his stories, Eisner banalizes them, making them too direct, eliminating ambiguity and alternative interpretations. As will be shown in the course of the analyses, figuration, along with autofictional hints and adult concerns, are sometimes conveyed in more indirect ways and interwoven with other elements of the narrative in the comics discussed later. The *Contract with God* trilogy itself, however, remains closed. While the next book, *C'était la Guerre des Tranchées*, also does not offer much room for further readings, its second part contains some possibilities for greater openness, conveying the comic's pacifist message on several levels instead of directly.

COLLECTIVIZED WAR EXPERIENCES: *C'ÉTAIT LA GUERRE DES TRANCHÉES*

Born in 1946 in Valence, Tardi began his career with the popular comics magazine *Pilote*, which ran from 1959 to 1989. Contributing to *Métal Hurlant* later on, Tardi's earliest collaborations were with Moebius, whose influence is most evident in Tardi's layouts and possibly the surreal moments that infiltrate realistic settings. Whereas the visual renditions of characters are comparable to those of the fellow Frenchman and contemporary Francis Masse,[22] Tardi's individuality stems from a distinctive combination of the comics and cinematic conventions of his era. Mentioning Jacques Tardi's and Alberto Breccia's works as exemplifications of the *bande dessinée moderne*, comics scholar Jacques Samson describes their modernity as something that "concerne la singularité d'une *semiosis* qui n'est réductible à aucune sémiotique générale, car l'artiste moderne crée lui-même sa propre 'sémiotique'" (concerns the particularity of a *semiosis* which cannot be reduced to any general semiotics because the modern artist creates his own "semiotics").[23] Tardi's style remains distinctive and more or less consistent over the years. Its persistence in all his works irrespective of their content—ranging from historical fiction to thrillers embracing the unreal—indicates the span of its signifying scope while also acting as a kind of commentary depending on the story being told. This is evident in the contrast between *La Guerre* (1993) and the *Adèle Blanc-Sec* adventures analyzed later. While *La Guerre*'s caricaturizing drawing style serves as a poignant contrast to the story being told, the same style highlights the exaggerated sensationalism of the plot twists in the *Adèle* stories, which both imitate and mock popular literature.

The antiwar sentiment is summed up by the title page bearing the French Croix de Guerre with blood trickling in the background. The very first paragraph of *La Guerre* aptly sums up the book's approach by declaring that it is not the work of a historian and that "[i]l ne s'agit pas de l'histoire de la Première Guerre mondiale racontée en bande dessinée, mais d'une succession de situations non chronologiques, vécues par des hommes manipulés et embourbés ... Il n'y a pas de 'héros,' pas de 'personnage principal,' dans cette lamentable 'aventure' collective qu'est la guerre. Rien qu'un gigantesque et anonyme cri d'agonie" (this is not about the history of the First World War recounted in comics, but a series of non-chronological situations lived by manipulated and bogged down men ... There is no "hero," no "main character" in this deplorable collective "adventure" which is war. Nothing but a gigantic and anonymous cry of agony).[24]

Nonetheless, Tardi also acknowledges the help of Jean-Pierre Verney, a historian specializing in the First World War, who supplied details regarding military protocol, uniforms, and weapons. Proving Tardi's continuing fascination with this period, the two initiated a two-volume series, *Putain de Guerre*, on the same topic in 2008. The artist's comics on World War I were inspired by his grandfather's memories of Verdun, which were related to him by his grandmother.[25] Tardi also mentions war literature, such as Louis-Ferdinand Céline's *Voyage au Bout de la Nuit* and Gabriel Chevallier's *La Peur*, as lasting influences.

The first nineteen pages of the book were initially published in 1983 as an independent episode called *Trou d'Obus* (*Bombshell Crater*). This book, in keeping with Tardi's trademark chiaroscuro style, is entirely in black-and-white, prompting Jacques Samson's claim that references made by the technique, the "évocations stylistiques inutilisées—gravures d'époque ou imageries d'Epinal" (unused stylistic evocations—contemporary engravings or Épinal prints) is one of Tardi's modern contributions.[26] Although the regular *bande dessinée* format is maintained, the page count of 120 is much higher than normal (albeit close to the size of black-and-white albums in the first half of the twentieth century). Also unusual for comics are the appended bibliography and discography. The layout generally adheres to three tiers per page and is particularly consistent in the second section. This arrangement of three page-wide panels per page is maintained until the end of the book, imbuing the events with a sense of immensity. Since page-wide panels are unusual in themselves, their sporadic rupture is all the more striking, punctuating the narrative flow and even bringing in a staccato rhythm.[27] The trinity formed by the three horizontal panels per page is a formal motif in the book that recalls the tri-colored French flag and adds a touch of irony to the anti-patriotic narratives.[28] Furthermore, many of the images in the panels themselves follow the classic principle of structuring compositions so that the main action and characters form a triangle at the center of the picture plane.

The first description uses a simile for the bangs shown in the preceding, silent panels and maintains the narrative distance present throughout the first section: "Les trois coups ont été frappés . . . comme au théâtre . . ." (the three shots were fired . . . like in the theatre . . .).[29] Speech balloons only appear after ten pages for a short conversation, before reappearing ten pages later for an even briefer exchange.[30] Distance from the events is likewise maintained by the lack of smooth transitions, making the panels resemble photographic stills rather than a continuous sequence of events. This is most evident in the depiction of a dead man accompanied by the narrator's matter-of-fact comment: "Sur cette image, au 1er plan, un soldat mort: le 2ème classe, Binet" (In this image, in the foreground, a dead soldier: second class, Binet).[31]

From this point onwards, the narrator takes up the story of Binet but the man himself does not say a word. Even the images keep him at a distance by avoiding close shots of him. It is this persistent third-person perspective that brings in an element of poignancy as with the scenes showing Binet waiting through the night for a fellow soldier, Faucheux, who had been sent to an outpost that had stopped communicating. The top tier comprises of two partially curved, smaller panels which depict perspectives of the watching Binet upon opposite ends of a deserted landscape resembling C. D. Friedrich's *Abbey in an Oak Forest/Monk's Funeral in Oak Grove* (1810).[32] Such partially curved panels are frequent and recall Moebius's radical frames which usually form a decorative layout. Yet Tardi's panels distinguish themselves from Moebius's radical forms by complementing the action more often and becoming, consequently, more rhetorical.[33]

While preserving the same theme, *La Guerre*'s second section narrates a more open story by incorporating shifting but interlinked perspectives of different soldiers, using figuration and balancing the narrative burden between words and images (instead of placing most of it on the words, as is the case in most of the first section). Maintaining the setting but not the names mentioned before, the second section of the book commences with a famous quote by General Rebillot from the *Libre Parole* of 13th December 1914: "Il était temps que vînt la guerre pour ressusciter, en France, le sens de l'idéal et du divin"[34] (It is about time that war came to resurrect the sense of the ideal and the divine in France). Such intertextual incorporations of actual quotations raises, as Matthew Screech has pointed out, *la question du réel* or the blurring of reality and fantasy.[35] Brought up by the inclusion of Rebillot's words, *la question du réel* is dealt with grim irony throughout the book, making it contrast glaringly with the romanticism of war in other works.[36] It can also be seen as a means of embedding personal recollections in collective memory. This interaction between fact and fiction entails work from the reader, but also allows the comic's structure and references to be open and flexible according to the reader's interpretations, which are likely to remain interlinked.

Recalling the introduction of movie titles in older films or trailers, the title of the book (and the second section) appears after Rebillot's words in a narrative caption accompanying a panel showing a bomb blast on the first page: "Les obus éventraient le sol torturé à l'intérieur duquel se terraient des milliers d'hommes qui avaient creusé la terre et y avaient aménagé des abris. C'était la guerre des tranchées"[37] (The shells ripped the tortured ground where millions of men who had dug the earth and converted it into shelters were hiding. It was the war of the trenches).

Compared to the episode on Binet, the second section is more macabre, unfolding in a darker, squalid landscape overgrown with barbed wire and wooden stumps and replete with vivid depictions of human suffering. Time moves back and forth with the brief sequences on different characters following them from their pre-enlistment lives to their death. However, characteristic of the second section's inversion of Christian symbolism, the two-paged sequence on the soldier Gaspard ends with his last moments in no man's land unfolding before a sculpted cross from which the small, suffering Jesus has come loose and fallen upside down, while a uniformed skeleton leans against the pedestal.[38] Visual and verbal comments against the Christian propaganda during the war appear with increasing frequency in the course of the section as with the panel showing a dead body clinging to barbed wire, which is accompanied by Abbé Sertillanges's declaration in the *Madeleine* of 27 September 1914:

> Va, petit soldat! Ta fatigue, tes blessures, ton angoisse d'exilé, ta mort même, tout cela est à haut prix. Nous te plaindrons, nous t'aimerons, si Dieu veut, nous te pleurerons ... nous dirons, en demandant que le ciel contresigne et transpose: Mort au Champ d'honneur![39]
> (Go on, dear soldier! Your fatigue, your wounds, your anguish of the exiled, your death itself, all of this has a high price. We will mourn you, we

will love you, if God wills, we will grieve for you ... we will say, requesting heaven to countersign and implement it: Death in the Field of Honour!)

The panel thus indicates the failing rhetoric of patriotism and religion in the face of reality without directly stating it. Furthermore, on the penultimate page of the book, the depiction of a soldier holding up a shirt stained in the middle by blood recalls the image of Christ on Veronica's veil, suggesting that the *vera icon* of the twenty-first century is a bloody, amorphous form clinging to a filthy shirt.[40] The motif of the toppled, suffering Christ also appears in the last and longest sequence in the book, narrated by the soldier Ducon. The three panels showing Ducon's conversation with the dying soldier alternate between a cross and Ducon's face against a flat, grey background.[41] Representing the fallen man's perspective, the middle panel along with the cross is inversed, which also ties up with the soldier's question: "Qu'est-ce que tu penses d'une religion qui a pour réclame un type à poil, torturé, cloué sur deux bouts de bois?" (What do you think of a religion, the *réclame* of which is a naked, tortured guy nailed to two bits of wood?)[42] Similarly, Ducon's own near-death experience occurs near a tombstone with a cross and a suffering Christ in the background. Ducon's outburst against the atrocities of war begins after the gassing that lands him in the infirmary. This condemnation continues for over twelve pages, in which facts about the mass atrocities of war appear in panels to corroborate the captioned words through war scenes that function as illustrations (rather than contributing further towards the narrative), similar to the images in the comic's first part.[43]

Nonetheless, the differences between the two sections indicate a development towards more sophisticated word-image narration. While the underlying structure of concentrating on the memories of a particular soldier until his death is retained, achronological shifts recur in the second section, merging more sordid details with hallucinatory horror.[44] Coupled with the morbidity of the depictions, the characters' reality and imagination are unsettlingly intertwined, as in the case of the horse with amputated forelegs rotting in the branches of a leafless tree.[45] Six pages later, Ducon encounters the creature again. Seeing how only the head and hind legs of the horse remain, he remarks that "on pouvait faire mal aux hommes et aux bêtes" (one could do evil to men as well as animals), thus indirectly capturing the magnitude of the war.[46]

Other themes and events of the narrative are likewise suggested through the use of indirect, unusual word-image relationships.[47] The panels narrating Soufflot's evacuation due to a self-inflicted injury, for instance, focus on a tank persistently trampling over barbed wire and a dying soldier. Instead of illustrating the details narrated by the text, this conveys the more abstract notion of the war's continuing devastation. In such cases, the images increment the words' field of signification by visually underscoring the massive loss of life in spite of the verbal narrative of survival. Notably, the distance maintained by the images, primarily through their perspective but also through their composition, which is closer to the stasis of traditional prints and illustrations than the dynamism of comics images, is purposeful: in the sequence with the dying soldier in no man's land, the distanced perspective of the narrative reflects the other soldiers' emotional detachment from the dead man whom they must remove from the field at the cost of their own lives.[48]

While the first section's brief narrative protests without generating empathy, the second section is rendered more open through the balanced division of the storytelling between words and pictures, the use of varied, dynamic images, some figuration (notably the crucifix), and the inclusion of references, all of which pave several interpretational paths within the interlaced narratives of the soldiers. This occurs through two main ways: firstly, the more indirect narration dependent on both words and images entails greater reader involvement and opens gaps for different interpretations; secondly, the direct and implied intertextual references, such as those to the General Rebillot, bring in an additional level of reality, whereas the reference to Céline binds the soldiers' stories with other experiences of war in literature and thus expands their scope. However, since war literature is only mentioned in the introduction and the bibliography, the references remain more superficial than in the *Nikopol* trilogy analyzed later where Baudelaire's verses are incorporated in the protagonist's dialogue and the story world itself establishes parallels to Baudelaire's literary and personal context.

While *La Guerre* distributes the actual experiences of the artist's grandfather across several deindividualized lives in order to create a collective biography of World War I, the biographical comics that will now be turned to concentrate upon the lives and works of the literary personalities Saint-Exupéry and Lovecraft, as well as the philosopher Deleuze.

BIOGRAPHIES OF LITERARY AND PHILOSOPHICAL FIGURES
Saint-Exupéry: Le Dernier Vol

Regarding rhythm as the most prominent feature of the *bande dessinée*, the psychoanalyst Serge Tisseron considers Hugo Pratt (1925–95) its master.[49] Traveling extensively, Pratt had worked with the Latin American comics artist Alberto Breccia during the 1950s. Both Breccia and Pratt were members of the "Group of Venice," which included other Italian expatriates such as

Dino Battaglia and Giorgio Bellavitis, who is renowned for his painterly images and expressionistic chiaroscuro.[50] Also incorporating literary figures in his comics stories, Breccia made a short fictional comics series, *Perramus* (with Juan Sasturain in 1983), on the Argentinian writer Jorge Luis Borges.[51]

Saint-Exupéry: Le Dernier Vol (*Saint-Exupéry: The Last Flight*), from 1995, adheres to the traditional, large *bande dessinée* format but has eighty instead of the usual forty to forty-eight pages.[52] The comic is a selective, achronological biography, where dreams, memories, and reality merge within the brief diegetic present of the story. True to its title, the book depicts the writer Antoine de Saint-Exupéry's last flight in which he was probably gunned down by enemy planes. The book preserves the uncertainty of his end, for the plane merely recedes into the horizon in the last panels, with the waning Saint-Exupéry declaring: "La mort c'est . . ." (Death, it's . . .).[53] Beginning on the same day on which he disappeared, the lapse of real time in the story is only twelve minutes, with the passing of each minute meticulously indicated by a laconic caption. Within these twelve minutes, Saint-Exupéry wanders through various events of his past that are evoked by a random word said or thought in the story's present. Always returning to the temporal and spatial locus of the Lightning P38 flying over southern Europe on a midday in 1944, the story shifts to South America to recount Saint-Exupéry's first meeting with his eventual wife, Consuelo, to Spanish Morocco during the war, Egypt, Saigon, Guatemala, New York, Madrid, as well as the clouds themselves. As his disappearance edges nearer, the reminiscences become more and more delusional, eventually transforming into mystical interfaces allowing him to communicate with his lost loved ones instead of only repeating the past. Throughout the comic, the impending doom looms in the form of the German warplanes, becoming increasingly repressive and culminating in their firing, which is interspersed with memories of the Spanish Civil War. It is only when Saint-Exupéry enters a black cloud that the Germans disappear and his final struggle is within himself.

While preserving its characteristic messiness, Pratt's sketchy renderings of the protagonists of *Saint-Exupéry* and *La Ballade de la Mer Salée*, appearing on their respective covers, are revealing portraits. For *Saint-Exupéry*, the random lines are significantly more aggressive since the thick black, felt pen marks, concentrating on Saint-Exupéry's torso and splashed randomly around him, signal the violent end of the book. Similar thick lines characterize Pratt's style in other late works such as *Morgan* (1999). This later style—thicker and messier lines with overemphasized outlines, using some shading but tending towards flatness—is similar to Tardi's newer *Adèle* adventures and comes across as a distortion of the *ligne claire*. Additionally, the drawings are more reduced and flattened than those for the *Corto Maltese* series and the inclination to aestheticize the protagonists is also suppressed.[54]

The dramatism of the earlier stories with the accompanying chiaroscuro is also absent in Pratt's last works. This is largely due to the evocative colors, which, like the arrangement of the book, adhere to a basic, recurrent palette. Brown and blue dominate the two main settings for the book—the desert and the sky—with the vastness of both spheres and the consequent sense of eternity becoming the main motifs. Since the brown of the desert is also reminiscent of the early, brown-and-white photographs from Saint-Exupéry's youth, the color consolidates the theme of memory. Both time and space are molded by Saint-Exupéry's thoughts and emotions. The intertwining memories are thus extrapolated onto the structure itself and the main theme of the story, memory, is consequently incorporated in the flow of the comic. The reader's imagination is given leeway for piecing together Saint-Exupéry's past and speculating over unanswered factors, such as his relationship with Consuelo and the reasons behind the deaths of the Aéropostale pilots.

The multiple levels of significance are accompanied by a simple layout with contrastingly complex transitions of content, such as the subtle shifts between reality and imagination. The comic relies on an expansive page layout with three tiers and generally two panels per tier, which can be classified as rhetorical according to Peeters's scheme since the words are dominant but the images go beyond merely illustrating them and make additional contributions to the narrative.[55]

The radio, which is the most prominent medium depicted in the comic, not only indicates the urgent invasion of reality and signals impending doom but also represents the distanced communication that is considered characteristic of the modern era.[56] Since the first time lapse is preceded by unexpected radio messages, the radio functions as an ambivalent node between reality and fantasy.[57] This is particularly evident during Saint-Exupéry's hallucinated conversation with his friend and fellow pilot Jean Mermoz as he flies to his death because the chaos of radios converges into "Radio Clouds" calling out, "... eh vous deux ... ici radio nuages! Vous êtes perdus!" (... hey you two ... Radio Clouds here! You are lost!).[58]

The main theme of personal memories—which also unfolds on a metafictional level through allusions to the problematics of recounting and thus reconstructing them—is broached by Saint-Exupéry's very first words in the book, where he muses over the last time he saw his mother. Memories, being regularly resurrected in the book, play an important role for both the protagonist and the narration of his story.[59] Exemplifying the metafictional merging of a writer's life with his writings, the Little Prince's appearance signals two other important themes, namely, the infusion of reality with artistic imagination and the intimate relationship between a creator and his creation. The extent to which Saint-Exupéry is the Little Prince, as well as the extent to which the Little Prince is a source of solace for him, highlight the connection between the artist and his work.[60] This also feeds into the complexities of individual identity suggested before Saint-Exupéry's disappearance: as several, identical LP 38's emerge from the black clouds, he exclaims, "Dieu du ciel, mais combien sommes-nous?" (Oh God, how many are we?)[61] Following the witnessing of his friends' deaths, Saint-Exupéry's multiple selves, represented by the planes they fly, evoke the senseless loss of lives and destructive capabilities of the industrial world, and modern society's tendency towards deindividualization.[62]

In keeping with Saint-Exupéry's known experiences, the book is also concerned with the theme of love and its failure. This is introduced early in the story by Mermoz's summarization of Saint-Exupéry's novel *Courrier Sud* (1929) as "[u]n journal intime sur l'impossiblité d'aimer" (an intimate journal on the impossibility of loving), which foreshadowed the theme of unrequited love in *Le Petit Prince* (1943).[63] Marital problems and the conflicting emotions aroused by Consuelo make up the most troubled portion of Saint-Exupéry's memories and thoughts. Although *Le Petit Prince* is mentioned only once in the book, the earlier, heavily autobiographical *Courrier Sud* appears twice.[64] By including these references, the comic functions as a node where Saint-Exupéry's (fictionalized) memories and his writing freely interact.

Pratt's creation of a biography for Saint-Exupéry is apt for numerous reasons. Firstly, both Pratt and Saint-Exupéry were storytellers relying on words and pictures. Although Saint-Exupéry's *Le Petit Prince* resembles an illustrated novel, it is more inherently dependent on its few pictures and their significant placement than typical illustrated books: in contrast to the pictures in most illustrated books, which complement the text without being essential elements of it, Saint-Exupéry's drawings play a role in the story itself. Moreover, as will be shown in the next section, Pratt's repertoire of adventure stories, by unfolding in the first few decades of the twentieth century, employs a contextual framework which is close to that of Saint-Exupéry's life.[65]

As in *Saint-Exupéry*, givens of the human condition, particularly mortality, are also a central concern in *Salut, Deleuze!* but are dealt with in a very different manner with the story being subordinated to philosophical dialogue. Although the biographical facet is insinuated to a far greater degree than any other book discussed here, both *Salut, Deleuze!* and *Saint-Exupéry* demonstrate the potential of abstracted drawing for narrating and visualizing profound ideas, opening up interpretational possibilities while creating distinctive aesthetic atmospheres.

Salut, Deleuze!

Salut, Deleuze! (1998) is a collaboration between Jens Balzer (b. 1969), the literary editor of the *Berliner Zeitung* who is also associated with the Arbeitsstelle für Graphische Literatur at the University of Hamburg, and the artist Martin tom Dieck (b. 1963). Their interest in comics theory is evident from the special issue of the literary journal *Schreibheft* edited by them.[66] Tom Dieck belongs to the group of artists who have recently earned considerable recognition in Germany and abroad through various promotional ventures such as comics festivals, exhibitions, as well as the regular publication of brief comics in newspapers, most notably in *Le Monde diplomatique*. Accounting for their self-reflexive comics, Balzer and tom Dieck regard words and images as paradoxical channels of expression whose constant tussle lies at the core of comics, making the medium essentially modern but also complex:

> Durch ihren zusammengesetzten Charakter besitzen die Comics eine Affinität zu Überlagerungen, Mehrdeutigkeiten und Vexierbildern. Aus diesem Grund sind sie in einem ursächlichen Sinne *modern*: ihre Zerstreutheit ist das Wahrnehmungsbild einer unaufhebbaren Unruhe. Sie sind Teil einer Ästhetik, die das Bild vom Ganzen nur in der Disharmonie kennt.[67]
> (Through their composite character comics possess an affinity to layers, multiple meanings and visual riddles. It is because of this that they are *modern* in a causal sense: their dispersed nature reflects an insurmountable restlessness. They are part of an aesthetic which reveals the image of the whole only through disharmony.)

This disharmony makes room for openness through the disjunctions between the panels as well as between words and images which create greater room for interpretation. Although *Salut, Deleuze!* is followed by *Neue Abenteuer des Unglaublichen Orpheus [Die Rückkehr von Deleuze]* (*New Adventures of the Unbelievable Orpheus [The Return of Deleuze]*, 2001), the sequel is unannounced in *Salut, Deleuze!*[68] The only hint is that the *Neue Abenteuer des Unglaublichen Orpheus* is also the title of the first book read by the ferryman, who repeatedly transports the comic's protagonist Deleuze to the other side.[69] First published in the form of short stories in the alternative comics magazines *Boxer/Strapazin* and *Lapin*, the first collected edition of *Salut, Deleuze!* was issued in French by Fréon in 1998. Since the story forms a sequence of nine pages that is repeated five times, each nine-paged set is ideal for being published separately. In doing so, it creates what Eco calls an "aesthetic rhythm," comparable to the obvious, deliberate repetition in *Peanuts*.[70] The story's repetitive structure follows Deleuze as he is rowed across the Lethe by a bandana-wearing ferryman and abruptly ends when he meets up with the trio of intellectuals—Michel Foucault, Roland Barthes, and Jacques Lacan—on the opposite shore.[71] Several citations, mainly from the poststructuralist thinkers, Foucault and Deleuze, as well as other major philosophers, particularly Nietzsche, recur throughout the book.[72]

Instead of presenting an actual event from Deleuze's life, *Salut, Deleuze!* focuses on an event rich in mystery and figurative connotations: death. The structure is a literal embodiment of Deleuze's treatise, *Différence et Répétition* (1968). Foreshadowing the understated figuration in the book, subtle repetition is already incorporated in the form since the frames of the regular, steady layout of four panels per page are mirrored by the format of the quadrilateral forty-nine-page book. This visual rhythm is reinforced not only by the vivid gestures but also by the repetition of actions. Yet, by containing words—and to a lesser degree, actions—that are not always identical, the dialectic between repetition and sameness has been simplified and transferred to the comics medium, whereby the words incorporate the difference in repetitive images that only undergo minor alterations. It is through this variation that the narrative develops and attains a conclusion with Deleuze presumably being left at the other side. *Différence et Répétition* also becomes the main theme of Deleuze and the ferryman's conversations and the book is shown sitting on the ferryman's table.[73]

The story's sequences have the same outline; they open with Deleuze in the indefinite landscape of a deserted roadside, with smoke from a departing vehicle in the background. Amidst abstracted tufts of grass and a clear sky, he remarks to the reader that the place is more beautiful than he had thought. He knocks at the tiny hut belonging to the ferryman—who usually grumbles about Deleuze being late—and after he has placed the money on a table near the ferryman's book, they hurry to the boat. Since it is already night the ferryman urges the philosopher to bring a lantern, an act which symbolizes philosophy's aim of shedding light on the mysteries of human thought and existence. In the course of their conversation, Deleuze has to take over the oars because the ferryman wants a beer. They converse, and the ferryman asks the philosopher for his last words because he collects them. At this point, they are interrupted by Barthes, Lacan, and Foucault, also carrying lanterns and hailing Deleuze from the river's bank. The last page follows the ferryman rowing back to his hut and resuming his reading.

The slight changes within this recurrent outline of the sequences essentially revolve around Deleuze and his conversations with the ferryman, with Deleuze changing opinions as well as actions. The first of these is his exchanging his post-philosophy pastime of growing herbs with the cultivation of rhizomes, which leads him to contradict his earlier declaration on the importance of light since rhizomes can thrive without light. Rhizomes, moreover, directly visualize Deleuze and Félix Guattari's metaphor for illustrating the complexity of contemporary signification systems. Correspondingly, the wild growth at the beginning of the story and the rich vegetation discernible under the water the ferryman rows across to return to his hut in the last panels of the sequences also resembles rhizomes. In the second-to-last sequence, Deleuze perceives the night—visually as dark as ever—as being lighter than before, thereby indicating the proximity of an end and consequently incrementing the allusions to death in the comic. Furthermore, instead of appearing late at the ferryman's hut, he turns up early in the penultimate sequence and is punctual in the last one. Apart from his words, the major change in the ferryman's behavior is reading *Différence et Répétition* in all of the sequences except the first and last ones. By taking up his initial book on Orpheus's adventures, the ferryman confirms his rejection of Deleuze's philosophy.

The structural simplicity in *Salut, Deleuze!* is misleading due to the abstraction involved and the equally significant disjunctions or differences induced by the narrating words and images. Firstly, the repetitive, boundless space aptly conveys the eternity in which, according to the ferryman, they find themselves.[74] Additionally, the panel in which Deleuze and the ferryman trade places on the boat that appears in each of the sequences reflects the concept of sameness, emphasizing the essential commonality—the humanity—of the two characters. As Deleuze tells the ferryman, "Sie sehen nicht das eine ich in den vielen anderen. Die Wiederholung in der Differenz" (You do not see the one I in the many others. The repetition in the difference)[75] and later, "Sie müssen versuchen, dasselbe als Wiederholung zu verstehen!" (You must try to understand "the same" as repetition!)[76] Correspondingly, the two panels that show the hut door containing only a vague human-shaped darkness in its center into which speech balloons of the ferryman and Deleuze's conversation disappear, confound the presence of light and dark and obscure the identity of the speakers.[77] Finally, owing to the minimalist style, only slight modifications of the lines are required to convey changes in expression.

Alternating between minimalist white or black backdrops, all the panels have an impasto texture, discernible through the uneven flecks of white in the night scenes or the shading that becomes more prominent against white backgrounds. The lines are thin and rough, complementing the craggy shapes used for figures and objects. This shaky formal simplicity is relevant because the unsteadiness of the lines can be regarded as being indicative of the abstruseness of the ideas discussed, as well as the surreality of the story world.

The visual contrast between light and dark functions as a trope rich in figuration, as is often the case with similar, monochrome visual narratives.[78] Not only does it play with the associations of light with knowledge or the polarity of life and death but it epitomizes the notion of oppositional pairs and their interdependency. Furthermore, the light forms a halo behind Deleuze when he takes the oars and his conversation with the ferryman really begins, with the halo persisting until Deleuze waves the ferryman goodbye.

While the ferryman represents the average person, trying to comprehend philosophy in terms of his own experience, he is also Charon in a lighter setting, where Hades and heaven have been mitigated to a peaceful nothingness following death. Thus, both space and time in the story's liminal zone are repetitive, but indefinite. As the ferryman declares at the beginning, "Hier unten weicht die Zeit der Ewigkeit" (Down here time yields to eternity).[79] And, instead of the other intellectuals, it is the ferryman who tries to hold philosophical discussions with Deleuze and who ultimately has the last word: "Tod und Differenz sind wohl nicht füreinander geschaffen" (Death and difference are really not made for each other).[80]

The river Lethe, representing the vast space upon which most of the philosophical reflections in the comic occur and where time is frozen to a standstill, is a chronotope encapsulating Deleuze's transition from life to death, the point where he departs from the physical realm to exist purely in the realm of ideas. The Russian literary scholar Mikhail Bakhtin described the chronotope as "the intrinsic connectedness of temporal and spatial relationships that are artistically expressed in literature."[81] Owing to its fusion of space and time, the chronotope is seen as "ideally suited to discussions of sequential art forms."[82]

What makes *Salut, Deleuze!* stand out is its undidactic presentation of philosophical dialogue in a way that transforms the technical and stylistic conventions of comics, such as their use of repetition and black-and-white images, into metaphors. In addition, the dialogic form of the text recalls the classical form of philosophical arguments while echoing Deleuze's own dialogic style, which is most apparent in his lectures.[83]

The focus on the fictionalized and abstracted moment of Deleuze's death enables the narrative to explore broader concerns revolving around the meaning and relevance of Deleuze's concepts. Proving his familiarity with Deleuze's book, the ferryman mentions that his conception of philosophy, in opposition to Heidegger's view of death as the all-consuming, nihilifying fact, is "das Denken zu denken—über das Bewusstsein hinaus, ohne zu verzweifeln und sich auf den Körper zu verlassen" (thinking about thinking—beyond consciousness, without despairing and depending on the body).[84] Correspondingly, at the end of this sequence Deleuze's words are written above the panel showing the ferryman's return journey: "einzig diejenigen Toten wiederkehren, die man zu schnell und allzu tief begraben hat" (only those dead return who were buried too quickly and too deeply).[85] The remaining two return journeys are also captioned by quotes functioning as ambivalent commentaries on the discussions during those journeys. The penultimate sequence ends with Deleuze's words:

> Wenn die Wiederkunft das höchste, das heisst, intensivste Denken darstellt, so deshalb, weil ihre extreme Kohärenz am höchsten Punkt die Köhärenz eines denkenden Subjektes ausschliesst [. . .] cogito für ein aufgelöstes ich.[86]
> (If the parousia presents the highest, that is the most intense thought, it is because its extreme coherence at the highest point obviates the coherence of a thinking subject [. . .] cogito for a dissolved I.)

Combined with the proximity of death, the last line is particularly significant in corroborating a key point voiced by the ferryman and evinced by the minimalist drawing style: the sameness of human beings is reinforced by the ultimate deindividualization of death. Tellingly, the page depicting the ferryman's return in the book's last sequence does not show his hut, but a distant candelabrum followed by two black panels with the second one citing Nietzsche and connecting with the words on resurrection quoted above: "Nur wo Gräber sind, gibt es Auferstehungen" (Only where there are graves do resurrections occur).[87] The indefiniteness of the story's end can also be connected to Deleuze's comment that, in *Thus Spake Zarathustra*, "Nietzsche gave no exposition of the eternal return" and despite being raised twice in the book "each time it appears as a truth not yet reached and not expressed."[88] In addition, the image of the boat disappearing during its passage across Lethe can be seen as corresponding to what Deleuze called "third time" or "this formlessness at the end of the form of time, this decentred circle, which displaces itself at the end of the straight line."[89]

It is significant that, instead of using the traditional forms of philosophical argument, *Salut, Deleuze!* adopts the more accessible comics form. The pertinence of deconstructing Deleuze through comics is twofold: on one hand, the medium's presence functions as a self-reflexive comment on Deleuze's writings, above all *Différence et Répétition*'s concerns with the problem of representation (albeit on a more abstract level); *Salut, Deleuze!* embodies the notion that "the highest object of art is to bring into play simultaneously all these repetitions, with their differences in kind and rhythm, their respective displacements and disguises, their divergence and decentring; to embed them in one another and to envelop one or the other in illusions the 'effect' of which varies in each case."[90] On the other hand, parallel concepts also appear in theoretical writings on comics, already in the literary scholar Pierre Masson's suggestions that comics are based on the dialectic of repetition and difference.[91] Emphasizing the Derridean link, Groensteen also states that on the storytelling level "une bande dessinée est régie par le principe de la *différance*: sa signification n'est construite en totalité qu'au terme de la lecture" (a comic is governed by the principle of *différance*: its meaning can only be fully construed at end of the reading).[92]

Ultimately, it is the ferryman's view of life—asserting the finality of death and all humanity's submission to it—that persists since Deleuze is unable to reply to the ferryman's question, "Glauben Sie, bloss weil in der Wiederholung die Ewigkeit steckt, dass Sie selbst ein Teil davon sind?" (Do you think, just because eternity lies in repetition, that you yourself are a part of it?)[93] As Deleuze's shoulders sink dejectedly, the ferryman concludes his tirade with the sinister declaration: "Ihre Ewigkeit, das bin ich. Ich bin das Ende" (I am your eternity. I am the end).[94] Yet, despite the ferryman's pragmatic arguments against Deleuze's ideas, the end is left open, like most of the comic, for the reader to construe and reconstrue for himself. The ambiguity of the conversations and the intertextual quotes leaves considerable room for reading additional meaning into the comic. The comic's visual simplicity and repetition or rhythm highlight the medium's potential for complexity and openness by rendering the form relevant for the content and, going even further, by dissolving the distinction between form and content.

Unfolding during the passage between life and the afterlife, the comic affirms Deleuze's legacy, his continuation through his ideas. While also merging the life and works of the central figure, the next book presents its well-known protagonist in a way that takes the self-reflexivity discernible in *Salut, Deleuze!* to another level: the facts of H. P. Lovecraft's life are incorporated in a manner that renders them indistinguishable from his own works as well as the comics artist-writer duo's fiction. This time, the artist and the writer are a blatant part of the story being told, with the story's creation and narration occurring simultaneously, offering a metafictional path of interpretation that accompanies the ambiguities of the interwoven stories and the life of their troubled author.

Lovecraft

The German artist Reinhard Kleist's (b. 1970) works often experiment with both visual style and verbal content. Most of his books are one-shots and frequently concern artists from diverse fields.[95] Appearing in 1994, *Lovecraft* is one of Kleist's earliest comic books.[96] It is divided into two parts, with the first section being a fictional biography of the American writer Howard Phillips Lovecraft (1890–1937), who is hailed as one of the pioneers of fantasy, horror, and science fiction. As an originator of "weird fiction," resonances of Lovecraft impregnate the world of comics.[97]

Heralding the comic's creation of a biography through amalgamating fragments from diverse sources, the book begins with a quote from the opening, autobiographical lines of Lovecraft's short story, "The Outsider," narrating his solitary, unhappy childhood.[98] The accompanying collaged caricature of Edgar Allan Poe forms an associative link to the Dark Romantic fiction both authors are renowned for. The first section has been written by Roland Hueve (b. 1962), incorporating Lovecraft's biography by Lyon Sprague de Camp (himself a writer of fantasy and science fiction), as well as the short story, "The Statement of Randolph Carter" (1919).[99] A stage director by profession, Hueve has penned several books, and all of his comics have been drawn by Kleist. The second section contains Kleist's visualization of the short story, "The Music of Erich Zann" (1922). The pages are unnumbered, with both sections encompassing roughly forty pages.

The three-page preface takes the form of a dialogue. After one speaker has described the book as a comic, the other immediately asks about the number of volumes, indicating the rarity of one-shot comics. This section also provides the basic facts of Lovecraft's life. The claim, "Ich habe schon Skizzen und Bilder für Szenen aus diesem Leben. Aber es fehlt noch der Rahmen, der sie zusammenhält" (I already have sketches and images for scenes from this life. But the frame that binds them together is still missing), suggests that the diverse scraps of photographs and drawings in the collages at the beginning are part of a work in the making, rendering the comic permanently processual and, consequently, open to mutating readings.[100] The last page of the preface is another collage comprising of several painted objects pasted upon a black background against which the dialogue sums up "The Statement of Randolph Carter." Randolph Carter is introduced as Lovecraft's alter ego, thus justifying the short story's intertwining with its author's biography. Its metafictional relevance is underscored by the claim that "Randolph Carter" is "eine Parabel für die 'Lektüre' schlechthin" (a parable for "reading" itself).[101] Furthermore, the autofictional tendency of transforming authors into characters is foreshadowed by the dialogue's last lines, which reveal the two voices of the introduction as the writer and artist of the book:

> Wo bleibt Lovecrafts Biographie?
> *Wirst ja sehen.*
> Dann schreib mal.
> *Dann zeichne mal.*
> (Where is Lovecraft's biography?
> *You will see it for sure.*
> Then write it.
> *Then draw it.*)[102]

The story begins with the artist despairingly trying to piece together Lovecraft's biography. At the beginning, three voices are interwoven, characterized by different background colors in the captions: one for Kleist, the other for Lovecraft who claims to be Carter, and the third representing various people from Lovecraft's past. It is this voice of the past that Lovecraft adopts when later, in the graveyard during his mother's funeral, he meets Kleist (who himself begins to slide into the role of Carter). Kleist's complete involvement in the story is a metafictional comment on both the artist's entanglement with his creation and the power of gripping stories that fully engross the reader, often by making him take the protagonist's place. In addition, Lovecraft's insistence on being Carter underscores the autobiographical relevance of the character, which recurs in some of the other analyzed works with biographical and autobiographical elements, such as *Saint-Exupéry* and Moebius's *La Déviation*.

Due to its collaged, mixed media nature, *Lovecraft*'s layout and visual style in the first section recalls Dave McKean's works. Kleist, like McKean, tends to vary his style not only between stories but within them. However, while McKean's images for *Arkham Asylum* are more detailed, Kleist's lighter, frequently painterly panels usually have an unfinished sheen. This rudimentary, unfinished aspect is foregrounded when the narrative focuses on the artist's world, showing him pondering how to portray Lovecraft's biography. The black-and-pink color schemes' association with the inexplicable is established early in the book when Lovecraft's grandfather describes Abdul Alhazred's travels to uncanny faraway times and places through the mysterious book he was obsessed with. This theme of traveling through fantasies created by others—namely, writers and artists, but also musicians—is upheld throughout the book.

Kleist's rendition of "The Music of Erich Zann" contrasts strongly with the combination of biography, short story, and metafiction in *Lovecraft*'s first section. Adhering closely to the original text, "Erich Zann" does not contain any collages, resorting to the more typical tools of comics, such as drawing consistently in heavy black ink and the dominance of dramatic chiaroscuro effects. The occasional use of colors is limited to green for the music notes superimposed on the panels to portray Zann's music and the contrasting red splash representing the indefinable monstrosity that takes over Zann and his room.

In keeping with the inexplicability dominating Zann's story, clear panel divisions are absent through most of the comic. For the few occasions that frames are used, the lines are unsteady. Unsteadiness persists in the visual style: the two characters, the narrator and the musician, along with the spaces enclosing them, are always crooked. Likewise, the faces, rendered in a manner that sharpens the expressionism of rhythmic drawings, like those by Baudoin, are distorted. Once again, form (particularly the visual style and the layout) brings in an additional connotational layer through which the story is re-filtered, and which increases the work's openness.

The expressive visual style complements Lovecraft's impassioned language, particularly towards the climax and subsequent end of the story when Zann is completely possessed.[103] The sight beheld by the narrator upon looking outside the garret window, from which Zann had dragged him away during his first visit, is shown by Kleist as a double page splash in red with a single caption—"Oh Allmächtiger!" (Oh God Almighty!)—on the lower right edge of the page.[104] This adheres to Lovecraft's device of incrementing the affective power of his works by describing the intense impossibility of the horror provoked rather than the terrifying object itself.

The images in "Erich Zann" therefore aptly capture the story's tone and atmosphere. For both words and pictures, it is not complexity alone but the incorporation of comprehensible levels of meaning that brings in openness, which is further incremented through the symbiotic but suggestive word-image relationships. As *Lovecraft* proves, the signifying potential of ambiguous images can be effectively exploited on the level of content, as well as technique, especially when it functions figuratively.

While the next comic, *Mariko Parade*, tells its story in a relatively more conventional manner, it also utilizes the evocative power of the meaningful, stylistic variation of images. Authorial presence and the concept of a book-in-the-making are likewise major concerns, offering another perspective for interpreting the work that is linked to the main story. Furthermore, since both comics reveal the process of their making which ends with the stories themselves, *Mariko Parade* and the first section of *Lovecraft* are chronotopes of themselves: their spatial extension corresponds to the temporal progression of the narrative's coming into being. In *Mariko*, however, the ambivalence between fact and fiction is housed in the personal lives of its creators.

AUTOFICTION IN THE *NOUVELLE MANGA: MARIKO PARADE*[105]

Published in 2003, Frédéric Boilet and Kan Takahama's *Mariko Parade* covers 188 pages and is issued as part of Casterman's *écritures* series.[106] Tellingly, *écritures* has dimensions close to the B5 format usually employed for trade paperbacks. Originally favored by the underground comix, the format is also common for many comics adopting the book form.

Born in 1960, Boilet is a French artist active since the 1980s. His works often use realistic drawing styles and periodic, jumping transitions recalling film stills or photographs. During his sojourn in Japan between 2001 and 2008, he became more active as a manga artist or *mangaka*. Takahama, born in 1977, has been publishing since 2001 in the pioneering alternative manga magazine *Garo*, which targets adults and often contains comics dealing with serious subject matter.

Hinting at the cinematic affiliation, Takahama describes the *nouvelle manga* as a "manga d'auteur."[107] For Boilet, idealistically, the *nouvelle manga* sets itself apart from the commercially established genres by being accessible for everyone, regardless of culture and age group.[108] The term, *nouvelle manga* (originally *manga nouvelle vague*, which referred not only to the cinematic movement but also the *nouvelle bande dessinée* or the recent, alternative *bandes dessinées*) was coined by Kusumi Kiyoshi, editor of the monthly art magazine *Bijutsu Techo*, to describe the multifaceted nature of Boilet's works: graphically affiliated with the *bande dessinée*, they employ the narrative style of *manga*, with the themes and tone recalling alternative, art-et-essai French films.[109] A comparison with Boilet's earlier, pre-Tokyo works like *Le Rayon Vert* (*The Green Ray*), from 1987, with its more sensationalist, rapidly paced arrangement of perspectives and cases, highlights the change in narrative pace and mode in his *nouvelle manga*. However, in order to extend the phenomenon to a global scale, Boilet applies the term essentially to its content. According to him, the *nouvelle manga* attempts to bridge the distance between readers, creators and editors, and aims at being a universal comic about the everyday, which can be autobiographical or fictional, or both. The employment of manga as a feminine noun, in deliberate disregard of French grammatical conventions, also differentiates it from mainstream Western comics, which usually attract a male audience. Correspondingly, a large proportion of the manga exported to the West continues to be action-oriented, even though the genres taken up by manga are far more diverse in Japan.

One of Boilet's means of nearing reality is to incorporate both the physical attributes and the personalities of his models. The first book created through such a collaboration with his model was *L'Épinard de Yukiko (Yukiko's Spinach)*, which was published in 2001 by Ego Comme X, a French publishing house that inclines towards experimental and personal comics. Although *Mariko Parade* is *L'Épinard*'s sequel, Takahama's involvement as Mariko introduces a reciprocal artist-model-character nexus because this time both protagonists are based upon the two artists narrating the story. *Mariko Parade* incorporates the brief strips and illustrations that Boilet based on his muse between 1998 and 2002.[110] These six brief sketches are ensconced in the main story, "La Ballade d'Enoshima," drawn by Takahama and co-written with Boilet. The transitions to Boilet's briefer, older episodes are usually triggered by the protagonists recalling those works, or by parallel aspects between the present and the past. Sometimes the episodes are also visually present in the panels from the main story creating a gradual, visual transition into the older works while including the reader in the protagonists' experiences. Besides incrementing the diversity of styles in the comic, these brief insertions also provide insight into the characters' past: "Les Petites Vestes de Boilet" (Boilet's small jackets), for instance, narrates Boilet's first encounter with Yukiko, his lover and model, who becomes Mariko in the second story.

The story begins with Mariko and Frédéric on a train to Enoshima, with Mariko rereading *L'Épinard* and remarking that she has changed. The first of many self-reflexive references to the making of a comic based on their lives appears when Frédéric shows her the drawings he wants to include in *Mariko Parade*, which leads to "Les Douze Chimères du Zodiaque" (The Twelve Chimeras of the Zodiac) episode with its series of twelve drawings forming full-page splashes.[111] After their arrival in Enoshima, Frédéric takes over the narration. Written across the panels, his thoughts, which alternate with his conversation with Mariko in the diegetic present, transform the panels into stills.[112]

Most of Boilet's brief episodes (with the exception of "Les Chimères") were originally published in Japanese as manga. Nonetheless, by depicting only the passage of time and being devoid of violent action and major events, those episodes, like all of *Mariko Parade*, stand apart from mainstream manga. Their unsensational realism aims at generating the reader's empathy, in the vein of television series and films with "soft" themes that are, at least superficially, closer to the lives of their viewers. Additional details, such as Frédéric's enthusiasm for the French footballer Zidane or his reference to

John Lennon and Yoko Ono as the "dieux du love and peace," situate the story in a world that is relatable for adult readers.[113]

One prominent feature from manga in *Mariko Parade* is the abundance of exaggerated emotions conveyed by caricaturized figures. These appear in both Boilet's and Takahama's panels, although the manga tendency of shifting to childlike stick figures is more perceptible in Takahama's story. Appearing in individual panels, they usually lighten an intensely emotional moment or illustrate one of the protagonist's sarcastic thoughts.[114] On the other hand, a similar sketchiness also characterizes the depiction of past events, with the very first instance recalling Boilet photographing Mariko for his illustrations in "Les Chimères."[115] As indicated by the regular inclusion of the environment, aspect-to-aspect transitions typical for manga abound in the main story by Takahama. In contrast, Boilet's panels are usually involved in simpler action-to-action or moment-to-moment transitions that preserve most of the elements of the previous panels.

Individual variations in style aside, the comic's two distinctive drawing styles are those of Boilet's episodes and Takahama's "La Ballade." The contrast between the two artists is discernible in the panel that appears soon after Frédéric begins his overhead narration in "La Ballade" and asks Mariko whether she remembers the first time they met, which is accompanied by a single panel by Boilet showing Mariko admiring his sketches of her.[116] Boilet employs a rotoscopic style that hovers between photographs and realistic drawing, exuding the spontaneity and realism of a snapshot while emphasizing its drawn essence. In lieu of clearly defined lines, Takahama relies more on grey shading that suggests features instead of outlining them. This is suitable for the comic's intimate theme and emotionally intense atmosphere. Moreover, the grey tones make the panels look as if they had been drawn on faded photographs, thus creating a link to Boilet's style. The tendency of manga to become sketchy and cartoon-like is relegated to backgrounds, which are frequently formed by hasty, vague lines, emphasizing their rough, drawn essence and alluding instead of imitating.[117]

Weaving the past—which is indicated by Boilet's visual style—and following the emotional ups and downs of the protagonists' relationship, the practical aim of the trip is fulfilled by Frédéric at the end of the story: alone, he makes the desired cover picture for the completed book that was supposed to be an authentic token of their relationship. It was this desire for "de vraies photos [. . .] pas seulement des documents. Des photos qu'on pourra garder" (true photos [. . .] not only documents. Photos that one can keep) that made Boilet use his analogue camera during the trip.[118] The cover image, which is also *Mariko Parade*'s cover, shows Boilet lying down in the sand next to an outline of Mariko's figure, who is wearing a *yukata* (summer kimono) with hydrangeas. This drawing-photograph crossover asserts the sense of transience in Frédéric and Mariko's relationship that permeates "La Ballade."[119] Nevertheless, it simultaneously affirms the power of images and their ability to preserve and resurrect memories, much like the slides at the beginning of "Les Ampoules" (The Blisters) that reenact Mariko's performance for Boilet in spite of his absence at the actual event.[120] Hence, while exemplifying the comic's reference to other media, the photographic element also enhances the story's theme of transience. Since both of these aspects are not blatantly stated, it is up to the reader to choose the possible meanings and connections that not only complement the main story, but can also become part of it.

One of the comic's most prominent tropes are hydrangeas, which embody transience while also alluding to the two artist-protagonists' disparate backgrounds through the different cultural connotations attached to the flowers. The insertion of such figurative language takes advantage of the fact that readers have the freedom to read the book at their own pace and muse over its contents. Originating from the realm of literature, tropes are relatively rare in comics and other popular fiction due to their temporal and cognitive demands. Yet *Mariko Parade*'s very first panel is a close-up of hydrangeas. In the course of the story, these flowers establish themselves as the quintessential motif of the book, signifying the changing emotions of the two protagonists and their different cultures.[121] The Japanese symbolism attached to the flowers is only clarified towards the end by the landlady of the guesthouse who, in response to Frédéric's remark that the flowers have changed since their arrival, points out that hydrangeas change color when in season because of which for the Japanese—in complete contrast to the Europeans—hydrangeas stand for inconstancy and indecision. Ultimately, the flowers end up signifying the transience of Frédéric and Mariko's relationship, their becoming more distant. Corresponding to the change and uncertainty embodied by the flowers, the comic does not have an unequivocally happy ending, but a more tentative, realistic one.

The faint reflection of Mariko engrossed in *L'Épinard de Yukiko* on the first page of *Mariko Parade* reveals that the hydrangeas are seen from a train window. Although most likely not a reference intended by the artists, the train in the story seems to function as Foucault's *hétérotopie* or heterotopia since "c'est un extraordinaire faisceau de relations qu'un train, puisque c'est quelque chose à travers quoi on passe, c'est quelque chose également par quoi on peut passer d'un point à un autre et puis c'est quelque chose également qui passe" (it is more of an extraordinary bundle of relations than a train, for it is something through which one goes, it is also something through which one can move from one point to another and moreover it is something that itself goes by).[122] Being a place of incessant change, the train in *Mariko Parade* suggests the transience of emotions and foreshadows a change in the protagonists' relationship.

Likewise, the cemetery, which becomes prominent in the second half of the book, is another kind of *hétérotopie* with darker connotations: "Les cimetières constituent [. . .] 'l'autre ville', où chaque famille possède sa noire demeure" (the cemeteries are [. . .] "the other city" where every family has its dark abode).[123] Already during their first walk on the island, the cemetery had caught Frédéric's eye.[124] And, aptly enough, while the cemetery escaped Mariko's sight, Frédéric noticed it at a time when, troubled as always by a sense of uncertainty, he was thinking about the eventual end of their relationship. Later, however, when they pass through it to get to a small, secluded beach, the cemetery underscores their closeness.[125] Thus, although the cemetery amalgamates Frédéric's dread of a breakup and the feeling of being too old for Mariko, it also gives him ambiguous reassurance, especially during his last day on the island, when it plays a role in inspiring the cover photo by reinforcing the motif of hydrangeas, which had also been placed on several graves.

Notably, both themes of transience and self-referentiality are emphasized by the allusions ensconced in the visual techniques. The album is mostly in black-and-white. In "La Ballade," color is used exclusively for the hydrangeas in the last few pages to highlight the changes the flowers undergo.[126] The gutters are kept black throughout the book, even though the interstices in Boilet's episodes were originally white. Although artists such as Pierre-Yves Gabrion have already used black gutters (in *L'Homme de Java* from the 1990s, for instance),[127] the shading in "La Ballade" enhances the photographic connotations of the gutters framing the panels through softening the edges of the images. While Takahama frequently employs such gutters in her other books, including *Kinderbook* and *L'Eau Amère* (*Bitter Water*), they are slightly thicker and consequently more dominant in *Mariko Parade*. In "La Ballade" such gutters give each panel the appearance of a snapshot, making the book resemble a photo album of memories and consequently preserving the reference to the possible, actual lives of the artists. Every action occurring in the diegetic present immediately becomes a part of the past, recorded in the book and accentuating the sentimental mood and the processual nature of the comic. This predominant visual style complements the action because Frédéric spends most of his time taking photographs of Mariko not only for his art but also in a desperate attempt to preserve cherished moments. Owing to its nuanced lighting, "Histoire Presque Sans Paroles" (Story Almost Without Words) gives a similar impression. While the thin panels with moment-to-moment transitions in Boilet's other sketches also recall photographs (as in "Les Petites Vestes"), Takahama's panels, due to their atmospheric nature, have the appearance of more personal recollections.[128]

As mentioned above, one of the main reasons behind transforming the author into the protagonist is to generate a more authentic effect. Stories like *Mariko Parade* consequently stand apart from mainstream comics due to the piquant possibility of being true and their proximity to ordinary life. Since the comic also narrates its own making, metafiction and self-reflexivity are intertwined, bringing in openness through the media-awareness that is generated.

The book's several visual references to photography and film, ranging from rotoscopy to the techniques familiar to the fine arts, such as mixed media and painting, are also significant because they reflect comics' links and differences from other media. Although allusions to film and photography were discernible in Boilet's early works as well, they involved the more basic, familiar employment of drastic perspectives and panel layouts in *Rayon Vert*, with rotoscopic drawing becoming more dominant after his move to Japan. In addition, typical cinematic conventions that are common to most comics and manga (the pioneering mangaka Tezuka, after all, had been inspired by Disney animations) are used throughout the comic by both artists, particularly for perspectives and transitions. These include the alternation of *en face*, single shots of the two protagonists during their conversations,[129] and close-ups that intensify intimate moments and also increase the involvement of viewers/readers, as during Mariko and Frédéric's second night on the island or the moment of their parting.[130]

However, as indicated by the original term of *nouvelle manga vague*, some similarities with the French New Wave are discernible that are uncharacteristic for comics or manga. The focus on Mariko during some of their talks gives the impression that Frédéric is holding the camera—even a film camera in the case of continuous panels. Thus, beginning with the structure itself, the story is marked by the *auteur*, or more precisely two *auteurs* with their characteristic visual styles. Along with the arrangement of the panels, the monochrome but atmospheric tones in the main story also recall films. The dimmed ambience in Takahama's night scenes, for instance, is evocative of films, contrasting with the clarity that comics usually thrive on.[131] Additionally, the main narrative's measured pace is comparable to the *nouvelle vague* or the New Wave's preference for real time. That the story itself is in the making, laying the process of its creation bare, is yet another similarity. Likewise, the shifts to Boilet's episodes, as well as the flow of the episodes themselves (particularly "Les Chimères," "Les Petites Vestes de Boilet," and "Les Ampoules"), recall the discontinuous jump cuts favored by the New Wave.

On a related note, the *nouvelle manga* also illustrates the commonalities that exist between experimental comics and the *nouveau roman*. Alain Robbe-Grillet, who wrote about the general traits of the New Novel, also collaborated with such New Wave directors as Alain Resnais in movies including *L'Année Dernière à Marienbad* (1961) and *L'Immortelle* (1963). Far from being a theory unified by a set of principles, the New Novel is "an exploration" through which authors try to bring out hitherto ignored possibilities of the medium and focus upon the process of becoming.[132] This also holds for *Mariko Parade* and other comics indulging in experimentation.

Yet, while borrowing techniques from, or referring to, other media, *Mariko Parade* also underscores the uniqueness of its images through their unusual arrangements and renditions, highlighting their relative freedom and constraints, as in the case of the color seeping in the toned, black-and-white images for showing the change in the hydrangeas towards the end of the comic.[133] The comic consequently exemplifies how the potential of word-image narratives is constantly being explored and extended, thus calling for analyses that account for a variety of media traditions, extending from the purely visual and literary to mixed media, while accounting for possible cultural nuances.

The comics discussed here display a variety of fictionalized biographies and a corresponding diversity of means via which they are incorporated into comics. The biographies can be grouped under two main types: those incorporating aspects or memories from the artists' own lives, such as *La Guerre* and *Mariko*, and those retelling the stories of literary and philosophical figures, such as *Saint-Exupéry* and *Salut, Deleuze!* The tension between fact and fiction is prominent in all of the comics, leading to openness when used suggestively or figuratively, as in the case of its self-reflexive thematization, which, through underscoring the presence of the media transposing the events (*Mariko*, *Lovecraft*) contributes towards openness. This tension can be partially traced to the nature of pictures and, above all, caricatures, which, for all their distortions, are grounded in reality and facts. In addition, many of the comics illustrate different possibilities for generating openness through experimenting with visual and narrative techniques to create ambiguity and thus entice the reader to look further (as with the collages in *Lovecraft*, or the intertwining of Saint-Exupéry's biography, memories, and fiction).

Differences from the stereotyped notion of comics are already apparent in *Contract*'s focus on adult life and the packaging of the stories in book form. Just as autobiographical aspects of Eisner's life permeate *Contract*, references to the artists' personal lives can also be found in the works analyzed in the coming sections, even though they are subordinated to other concerns as in the case of *Le Voyage*, where autobiographical hints remain in the background of the main character's surreal adventures.

Already the graphic novels that are traced back to the underground comics of the 1970s often contained autobiographical or autofictional material, such as Justin Green's *Binky Brown meets the Holy Virgin Mary* (1972). Also partially autobiographical were the woodcut novels from the early twentieth century including, for instance, Frans Masereel's *Mon Livre d'Heures*, which is discussed later in this book. Even today, most of the widely acclaimed comics or graphic novels are rich in autobiographical details, such as Art Spiegelman's *Maus* and Marjane Satrapi's *Persepolis*, both of which adopt the allusive potential of abstraction to enhance their emotional density in lieu of turning to elaborate artistic techniques. While *Salut, Deleuze!* also uses the figurative potential of abstraction, it does so for broader philosophical concerns. As suggested at the section's beginning, themes based on biography and memory acquire potency and even a certain, false sense of authenticity due to the indexical nature of images, which is enhanced by the distinctive visual style of each comic. As further underscored by the comics in the remaining sections, the signifying potential of the style brings in additional connotations in more open works.

CHAPTER TWO

Adventure and Superheroes

The epic roots of adventure stories or thrillers are traceable from the *Odyssey* and *Iliad* to the medieval romances. The early instances of Western European literature, the *chansons de geste*, narrated adventures with larger than life heroes and their equally remarkable deeds. These key works of literature amalgamate several functions—ranging from creating and preserving a collective consciousness to instruction and entertainment—that continue to play a dominant role in cultural productions. Larger than life, ageless heroes, comparable in varying degrees to the knights of medieval romances, are to be found in the first three comics in this section (*La Ballade de la Mer Salée, Arkham Asylum, Sandman*), which recount only one of their protagonist's many adventures, but which are not part of a long-running series. That several stories with the same protagonist continue beyond the comics analyzed here can contribute towards openness since the range of adventures attached to the character flesh out his world, while being dispensable for the actual story being told by these comics, which remain complete on their own. Given that the portrayal of characters in the comics analyzed here often unfolds through allusions to the characters' psychological states instead of direct descriptions of them, interpretational work from the reader is called for.

As in the previous section, the more recent works can be seen as expanding and intensifying the potential for openness discernible in the earliest comic, *La Ballade*'s encapsulation of its story in book form. *La Ballade* is followed by *Arkham Asylum* and *Sandman: Preludes and Nocturnes*, which overturn the conventions of the typical superhero comics that have flourished in America since 1938 with the advent of Superman. Although *Arkham* and *Sandman*, like *Le Voyage*, the last comic analyzed in this section, also contain elements of fantasy, their presence here is based on the predominance of the adventure in which the protagonists are involved, since all of them undertake a difficult journey or quest.

Given that the journeys in *Sandman*, *Arkham*, and *Le Voyage* unfold on both psychological and physical planes, these comics also demonstrate the preference for incorporating psychological themes, which has incremented in comics from the mid-1970s onwards on both sides of the Atlantic. In addition, *Arkham* and *Sandman* exemplify the increased intricacy and even a kind of poetry in storytelling within the superhero genre, whereas *Le Voyage* brings out the visual lyricism of sequentiality and surreal art imitating gestures. *Arkham*, one of the most intricate works analyzed here, generates openness through the visual layers incorporated within each panel, the complex characterization and story structure, as well as references to other works and ideas (which, however, are at times too obscure or esoteric to contribute towards opening the comic). In *Le Voyage*, the adventure unfolds in the internal and external worlds of the protagonist, and is conveyed through a lyrical variation of the monochrome, formulaic style of comics. The openness discernible in the latter three comics, which is generated through pertinent, often experimental visual styles, figuration, and intermedial references, expands on features already discernible in *La Ballade*, such as its cohesive story, inclusion of literary references, and the insertion of some ambiguity in the characters and images.

Hugo Pratt's *La Ballade* is possibly the earliest consecutive comics adventure story to be published and widely distributed. Although most of the works analyzed in this book contain full-length stories that attain some kind of a resolution, the extent to which the stories told are inscribed in a series reveals their proximity to the formulaic, commercial tendencies of mainstream comics. Being part of a series, however, does not automatically have a negative impact on a story's openness since openness depends on the extent to which the story is complete and independent of the next installment in the series.

A NAUTICAL ADVENTURE: *LA BALLADE DE LA MER SALÉE*

In his obituary for Pratt, Umberto Eco mentions that creators of stories that attain mythic proportions need not be brilliant writers but they need to resurrect archetypes through their prototypical characters.[1] Given that myths are long-lived, whereas literature is constrained to temporal tastes, the very archetypal quality of characters such as Corto Maltese and Superman is the reason behind their prominence in the collective consciousness. There is, however, a difference between the myths of yore and those of contemporary popular culture, which is explained by Eco as follows: the influence of the novel, its tendency of telling new untold stories with identification potential and character development is balanced in popular culture against the mythic character's immutability and predictability.[2]

Pratt created successful comics series for journals in Argentina, Italy, and France. Bearing in mind his literary preferences and itinerant lifestyle, it is not surprising that he also created a *bande dessinée* version of Robert Louis Stevenson's *Treasure Island*. Corto Maltese's debut adventure, *Una Ballata del Mare Salato* (*The Ballad of the Salt Sea*), was originally published in the late 1960s in the Italian comics magazine *Il Sergente Kirk* between 1967 and 1969. It appeared in the French daily newspaper *France-Soir* as *La Ballade de la Mer Salée* between 1973 and 1974, only to be published a year later by Casterman as a comic book. Covering 116 pages and recently issued as part of Casterman's series for "les grands romans de la bande dessinée," its length is more than double that of conventional comic albums.[3] Its format in this series is likewise slightly larger and broader than that of most *bandes dessinées*. Although comprising of adventures, based on the timeless motif of *l'érrance* or wandering, Corto's world stands apart due to its strange mix of real worlds with imaginary ones: "Évoluant toujours aux frontières de contrées aussi évanescentes que précisément décrites, Corto, gentil *desperado* à la triste figure, n'a pas son pareil pour nous perdre dans des espaces-temps où régnent magie" (always evolving at the borders of regions that are as evanescent as they are precisely described, Corto, charming *desperado*, melancholic figure, does not have an equivalent for immersing us in the space-time where magic reigns).[4]

Corto Maltese is a vagabond sailor of mixed origins, born in Malta and sailing across the world. Although most of his adventures unfold during the First World War, the war is essentially a background or contextual element. He makes his debut in *La Ballade*, in November 1913, tied to a raft in the middle of the Pacific Ocean when he is discovered by Rasputin, an old acquaintance and a pirate answering to the mysterious Monk headquartered on the hidden island of Escondida.[5] Although Rasputin looks like his historical namesake, his only similarity to him is a cruel, unpredictable, and deranged nature. In *La Ballade*, Rasputin has the good fortune to stumble on two other castaways, Pandora and Caïn Groovesnore, who are members of a wealthy family from Sydney. The story revolves around the two children's struggle to return home as they fall into the hands of different groups with conflicting interests. Corto, the Melanesian Cranio, the Maori boy Tarao, and the German naval commander Christian Slütter are the few people who are sincere towards the young adolescents throughout the story.

Pratt's drawing style is animated by casual, dynamic lines. There is ample use of shading and some realistic detail for his figures, depending on the scene. Comparable to Milton Caniff's style for *Terry and the Pirates*, which had greatly influenced him, Pratt's drawings retain a distinct, unfinished quality. Temporal and locational markers are accurately—though necessarily with some simplicity and abstraction—presented with Pratt's usual visual lyricism.

Although slight changes in the appearances of the main characters can be attributed to the carelessness of the typical fluid, often rushed style of comics, in Pratt's case they also complement specific moments in the story.[6] The abundant action is conveyed through the visual dramatization of bold viewpoints and chiaroscuro.[7] Gory details of the many deaths are, however, avoided. Although Caniff's influence remains discernible, it is difficult to pin down Pratt's characteristically individual style, especially since his travels familiarized him with several international trends. Rather than the harder American styles, Pratt's drawings recall the freer pencil of the major Franco-Belgian currents departing from the *ligne claire* (such as Underzo or Jijé's École de Marcinelle styles) and, above all, the art of Alberto Breccia. Influences of the heavily Americanized *fumetti* are also discernible. While Pratt's rough lines are harmonious with the hurried incompleteness of the images in many adventure comics (even though their characters and settings are usually drawn with considerable realism), his style is also particularly apt for Corto's context, for depicting the rough, unpredictable life of those at sea. The strong interplay between light and shadow also serves to obscure aspects that are unclear for the characters themselves.[8] Subsequently, Jacques Samson's description of Breccia's untidiness and incompleteness as heterogeneous plasticity—which makes his works processual and perpetually mutating—is also applicable to Pratt's images.[9]

The prevalent dramatism and exotic settings of the book are established in the first panel, which shows a Fijian catamaran on unsettled waters as the native deckhands see the Groovesnore children. Well-knit and straightforward, the story is interspersed with unexpected twists, but the hero perseveres through all hurdles, frequently with unbelievable luck and skill. Although its outbreak is relegated to the background, the First World War becomes more prominent in the course of the story, having direct consequences upon the character's lives, which climax in Slütter's death at the hands of the English. The story nonetheless has a happy ending because, by immortalizing him as a hero who died for his principles, even Slütter's execution is redeeming.

The songs of the sea, sung by the Maoris as well as the Melanesians, weave in and out of the narrative, bringing in not only an audible dimension to the story, but also commenting on it. Besides the natives' chants painting the aural atmosphere, environmental elements, such as the coconut palms and the seagulls, also form motifs through their—at times strategic—recurrence. The relationship between the words and images is kept at its simplest to enhance the smooth narrative flow.[10] The grid is likewise regular: the panels are arranged in four tiers per page, with two or three panels per tier. As always, short panels speed up the action, whereas the longer panels draw more attention to themselves and usually include distance or wide shots that show the setting. Since such panels are frequently unframed when depicting the ocean, they underscore its vastness. Likewise relying on cinematic conventions, conversations unfold through alternating shots of the speakers, as well as two-person or group shots. The frequent change of angles and viewpoints strengthens the sense of persistent activity. Despite the narrator's limited words, his rapport with the reader is assumed, as when Slütter re-enters the story and is introduced as "notre vieille connaissance" (our old acquaintance).[11] This is one of the simpler means commonly used by comics to include readers. Hence, apart from the expressive visual style, which becomes suggestive on certain occasions, the more typical comics tools facilitating unambiguous narration are used.

Series of voyages, with each voyage leading to a fresh adventure, along with the setting of unexplored islands, have been recurrent structural elements for adventure tales since the Greek epics. The island is also a familiar situational prototype in literature and popular culture, serving as a place where characters acquire a deeper understanding of themselves and their place in the world. Thus, Cranio informs the newly landed Japanese troops that the island was once taboo for the natives and was used for the initiation of young men into magical practices. The island also functions as a secluded microcosm that indirectly comments on events unfolding elsewhere during the turbulent years from 1913 to 1915. Furthermore, like the train and the cemetery discussed above in *Mariko Parade*, the boat was also a heterotopia for Foucault who described it as "la plus grande réserve d'imagination [. . .] l'hétérotopie par excellence" (the largest reservoir of imagination [. . .] the heterotopia par excellence).[12]

Additional significant visual motifs include the many seagulls, which can be seen as symbolizing the ideal of personal freedom and by extension, the itinerant, pacifist Corto.[13] The seagull is also related to the darker solitude and regret symbolized by the pointlessly killed albatross in S. T. Coleridge's famous poem, which is cited by Caïn.[14] Moreover, the seagulls often express the story's emotional atmosphere.[15] The bent palm trees likewise allude to human fate being molded by the winds of fortune. Introducing the situation in the very first panel, the Pacific Ocean persists, visually as well as verbally, throughout the book. Witness to all of the drastic twists in the story but remaining unchanged itself, its characteristic capriciousness being eternal, the ocean is a chronotope embodying the story's flow.

Though an adventure like many other popular comics, the story breaches multiple thematic issues, including the unpredictability of fate personified by the ocean, as well as despotism and its parody through the Monk and Rasputin: the pomp and ceremony accompanying the Monk is travestied in Rasputin's attempts to become king and the wearing of a ridiculously large fruit crown.[16] Through his attempts at camouflage and self-erasure, the Monk also illustrates the issue of lost or transformed identity. Caïn's question, "Qui êtes-vous Moine?" (Who are you Monk?), is followed by a silent panel with a medium shot of the Monk. A long shot encapsulating the silhouettes of both against the unobstructed horizon reveals his answer, "Qui sait . . . laisse tomber Caïn" (Who knows . . . let it be Caïn).[17] Although it is suggested that the Monk is an uncle of Caïn's who disappeared, the Monk's identity is never revealed.

The homonymy—or, to use McHale's term, partial trans-world identity—of the main characters is an effective means of embedding intertextual space and further opening up the work.[18] According to Eco "the mere mention of [. . .] mythical characters opens up a whole new field of suggestions for the imagination."[19] Such references offer the possibility of linking the characters with their other literary and mythical counterparts. Stemming from different myths, Caïn and Pandora are proverbial prototypes of the selfish, destructive capacity of humans. Though these tendencies exist in the two characters, they also reflect the ongoing war itself.

Literary references are present in the comic from the beginning; the panel introducing Rasputin shows him reading Bougainville's *Voyage Autour du Monde*.[20] Notably, when Caïn quotes from Coleridge's "The Rime of the Ancient Mariner,"[21] he selects a passage that reflects the protagonists' conditions and the commencing war in the background:

Alone, alone, all, all alone,
Alone on a wide wide sea!
And never a saint took pity on
My soul in agony [. . .]

The many men, so beautiful!
And they all dead did lie:
And a thousand thousand slimy things
Lived on; and so did I.[22]

Towards the end of the book, the concept of heroism is brought to the foreground by comparing the characters' trials and actions to those of the epic heroes. For instance, watching Corto say goodbye to the vessel that brought him to Escondida, Caïn likens him to Jason alone with the Argo in the forest.[23] Through such references to literary, mythical, and historical stories, Pratt's adventure comics contain some room that allows for further interpretation. Furthermore, proving the influence of the cinema—especially the film noir of the 1940s—Pratt, like Eisner, is a skilled manipulator of chiaroscuro, particularly for exploiting its dramatic potential; in the comics considered here Pratt also makes use of its potential for creating ambiguity.

Having looked at a long comics narrative, its use of visual motifs, references to other texts, and ambiguity (mostly on the visual level), it is now time to examine the additional possibilities of openness in comics generated through greater experimentation by the next generation of artists and writers.

THE SUPERHERO UNDONE: *ARKHAM ASYLUM*

Born in 1960 in Scotland, Grant Morrison began writing for comics in the late 1970s, starting with the short-lived experimental comics magazine *New Myths*. He is known for bringing in a distinctive edge to popular American superhero series, including DC Comics' *Animal Man*, *The Justice League of America*, and *Superman*, as well as Marvel Comics' *The New X-Men* and *The Fantastic Four*. He has also initiated his own series, such as *The Invisibles* (1994–2000). Born in 1963 in England, the artist Dave McKean's work as designer, photographer, and painter leaves a strong mark on his comics. Exemplifying McKean's fusion of art and design, his pages for *Arkham Asylum*, like the panels arranged within them, are often detailed compositions, incorporating a variety of artistic techniques, such as painting, drawing, and collages. As emphasized by the Vertigo series editor Karen Berger in "Changing the Face of Comics," her afterword to *Arkham*, the comic was made before the onset of computer graphics technology and thus entailed considerable involvement from the artist for the making of each panel.

Issued as a one-shot in 1989 and "recommended for mature readers," *Arkham Asylum* covers 216 pages, with the main story running 128 pages and the subsequent script kept unnumbered, which is common to many comics and can be seen as rejecting the linearity and order imposed by paginated books. The comic's subtitle, "A Serious House on Serious Earth," quotes from the last verse of Philip Larkin's poem, "Church Going," expressing the bitter sarcasm seeping through most of the comic which unfolds in a lunatic asylum:

> A serious house on serious earth it is,
> In whose blent air all our compulsions meet,

Are recognized, and robed as destinies.
And that much never can be obsolete,
Since someone will forever be surprising
A hunger in himself to be more serious,
And gravitating with it to this ground,
Which, he once heard, was proper to grow wise in,
If only that so many dead lie round.[24]

While complementing the comic's caustic tone, Larkin's poem also hints towards the metaphorical scope accorded to the asylum, especially its role as a microcosm for the real world. This emphasis on the fine lines between the real and unreal, madness and sanity is maintained throughout the comic.[25] The accompanying psychological concerns show how comics can succeed in conveying nuances of character through suggestions rather than descriptions.

The protagonist trapped in *Arkham Asylum*'s layered verbal and visual content is none other than Batman. One of the numerous superheroes created during the Golden Age of comics from the 1930s, Batman remains popular to the present, starring in several blockbusters and acclaimed graphic novels, such as Frank Miller's *Batman: The Dark Knight Returns* (a four-issue series from 1986). A billionaire exploiting his athletic capabilities and aided by high-tech gadgets, Batman is one of those superheroes who lack supernatural powers but achieve the extraordinary through the sheer extension of material possibilities. His creators, the artist Bob Kane and the writer Bill Finger, had been inspired by characters such as Zorro and the Shadow. In complete contrast to the bright tights and capes of other superheroes, darkness was a part of Batman's costume and—to a limited, varying extent—his character since the beginning. In *Arkham Asylum*, the darkness of Batman's personality becomes the narrative's focal point and is complemented by greater visual obscuration than usual. Persisting essentially as a shadow, Batman's face is never shown. His creation of a superhero alter ego and the consequent dehumanization is attributed to a childhood trauma, which is brought to the surface by his adventure in the asylum. Such realistic character portrayals, where the polarities of good and bad are subdued, render characters more ambiguous and approachable to their readers.[26] In contrast to Batman's somber form, depictions of the Joker in electric shades of green, blue, and red explode across the page, complemented by a distorted, magnified face with bulging eyeballs and equally exaggerated physique. Having transformed one of Batman's main enemies into a transvestite, Morrison claims that the Joker's attitude in *Arkham* mocks pop icons such as

Madonna and Marilyn Monroe. However, like many of Morrison's allusions, this is not obvious. Since the connections between the allusions are also not always discernible, the full potential of those references is not exploitable. Thus, the comic, while being open, is not as open as it could have been had all of its references been less obscure.

Of all the villains, Two-Face has undergone the greatest degree of alteration, changing from a vicious enemy to an indecisive, nervous wreck after being deprived of the scarred dollar coin that had helped him decide. Visually, however, it is Clayface who has been drastically transformed to personify the extreme of filth and disease. That the first narrator in *Arkham*, Amadeus Arkham, had not appeared in a Batman adventure before brings in a fresh perspective.[27]

The double-page collage in between the comic's opening credits describes the work as a passion play, "[a]s it is played to-day," containing a Latin-cross floor plan for a church and pictures of rusted nails auguring the Christian symbolism that is conflated with several other symbolic realms in the comic.[28] On the second page, the use of "Icaronycteris (Icon)" as a title for the picture of a fossilized skeleton of the extinct genus of bats, Icaronycteris, signals the recurrence of occult symbols for life, death, and regeneration in the comic, particularly the motif of the scarab beetle. Such symbols, along with the intertextual and intermedial references, make it possible to read further into the story.

The most striking visual aspect of *Arkham Asylum* is the collage. A collaged structure prevails throughout the book not only on the level of the image but also with regard to its insertion; the panels are frequently placed upon a background which in itself is a larger panel depicting action. In this way, two simultaneous happenings are narrated, with the one in the background remaining more obscure, entailing further interpretation and increasing the story's ambiguity. While the employment of background images is common in superhero comics, the collages within and between the panels in *Arkham* create transitions that are often allusive, especially through the use of recurrent symbols, such as the asylum's blueprints. Maintaining the affiliation to superhero comics, the panels are diversely shaped and arranged. A particularly recurrent layout is that of unevenly juxtaposed, thin, high rectangular panels where the thin forms increment the speed of the action, as when Two-Face tosses his coin to decide Batman's fate. The allusive potential of the collaged images contributes towards increasing the comic's openness: the collaged structure creates suggestive connections between panels and superimposes the actions unfolding in the story world with symbolic images, such as the scrap of white lace, referring to Arkham's and Batman's mothers, and the bat itself, which represents the dark thoughts tormenting not only Batman but every one of the asylum's inmates. The juxtaposition of fragmented drawings, paintings, photographs, and collaged objects also enhances the uncanniness of the story, thus complementing the comic's blurring of physical and psychological realities while bringing in additional intermedial and self-reflexive references.

McKean's visual narrative skill is also evident in the framing and perspectives that he uses to imbue Morrison's thumbnails containing the preliminary sketches for the comic with dynamism and suggestiveness. A considerable portion of the storytelling, particularly the interlinking of the various characters and their narratives, is accomplished via pictorial cues, such as the Joker card that Arkham notices on the floor or his mother's lace wedding dress, which is worn by both him and his successor in the asylum, and which reappears as a scrap in several places, including the double page at the end of the comic with Batman's and the Joker's diary entries. Another image established as a motif in the collaged background is the cutoff clock. Besides the obscure symbolism attributed to it by Morrison (who claims that it is part of the vescica piscis shape, which forms the basis of the asylum's architecture), the cutoff clock also symbolizes the comic's mélange of temporalities.

Some figuration—such as the Mad Hatter's layered remark, "Sometimes I think the asylum is a *head*. We're inside a huge head that dreams us into being"—introduces a metafictional allusion that holds for the entire book.[29] Arkham also contributes to the metaphorical implications of the asylum by describing it as "an orgasm, hungry for madness. It is the maze that dreams."[30] Arkham's belief that his (and his mother's) worst enemy was the bat is shared by Charles Cavendish, the doctor in charge of the asylum in the comic's diegetic present. Heavily influenced by Arkham's writings, Cavendish eventually launches a plan for killing Batman, and it is while facing a delusional Cavendish that Batman is pushed to brokenly claiming, "I . . . I'm just a *man*," the universal dimensions of which are underscored by a crumbling Ecce Homo rendition of Christ in the background.[31] These allusions converge to highlight the ordinary, everyman facet of the superhero.

The book ends with what Morrison calls "a visual echo of our beginning," namely, a penciled version of the two chimneys on the asylum's roof, this time incorporating several symbols of the tarot and Egyptian mythology.[32] The inclusion of Anubis, the Egyptian god of the afterlife serves to "identify [. . .] the Asylum as a place of trial and judgment," which is why he also loomed above the Joker when Batman was about to enter the asylum at the comic's beginning.[33] Exemplifying the range of references to other works and their frequently loose juxtaposition, the penultimate page contains one of the many references to *Alice in Wonderland*, used this time to allude to the nightmares plaguing Arkham's daughter.[34] Diverse symbols are thus often meshed in abstruse ways as summarized by Morrison in a footnote at the beginning of his script for the comic:

> The story is woven tightly around a small number of symbolic elements, which combine and recombine throughout, as if in a dream:
> The *Moon*, the *Shadow*, the *Mirror*, the *Tower* and the *Mother's Son*.
>
> The construction of the story was influenced by the architecture of a house—the past and the tale of Amadeus Arkham forms the basement levels. Secret passages connect ideas and segments of the book. There are upper stories of unfolding symbol and metaphor. We were also referencing sacred geometry, and the plan of the Arkham House was based on Glastonbury Abbey and Chartres Cathedral. The journey through the book is like moving through the floors of the house itself. The house and the head are one.[35]

As already mentioned, many of the symbols are difficult to decode, with only a few proving crucial for the story. In the case of Arkham's mother, for instance, a panel portraying her with white dogs on each side of her bed does not easily evoke her link with Hecate. In such images, "the ritual power of the image" promised by Morrison risks dissolution through obscurity. However, even though many of the details described by Morrison are not visualized, since McKean's style obscures more than it clarifies, the visual ambiguity and figuration serve to increase the comic's openness instead of giving in to the obscurity which Morrison's references tend towards.

In his script, Morrison's summary of the intertextual background, ranging from Lewis Carroll and Aleister Crowley to C. G. Jung and quantum physics, also includes contemporary Surrealist filmmakers and animators such as the Quay Brothers and Jan Švankmajer.[36] The latter's work is comparable to the East European artists Franciszek Starowieyski and Stasys Eidrigevičius, who have been a source of inspiration for McKean. Since the script for *Arkham* also recalls those for films, and the collaged scenes are often referred to as montage scenes, comics' proximity to films is once again underscored. Although it is only after reading the script that the complete range of references in the "Feast of Fools" splash becomes apparent,[37] a vaster, more accessible range of visual, intermedial references, which are usually unmentioned in the script are ensconced in McKean's collages, such as the line of écorché heads by Andreas Vesalius that appears when Batman questions the psychoanalyst Ruth's curative methods.

The main characters also embody the story's themes of psychosis and identity and its relevance for modern or postmodern life.[38] It is already evident in Batman's first scene that the self-confident superhero has been replaced by an insecure, traumatized being when he says:

> Afraid? Batman's not afraid of anything.
> It's *me*. *I'm* afraid [...]
> Sometimes I ... *question* the rationality of my actions.
> And I'm afraid that when I walk through those asylum gates ... when I walk into Arkham and the doors close behind me ... It'll be just like coming home.[39]

Not only is the difference between Batman and his villains decreased in *Arkham Asylum* but the focus on their mental imbalance mitigates, or at least nuances, their evilness. Morrison adds in the script that the asylum inmates represent different personal, psychological states that Batman must confront. Hence, besides the symbolic characterization and the multilayered images, another aspect contributing towards *Arkham Asylum*'s openness is its focus on the protagonist's inner turmoil, which plays a key role in the story and unfolds on an allusive level instead of being fully spelled out. While many of the exact references are only unveiled by the script,[40] the broad significance of Batman's quest is obvious in the main story. Also functioning as a psychological journey, this quest blurs the superhero's struggle between good and evil, imbuing absolute values with ambiguity.

In stark contrast to the other works discussed in this book, both *Arkham* and the next comic, *Sandman*, are replete with explicitly violent images which can be interpreted as a legacy of the superhero genre that both authors chose to retain.[41] In his transformation of the Sandman, Neil Gaiman also introduces a more psychological dimension to the story but transposes the tale into a mythical realm.

FURTHER OBSCURATION OF THE SUPERHERO: *SANDMAN*

Born in 1960 in England and currently residing in the United States, Neil Gaiman is renowned for his *Sandman* series, which is also his longest comics series to date. Published between 1989 and 1996, the *Sandman* books helped launch DC Comics' Vertigo imprint, which is known for its alternative comics. Gaiman has also published novels for adults, beginning with

Good Omens (1990), which was co-written with Terry Pratchett. Foreshadowing later Japanese collaborations, Gaiman adapted the English screenplay for Hayao Miyazaki's hit anime *Princess Mononoke* (1997). Most of the *Sandman* covers were made by Dave McKean, with whom Gaiman collaborated on graphic novels such as *Violent Cases* (1987) as well as the TV miniseries *Neverwhere* (1996) and the fantasy film *Mirror Mask* (2005), in which each shot—as with McKean's panels—merges a broad range of media references.

The *Sandman* series reached its conclusion in its tenth volume, *The Wake* (1996), which deals with the aftermath of Dream's death. Supplementary volumes contain tangential stories, such as *Endless Nights* (2003), comprised of seven, independent narratives about the Sandman and his siblings, the other Eternals. Drawn by different, internationally renowned comics artists such as P. Craig Russell, Milo Manara, and Miguelanxo Prado, the volume highlights the autonomy of each work and the collection's diversity. The early *Sandman* volumes are complete stories on their own and do not end on cliffhangers with the promise of resolving them in the next issue, as is the case with many serial works, such as the *Adèle* adventures discussed below. While the artists change frequently, Gaiman remains the main writer for the *Sandman* books.

Like *Arkham Asylum*, Gaiman's *Sandman* is indicative of the eagerness to experiment and dislodge the stereotypes associated with superhero comics. Also an offspring of the Golden Age, the original Sandman—started in 1939 by Gardner Fox and Bert Christman, and taken up by several artists and writers in the course of the years, including Joe Simon and Jack Kirby in the 1970s—attracted only limited success before Gaiman's complete transformation of the character. The original Sandman underwent several metamorphoses, relying in the beginning upon sleeping gas while wearing a World War I gas mask and acquiring superpowers in the later series.

Although he does possess supernatural powers like any other superhero, Gaiman's Sandman is more elusive: as one of the Eternals, who personify universal notions—Death, Destiny, Desire, Despair, Delirium, and Destruction—he and his siblings have several visual forms, freely mutating in concert with the artists' styles. While the naming of characters after abstractions is not unknown in the superhero world, these allusions are usually superficial and rarely mold the narratives to the extent discernible here.[42] The Sandman himself has various names, including Dream and less frequently, Morpheus. By personifying an abstract notion, Dream, unlike Morrison's Batman, is more remote from the reader and possibilities for empathy would consequently have been limited. To prevent this, and much like the ancient gods, Dream has several human aspects, including his indulgence in emotions such as anger, resentment, a profound feeling of loss, as well as a sense of familial affinity to the other Eternals.

The story world itself is hinged between dream and reality where time is indeterminable. These dream realms are chronotopic not only because of their confluence of time and space, but also because of their centrality to the story. Although the narrative focuses on Dream's timeless realm, links between happenings on the spiritual plane and the earthly, contemporaneous world are recurrent, starting with the "sleepy sickness" that takes over the world during Dream's imprisonment at the beginning of the comic.

Unfolding in word balloons and narrative captions, the verbal style switches from poetry to prose. While *Arkham Asylum* builds upon the dubiousness already present in the original Batman, Gaiman's Sandman retains little more than the name of his predecessors.[43] His resurrection of the Sandman involves undoing typical superhero attributes such as double identity, crime-fighting, and special, inimitable weapons. However, instead of simple deletion, the protagonist is transformed through replacing the league of superheroes with a pantheon of fallible gods. Albeit restricted to his realm of dreams, Dream's powers near those of a god. Since Dream does have his dark side—such as the refusal to forgive his former lover, Nada, even after eons—the good-evil division is less polarized, even though there is no doubt that Dream is on the right (or at least neutral) side and contributes towards maintaining order in the world.

Strengthening its intertextual link with previous comics, the protagonist of the original comic book Sandman, Wesley Dodds, is shown in the first episode of the series as a replacement for Dream after Dream's imprisonment in 1916,[44] which provoked the decade-long "sleepy sickness" and which was a mistake, since the wizards were after his sister Death.[45] Like Dodds, Dream wears a gas mask in his first appearance in the series, when he is summoned by the magicians who strip him of his powers; this "helmet" is one of Dream's three treasures (the other two being a ruby and a pouch of sand) the recovery of which is the main aim of the first volume's issues.[46] Having harmful properties that are less bloody and more psychological, the pouch of sand pushes Dream closer to the original Sandman of a folk tale popularized through E. T. A. Hoffmann's horror fantasy short story of the same name.[47] Corresponding to the properties of the pouch of sand, violence in the comic, while often attaining horrific vividness, ultimately unfolds on psychological and metaphysical planes, confounding time, space, and other givens of reality. This allows the stories to be interpreted in several, interlinked registers, functioning as mythical or abstract tales that also allude to the reader's reality.

Gaiman likens his conception of the protagonist to the making of a sculpture, beginning with a basic image that was then chiseled and fine-tuned.[48] Dream's costume was inspired "from a print in a book of Japanese design of a black kimono, with yellow markings at the bottom which looked vaguely like flames."[49] The fragile being clothed in a long coat, which often trails along the floor like a gown, presages that Dream is no regular action figure but will fight his battles on a different level. On the other hand, such a physique is common for many manga heroes. In an autofictional twist, most of the renditions of Morpheus in the first volume resemble Gaiman.

The *Sandman* series adheres to the same trade paperback format as the contemporaneous *Arkham*, and its first volume, *Preludes & Nocturnes*, extends across 235 pages. The first eight issues collected in this volume were illustrated and colored by different artists, beginning with Sam Keith, shifting to Mike Dringenberg, and ultimately Malcolm Jones III, with Todd Klein being the letterer for most of the issues. Contrasting with McKean's collaged cover and separators for the volume, the other artists adhere to the traditional, garish four colors and the realistic, dramatic mode of superhero adventures. Correspondingly, the layout is usually decorative or rhetorical (relying on the interaction of words and images). However, some layouts incorporate figurative elements, as in the last page of "Imperfect Hosts," which shows Abel talking about his relationship with Cain in widespread panels against a plain white background that is splattered with blood.[50]

Already McKean's cover for the first *Sandman* issue eschewed a comics tradition by not including a clear image of the main character.[51] Stating that the first volume's aim was "to explore the genres available," Gaiman links the episodes to a variety of popular genres:

> "The Sleep of the Just" was intended to be a classical English horror story; "Imperfect Hosts" plays with some of the conventions of the old DC and EC horror comics (and the hosts thereof); "Dream a little Dream of Me" is a slightly more contemporary British horror story; "A Hope in Hell" harks back to the kind of dark fantasy found in *Unknown* in the 1940s; "Passengers" was my (perhaps misguided) attempt to try to mix superheroes into the *Sandman* world; [...] "Sound and Fury" wrapped up the storyline; and "The Sound of her Wings" was the epilogue.[52]

The volume is correspondingly rich in numerous references ranging from pop culture to canonical texts which, while often pushing the stories closer to the reader's experience, also increase their interpretational scope. Like the literary references, the crossovers from comics universes are numerous. Arkham Asylum appears in the second issue, and Dr. Destiny is in possession of the ruby, the last piece of treasure that Dream has to recover. Even Etrigan, from the 1970s series *Demon*, appears in "Hope in Hell." Identical to Jack Kirby's creation, the creature hails from King Arthur's legends, according to which Merlin the magician conjured him from the depths of Hell to counter Morgan le Fay. However, since Dream mentions the City of Dis, the reference to Dante's *Divine Comedy* is unavoidable, making Etrigan also stand for Geryon, the beast before the eighth circle.[53] Adhering to Dante's configuration of hell, Dream encounters the Wood of Suicides soon after passing the gates, with the funneled structure becoming evident when he is on his way to meet Lucifer who,[54] echoing Gustave Doré's illustrations for *Paradise Lost*, is depicted like an angel (but also resembles David Bowie, thus retaining the tongue-in-cheek humor of comics). In the epilogues, Dream cites an ancient Egyptian death song, the "Dispute between a Man and his Ba" (ca. 1800 BC) as a paean to his older sister Death.[55] Furthermore, as already foreshadowed in the title "Dream, Dream a little of me . . ." the pop songs that are also incorporated often add ironic undertones.[56] John Constantine (the protagonist of the *Hellblazer* series), for instance, sings the Eurythmics' "Sweet Dreams," when Dream asks him for help with recovering the pouch of sand.[57]

The narrative self-containedness or autonomy of the issues in the first volume along with the suggestively titled segments resembling chapters which, while being familiar aspects of serialized comics (since each comics issue has a different title and not all series end on cliffhangers), also recall the novel's form. Beginning with Dream's imprisonment, they trace his escape and the recovery of his treasures, with each issue usually concentrating on one major task. The difference between these issues and the chapters in a novel is small. Although the epilogue does provide an appropriate end for the volume, it also introduces a new protagonist like any other comic striving for its series' continuation. The other *Sandman* volumes generally follow the same structure of bordering the volumes of collected issues with episodes serving as epilogues and prologues, which is a practical means of making books out of episodically published series.

The mystery surrounding the main figure and his story is a means of opening a text by encouraging multiple interpretations. The *Sandman* comics also exemplify the ability of pictures to concretize unreal spaces in compact forms and bring in their own silent but broad set of allusions and references. Although these spaces are solid and detailed in the *Sandman* volumes, they acquire abstracted nuances imbuing the images with multiple meanings in *Le Voyage*.

SURREAL ADVENTURE: *LE VOYAGE*

Born in Nice in 1946, but only able to realize his dream of becoming an artist in his thirties, Edmond Baudoin's first comic, *Civilisation*, came out in 1981. He has published numerous albums since then, most of which have been both written and drawn by him. The overlap between reality and fantasy is a recurring milieu in his oeuvre, as are major themes ranging from existential concerns to the role of art and the artist's presence in his works.

The story opens in a Parisian apartment with Simon having breakfast with his wife, Marie-Jeanne, and their son, Pierre.[58] As Marie-Jeanne insists that they cannot take their cat with them on their upcoming holiday, the top of Simon's head, which is open, changes, showing the cat reacting, being caged, and escaping, while Simon reluctantly agrees with his wife. Visualizing his psychological state, Simon's open head takes up increasingly horrific forms, which culminate in a pile of skulls during the crowded metro ride on his way to work. That the protagonist feels suffocated by his life is evident, and it only takes a small incident—his coming across a colleague crying over her dead cat—to make him run away from the office and the city. The rest of the book traces Simon's journey through the countryside, his encounters with various people, including Olivier, an itinerant puppeteer, and his friend Marc, a sailor confined to a wheelchair after an accident. Simon, like Olivier before him, falls in love with Marc's sister, Léa, who also has an open head when Simon sees her for the first time. Olivier and Simon end up resolving the awkwardness between them after being visited by Léa's ghost during a night out camping near the end of the comic. The story ends with Simon paying his son, whose memory haunted him throughout his journey, a visit. Throughout the comic, the real and the imaginary continue to interact with, and merge into, one another, like the people and elves in a story told to Simon by an old woman, Fanny, whom he met by chance.[59] Chance itself plays a key role in determining the directions taken by Simon's adventure to find himself.

Working mostly in black-and-white, the sensuous lines of Baudoin's forms echo the fluid, free movements of the contemporary dance that he is influenced by. This is particularly evident in the two pages devoted to Léa's dance for Simon, where the frames are momentarily removed, allowing her movements to take over the page, time and space without restrictions. While such a lyrical usage of the line recalls Matisse, it is more emotionally charged in Baudoin's case and is seen as a means of connecting with the reader:

> Dans *Essai sur le beau*, Töpffer affirme que toute imitation de la réalité est vouée à l'échec. Pour ma part, je me situe plutôt dans l'axe de la ressemblance. Je cherche avant tout à capter l'émotion. Dans ce que l'on raconte, dans ce que je raconte, seule l'émotion est importante, surtout pas ma vérité. Je pense souvent que lorsqu'on lit, on arrive toujours à une situation peu claire avec soi-même. L'universalité serait d'aller au plus précis des émotions afin que le lecteur puisse se les approprier, qu'il puisse y ajouter

la musique qu'il désire. Mais c'est aussi dangereux, car après il n'existe plus de distance entre lui et moi.[60]
(In *Essay on the Beautiful*, Töpffer affirms that all imitation of reality is destined to fail. For my part, I situate myself rather on the axis of resemblance. I try, before all else, to capture the emotion. In what one tells, in what I tell, only the emotion is important, not my truth. I often think that when one reads, one always reaches a situation with oneself that is relatively unclear. Universality would imply rendering the emotions so clearly that the reader may appropriate them, attach the music he desires to them. But this is also dangerous, because after that there is no longer any distance between him and me.)

Baudoin has been one of several French artists to be published by the leading Japanese publisher, Kodansha, and *Le Voyage* was first published in Japanese in 1995. The most obvious Eastern influence is in the frequent aspect-to-aspect transitions, as well as the general minimalism and higher frequency of mute panels. In addition, the inky, flowing quality of Baudoin's lines is evocative of Japanese calligraphy. Unpaginated, the French edition of *Le Voyage* is published by one of the main French publishers for alternative *bandes dessinées*, the artists' collective, L'Association.

Le Voyage forms a cohesive story tracing the protagonist's journey of self-understanding across more than 200 pages. The unassumingly surreal story of Simon connecting with new people, realizing life's possibilities, and finding a better way of living is told through a fairly steady layout of three tiers per page, with one or two panels per tier. Complementing both Baudoin's fluid lines and the subjective nature of the story, the panel borders are never straight.

Along with the cage mentioned above, stars are the objects that appear most frequently in Simon's open head, symbolizing dreaming and the desire to escape the everyday.[61] Baudoin explains that "lorsque je dessine ce personnage au crâne ouvert ce n'est pas anodin. Je sais bien que le lecteur va lire l'état de ce personnage puisqu'il va aussi sentir cet état. C'est cela la création" (when I draw this character with an open head, it is not insignificant. I know very well that the reader will read the state of this character for he will also sense this state. That is creation).[62] The open head therefore expresses the character's mental dilemma and untenability in the mundane reality of bourgeois city life. Besides the several metaphorical connotations of the open head, it also subverts a fundamental rule of drawing people that is rarely infringed upon, even in caricatures.[63] For all their fantastic metamorphoses, open human heads are likewise rare in works by the Surrealists. One exception is Francis Picabia's *Hera* (1928) where, from four heads, the large, all-encompassing male head is still fully outlined, and the other, overlapping visages are partially open. Indeed, Baudoin's drawings for *Le Voyage* share many similarities with the Surrealist movement, including the body's merging with its surroundings and the placing of unrealistic images in everyday settings, which subsequently offer alternative perceptions of reality.

Notably, the comic's last portion is described as an epilogue:

> Ici, il y a un encadré, c'est pour faire une transition. Dans les romans, les vrais, ça s'appelle épilogue.[64]
> (Here, there is a box, it is for making a transition. In novels, the real ones, this is called an epilogue.)

The phrase "les romans, les vrais" is metafictional since it raises the question of the status of comics. It is also in this epilogue that the separation between Simon and his wife is suggested through both visual and verbal metaphors. Pierre recounts a dream where his father was the king of dinosaurs and his mother the president of the world in 3000 AD, because of which they were unable to meet and Pierre had to visit them through a special rocket. As the boy points out that this is close to his reality, the father and son are shown from a distance sitting on a riverbank. This perspective is maintained through four long panels where two barges in the foreground, near each other, cross and part ways, symbolizing Simon and Marie-Jeanne's eventual failure at understanding each other and maintaining a connection.

Images are therefore also used to suggest events and happenings, in addition to psychological states. Being less precise than words, the abstract images leave it to the reader to discern the possible significance of the events as well as the characters. An early instance of the narrative dependence on pictures and visual figuration occurs when Simon asks Fanny about the purpose of life and she tells him that he is sure to know better than her and that he should look at her wrinkles. This is followed by a silent, one-page splash displaying her wrinkled face transforming into a tree. On the next page, both Simon and Fanny are shown with their heads open, from which images of anonymous bodies fly out and merge into one another over two thirds of the panel. As in many other places in the comic, actions and thoughts become indistinguishable.

The book's last page also brings in an apt intertextual comment since a tramp in the park calls Pierre a small prince, consequently evoking Saint-Exupéry's *Le Petit Prince*. While sharing many similarities with Saint-

Exupéry's story, since Simon is also a dreamer navigating through various terrains and trying to overcome a failed relationship in the background, the major difference between the two lies in the more blatantly psychological and personal nature of *Le Voyage*. Several events in the comic are rendered symbolic, interpretable as actual events unfolding in the story world while also functioning as metaphors representing the characters' thoughts. Furthermore, the theme of a mental journey is reflected by the title's possible reference to Charles Baudelaire's eponymous poem which takes up the Odyssean trope of the voyage. Tracing a despairing trip away from the ennui of the real, the poem evokes a spiritual journey comparable to that of Simon.[65]

Along with the literary allusions, stories within the main narrative reveal metafictional and self-reflexive elements that are relevant for the main story's themes. The first story-within-a-story is Olivier's tale of Pitou, "un homme qui a des étoiles dans la tête" (a man who has stars in the head) and who resembles Simon. As in all three instances of ensconced narratives in *Le Voyage*, the images focus essentially on the story's narrator and events, while the backgrounds are blank or minimalist. Such bareness of the panels, which limits them to the narrator's words and the main figures, echoes the simplicity of the verbal narration. The de-emphasizing of place and context in these stories imbues them with a sense of universality.

Of the books discussed in this section, *Le Voyage* is clearly the most subjective and possibly the most moving, in a way that is comparable to some of the fictionalized biographies discussed above. In contrast, the other comics do not aim at connecting with readers at such an emotional level, although they do contain identification potential through their interweaving of the broad themes of loss, memory, and identity. All of the last three comics—*Le Voyage*, *Arkham*, and *Sandman*—are open since they encourage the reader's cognitive involvement by offering several interconnected paths of interpretation, often through narratives and techniques that stand apart by avoiding or altering expectations regarding storytelling and the comics medium itself. Already *La Ballade* offers a complete story that, in avoiding the requirement of indefinite continuation imposed by seriality, is imbued with greater autonomy. Although part of a miniseries, the first *Sandman* volume is a structural whole: Dream has completed the quest for recovering his treasures, and although there is "[m]uch to restore, much to create," that would lead to very different stories, as the story being told is completed.[66] Notably, the mainstream visual style in *Preludes & Nocturnes* intensifies the divergence of the *Sandman* stories from other superhero comics since the genre expectations suggested by the style are subverted through the stories being told. A similar trend of altering or even subverting conventions to create openness can be traced in the comics incorporating elements of noir, black comedy, and crime, which will now be explored.

CHAPTER THREE

Noir, Black Comedy, and Crime

As already indicated by the comics of Eisner and Pratt, the influence of film noir is prominent in comics, especially visually through the use of chiaroscuro or black-and-white contrasts for dramatic effects. Adding to these technical aspects, the works described and analyzed in this section incorporate noir features in their stories, especially their narration and characterization. While noir visualization and varying degrees of black humor are discernible in all four works, elements of crime and mystery genres[1]—particularly the basic requirement of crime as a key element of the plot—are discernible in three of them (*Adèle Blanc-Sec*, *From Hell*, *Tohtori Futuro*).[2] The last two comics analyzed here, *Kuolema Kulkee Kintereillä* and *Tohtori Futuro*, parody the superhero genre by incorporating noir features and black humor, while also playing on the superhero genre's close interaction with science fiction and crime.[3]

The first two works discussed below, the *Adèle Blanc-Sec* series and *From Hell*, take up and alter the conventions of crime and mystery to varying extents. The strikingly different ways in which they achieve this enables one to gauge how degrees of openness are generated in comics. Incorporating multiple levels of meaning, *From Hell*'s story is ambiguous and calls for a discerning reader. Being both structurally complete and flexible, it is also narrated in a more allusive manner than the *Adéle Blanc-Sec* adventures.

The other two, more recent books, *Kuolema Kulkee Kintereillä* and *Tohtori Futuro*, incorporate noir aspects such as antiheroes and existential situations. While *Tohtori Futuro* subverts crime fiction, *Kuolema*'s subversion extends to science fiction clichés. Such subversion is self-reflexive in that it offers alternative ways of looking at familiar codes. In both comics, expectations, particularly those regarding the protagonists' heroism and the nature of the conflicts, are undermined. Going one step further than the ambivalent superheroes discussed in the preceding section on adventures, *Kuolema* and *Tohtori Futuro* depict the worlds of mortal superheroes deprived of their powers and reduced to a banality that is nonetheless imbued by the unreal. Black comedy, which is already rudimentarily present in *Adèle*, acquires a more self-reflexive facet in these two comics since they allow caricature to play with and comment on genre conventions.

Although *Kuolema* also subverts formal conventions of comics narration by frequently using indirect word-image relationships and transitions, it is essentially *From Hell* that merges a large range of tools that contribute towards openness in comics. These tools include varied word-image connections, expressive, ambiguous visual styles, the inclusion of self-reflexive, metafictional elements and intermedial references, as well as figuration. Important for openness is the embedding of these aspects in a structure that, while refusing to commit to a single narrative path, is not as loose as that of the *Adèle* series. Nonetheless, elements of parody—albeit not exactly subversion—are already discernible in the *Adèle* books.

THE EXTRAORDINARY AND NOIR: *LES AVENTURES EXTRAORDINAIRES D'ADÈLE BLANC-SEC*

Matthew Screech sees both Moebius's and Tardi's works as exemplifying Lecigne's *nouveau réalisme* in comics,[4] a darker trend which, in breaking away from the principles of the *ligne clair*, indulges in the undifferentiated depiction of thoughts, dreams, and actual events, whereby reality and unreality in the narrative are only distinguishable through context.[5] Screech differentiates between two kinds of *nouveau réalisme*: the first is exemplified by several of Moebius's comics (who is discussed in the next section) and *La Guerre*, where "the boundary between the real and the imaginary is blurred but [. . .] not erased entirely," and the second is discernible in *Les Aventures Extraordinaires d'Adèle Blanc-Sec*, where fantasy and reality are unabashedly merged.[6]

The first of Tardi's *Adèle Blanc-Sec* adventures, *Adèle et la Bête*, was published in 1976. The series continued to appear fairly regularly until 1985, when the sixth volume, *Le Noyé à Deux Têtes* (*The Drowned Man with Two Heads*), was published. It was taken up again after a hiatus of nine years with *Tous des Monstres* (*All Monsters*) and is published intermittently to date. A movie, loosely based on the series' earlier volumes and directed by Luc Besson, was released in 2010. Recent installments of the *Adèle* series such as *Le Labyrinthe Infernal* from 2007 have been published as albums and in the form of tabloid newspapers, with three sixteen-page issues per comic book.[7]

It is in the later *Adèle* albums that the coarseness of Tardi's line becomes more marked. Similar to the frequency of its publication, time in the series also progresses in gaps, skipping the First World War, during which Adèle remained frozen, and inching towards the 1920s. Although the title of the coming episode is usually announced at the end of each comic, Tardi declares that he never has a concrete plan for its development.[8] Consequently, the stories progress in a whimsical manner, leaving the structure too open to allow the comic to work as an open text: anything is possible in the story, and its interpretation can follow a variety of unconnected paths, much like the *Superman* comics or Ian Fleming novels described by Eco as closed texts.[9] The indefinite seriality is the result of the *Adèle* comics' homage to the *roman-feuilleton* or popular novel. This homage also works as a parody that, to a considerable extent, relies on the dissolution of strong narrative structures.

Establishing the series' visual and literary style, the first volume has the size of a typical large-format *bande dessinée*, with forty-eight pages. Like most of Tardi's books, the story is set in early twentieth-century France (*La Bête* opens in 1911) and centered in Paris. The implausible adventures therefore unfold in the contented ambiance of the Belle Époque, where only the extraordinary could have gone wrong.[10]

Beginning with an exterior view of the Muséum National d'Histoire Naturelle at midnight, the panels on the first page zoom in on a large cracking egg. It is this event, the birth of a pterodactyl, which triggers the story. Set loose in Paris, the uncontrollable prehistoric bird unwittingly causes havoc. The massive reward offered for its capture or photograph attracts Edith Rabatjoie, the daughter of a flailing aristocratic family, to the French capital. En route, she is kidnapped by Adèle, a writer of feuilletons and popular novels, who wants a flying machine created by Edith's father, for which she had already paid in advance, as ransom.[11] Adèle intended to use the machine to save Lucien Ripol, a close friend of hers, who had been wrongly accused of murder.[12] The plot gets increasingly tangled as more and more people with different interests get involved. The creature is eventually shot down by a pompous, fame-hungry hunter who loses his mind when the furious museum paleontologist points a gun at him.

Similar to a popular crime or mystery novel, the comic is full of unexpected surprises and twists, with the atmosphere becoming increasingly dangerous towards the end. Although the story eludes the plausible, it follows the model of detective fiction: the resolution of the mystery occurs only at the end of the book. Exemplifying the red herring device popular in thrillers, Albert—one of Adèle's two male assistants—reveals himself as a traitor and narrates how Edith Rabatjoie made her father's machine resemble the pterodactyl in order to rescue Lucien Ripol from the guillotine so that the police would be forced to arrest the banker's real murderer, Eugène Lobel, who had also killed Edith's brother. Albert then kills Ripol but is in turn shot by Adèle's other assistant, Joseph, albeit not fatally. Albert manages to slip away with the two bags stolen from the murdered banker that Ripol was able to recover. With everyone dispersing with the arrival of the police, Adèle ends up walking alone. She is picked up by a stranger, Simon Flageolet, who reveals that he too is interested in the two bags, which, contrary to everyone's assumptions, do not contain money. The comic ends at this point, promising to resolve the questions regarding the content of the bags and Albert's fate in the next issue. Ending in this way on a cliffhanger, the story remains inconclusive.

The drawings have been rendered in Tardi's distinctive style with its unsteady lines toying with the *ligne claire*'s simplicity and combining it with the dramatic lighting of thriller comics. Fantastic colors and contrasts persist throughout the book, such as the mustard yellow for the paleontologist's assistant Antoine's fantasy about Adèle, and magenta for Ripol's execution scene. To a certain extent, Tardi can be said to have appropriated and accentuated Edgar P. Jacobs's canonical palette and brought in the element of ludicrousness to the detective genre that most of Jacobs's works belong to. The marvelous and the fantastic also overlap in Jacobs's comics, evoking the Freudian *Unheimliche*, especially through the elimination of boundaries between life and death, for which resurrected zombies are the most popular example.[13] Such features caused Fresnault-Deruelle to distinguish between the *merveilleux noir*, which rejected the romantic notions of pleasurable fear, from the *fantastique* or "la subversion de vraisemblable" (the subversion of the probable).[14]

A popular device adopted by Tardi in *La Bête* is the use of newspapers to convey happenings and their impact. This device is not used as frequently as in Eisner's *Contract with God* trilogy and varies between newspaper briefs to hawkers' cries announcing the headlines.[15] The layout used is conventionally rhetorical: although the words are dominant, the narrative unfolds through an interaction between words and images.[16] Nonetheless, the form of the frames often fulfills a more decorative function, as with the partially curvilinear frames enhancing the shape of the depicted content.[17] While also reminiscent of Moebius's comics, such decorative layouts have been in use since the end of the nineteenth century or the beginning of comics as we know them (in *Ally Slopper* and *Little Nemo*, for instance). Even though a diversity of perspectives is maintained, the panels are closely connected and information flows smoothly, without creating ambiguities.

Correspondingly, the narrative captions, like the dialogues, are straightforward. Some of the storytelling burden is also carried by the pictures due to which visual details—such as the label for the pterodactyl egg and its gradual cracking, or the prying Albert outside the Rabatjoie house[18]—also play a narrative role. The visually reinforced ambiguity of identities (between, among others, Albert and Joseph) is not so much a theme but rather a device for generating confusion in the plot.[19] The lack of figurative density asserts the narrative's concentration on the direct portrayal of strange but unambiguous actions.

Although the series is named after Adèle, her character remains somewhat undeveloped. Belonging to the petite bourgeoisie, she incorporates the modernist traits of individualist and capitalist thinking that also prevail over her world where money and power are the principle motives for action. It is in the course of the series that some attributes establish themselves, namely, her pragmatism, self-sufficiency, and tomboyishness. The latter becomes increasingly evident in her appearance: the short, cropped hair and unidealized, matronly appearance of the post-World War I episodes contrasts with her earlier long-haired, slim figure. Reflecting the mentality of the period in which the series was created, during which women's liberation movements were underway, Adèle symbolizes the emancipated female.[20] On the other hand, Adèle's occupation as popular fiction writer is one of the similarities between Tardi and his creation, which is alluded to by the tabloid format used for later issues of the series.

Criticism of incapable authorities—beginning with the policemen in *La Bête* who are unable to resolve the pterodactyl problem—underlies the series and is another commonality with Moebius. Such criticism is more marked in *Labyrinthe*,[21] where the usually neutral narrative voice stating the time and place regards the towers of the Palais de Justice as "sinstres symboles de répression et de farce judiciare" (sinister symbols of repression and judicial farce).[22] This notion is embodied by the presence of a bloodthirsty police commissioner-turned-minotaur and the gangster-like rendition of the new commissioner.[23]

Even though *Adèle* has undergone certain changes over the decades, the series' albums have not become more open. While subversive elements persist in the antiheroes and the mocking of authorities, these aspects are conveyed directly and do not call upon the reader to seek additional meanings. Nonetheless, the latest volume of the *Adèle* series, *Le Labyrinthe infernal*, reveals some aspects that call for further analysis due to their experimentation with format, unconventional characterization, and the inclusion of some subversion, all of which can contribute towards openness when interwoven in a "closed" story structure.[24]

The publication of *Labyrinthe* in tabloid form in three installations underscores the series' affiliation to popular fiction. The new format also accentuates the coarser pictorial style. The palette is noticeably dismal, dominated by gray (the buildings, the Seine, and the sky) with brief spurts of glaring red (usually blood or monsters) and yellow (electric light) to provide contrast. This persistence of garish colors affirms the series' unabashed affiliation to popular culture.

In *Labyrinthe*'s opening scene, Adèle confronts the reader with the following declaration: "Ne croyez surtout pas que ça me fasse plaisir d'être ici!" (Do not by any means believe that it pleases me to be here!)[25] In this extra-diegetic commentary, she grumbles about her situation as a character in wacky adventures and accounts for her long absence. The stronger, de-romanticizing tendency of the later episodes is heightened by the introduction of Brindavoine, the anti-Prince Charming responsible for waking Adèle, who had been put to sleep by her last lover, a scientist hoping to preserve her life in spite of her murder. With his amputated arm and prosthesis, Brindavoine is a reminder of the violence of the First World War, which is a recurrent background element of the later books (reinforced, for instance, by the depiction of an amputee with a Croix de Guerre and the sign "Verdun" around his neck in *Labyrinthe*).[26] Similarly, Honoré Fiat, the illustrator of Adèle's feuilletons, suffers from an incurable war injury, albeit with unrealistic, in keeping with the series' title, "extraordinary," monstrous manifestations. *Labyrinthe* is replete with visual and verbal references to people and events from Adèle's past adventures that are elaborated in footnotes. However, as in *La Bête*, references to works beyond the series are limited.[27] The story itself also resorts to the formula of the previous episodes: the heroine is implicated in some kind of impossible adventure sprinkled with supernatural elements, and the problem is only partially resolved after several twists, which culminate in a climax and several questions that the next episode promises to answer.

Alternating between horizontally or vertically inclined quadrilateral frames and circles as inserts with extreme close-ups of the characters' faces, *Labyrinthe*'s layout is more uniform than that of *La Bête*. Furthermore, the panels depicting ringing phones are worth mentioning because of the aptness of their zigzagged edges for expressing the disturbance caused by the urgent, persistent sound.[28]

Like the ensemble of monsters, all of the gruesome acts, threats, and villains in the series are only half-serious, with Adèle remaining unharmed. This mockingly lighthearted tone is complemented by Tardi's drawing style, which nears cartoonish simplification without fully embracing it. In contrast to *La Bête*, *Labyrinthe* adds the science fiction theme of mutation to the monstrosity that is an indispensable aspect of the series. Calling the police commissioner-mutant a minotaur links it to the mythological roots of the labyrinth mentioned in the episode's title, but these references remain superficial. In keeping with the series mocking tone, Adèle calls the minotaur a cow, correcting her friend, an Egyptian mummy, who described it as an ox.[29] Similarly, while the hand is visually established as a motif, the scope of its connotations for the episode—as a metonym for man's doings, or as a symbol of amputation, for instance—is not mined.

Though the story hovers between dream and reality, the parallel to death and life is indicated by the presence of the resurrected mummy and Adèle's own defrosting. Rare in American popular fiction, this kind of *nouveau réalisme* has exercised considerable influence on Franco-Belgian *bandes dessinées*.[30] On the other hand, noir elements persist both visually and textually through the contrasting flat colors and antiheroes. Although some intertextual play is present through the combination of genres (particularly noir fiction and feuilletons) and elements of parody and subversion are likewise discernible, these aspects are not fleshed out, making the *Adèle* comics closed. The *Adèle* stories and art contrast starkly with the darker, more intricate plot of *From Hell*, with its frequently obscure, ambiguous drawings, rich figuration, and complex structure—all of which allow for several possible, interlinked interpretations, leaving the inconclusiveness of the Ripper case to be construed at the reader's discretion, albeit within the constraints set by the narrative.

NOIR HISTORICAL FICTION: *FROM HELL*

Born in 1955 in Glasgow, Eddie Campbell was involved in the alternative comics scene of the 1970s and 1980s, publishing his own fanzines and actively contributing to independent publications. Before *From Hell*,[31] one of his best known series was *Bacchus*, with which *From Hell* shares many stylistic similarities. Campbell recently created a "meta-memoir," *The Fate of the Artist* (2006), a disjointed collage of text and pictures narrating the artist's relationship to his world and its subsequent transposition to his art. Although currently occupied almost exclusively as a writer, Alan Moore had started out by drawing comics. Born in Northampton in 1953, he became an award-winning comics writer by 1982, going on to create several revisionist superhero stories such as *Watchmen* (1986–1987, drawn by Dave Gibbons). To date, he is regarded as one of the major figures exploring the potential of comics, largely through his critical and poetic stories. Esotericism, in an arguably more concrete form than in Morrison's works, is a recurrent component of Moore's stories, and *From Hell* is no exception.[32]

The comic first appeared as a limited series between 1991 and 1996 in the alternative, irregularly published comics anthology *Taboo*. The collected Knockabout Comics edition leaves out continuous page numbers and is somewhat unwieldy due to the number of pages, as well as its dimensions:

24.5 x 18 centimeters.[33] Subtitled "a melodrama in sixteen parts," the comic's fourteen chapters are bordered by a prologue and an epilogue, and concluded by two metafictional appendices. Emphasizing its contemporary relevance, the comic's central thesis is that "the 1880s contain the seeds of the twentieth century" in aspects ranging from philosophy and art to the sciences and international politics.[34] Officially, the book is classified under four categories: Graphic Novels, Horror/Jack the Ripper, History (of London), and Crime Noir. Also fitting the category of historical fiction—or historiographic fiction, due to its self-reflexive nature and bearing in mind Linda Hutcheon's distinction of events from facts[35]—the novel focuses on the infamous murderer, Jack the Ripper, who was active between August and November 1888.[36] That the case became one of the most notorious in the history of crime can be partially attributed to the confluence of media and political interests of that period, indications of which filter through the story's narration.[37]

An omnipotent third-person narrator is essentially absent from the narrative. This absence is supplemented by a long appendix, where Moore separates fact from fiction for each page, frequently evaluating the verisimilitude of the personages as in the case of the inspector Frederick Abberline, where he points out that "when we know the details of a person's life but not how he or she felt, then we must resort to fiction, unless we are to exclude feelings altogether."[38] Bringing in an element of instability, fictionalization for calibrating the insufficiency of facts is extended to the entire comic because "[a]s with much of the evidence surrounding these murders, the data is ambiguous, a shifting cloud of facts and factoids onto which we project the fictions that seem most appropriate to our times and our inclinations."[39] Consequently, the appendices delineate the process of the book's creation and, in keeping with the behind-the-scenes perspective, Moore also mentions the rare points on which he and Campbell did not agree. However, by placing the explanations—including socio-historical facts and metafictional aspects—at the end of the book as "Annotations to the Chapters," these comments are bestowed with secondary, disposable relevance because the reader is likely to concentrate on the main story. The appendices themselves are not didactic explanations; instead, they provide additional interpretational paths or deepen existing ones. For the later chapters, especially after the ninth one, facts become increasingly blurry even in the annotations. Self-reflexive criticism is also incorporated within the story, targeting, for instance, the sensationalism of the events, as with Abberline's comment after hearing a souvenir manufacturer's sales drive on the historical relevance of his monk-headed walking sticks: "Mark my words, in 'undred years, there'll still be cunts like 'im, wrapping these killings up in supernatural twaddle. Making a living out of murder."⁴⁰ That this also applies to the comic is difficult to overlook, and Moore himself calls it "a form of shamefaced apology from one currently making part of his living wrapping up miserable little killings in supernatural twaddle."⁴¹

Such a relativized mode of narrating history is in itself self-reflexive, mirroring the philosopher Giambattista Vico's understanding of fable, history, and myth as interlinked narratives. Declaring that "fables are histories" and that "memory is the same as imagination," Vico highlighted the fictional essence of history and, conversely, the historical relevance of fiction; the Greek word *mythos*, after all, means "true narration."⁴² Additionally, it is Vico's admirer Erich Auerbach who underscored the difference between clearly delineated and obscure diegeses and characters, with the latter having vaster, more universal signifying potential, which in turn require greater interpretational effort from the reader.⁴³ Correspondingly in *From Hell*, the interweaving of historical figures with mythical and fictional ones generates irresolvable doubt regarding the verity of the story without obliterating the uncomfortable possibility that the story might be true.⁴⁴ While acknowledging that the first victim, Polly's dreams portending her death are fiction, Moore adds that "the individual elements from which it is constructed are genuine."⁴⁵ Moreover, "*From Hell* has, if anything, been more thoroughly researched visually than it has in terms of content. Eddie's backgrounds are, more often than not, precisely referenced shots of the areas mentioned in the text."⁴⁶

Besides the persistent self-reflection, the book incorporates several intertextual references, not only in the quotes opening each chapter but also in the dialogues. The surgeon and prime Ripper suspect, Sir William Gull, talks about the life and work of William Blake and the architect Nicholas Hawksmoor, ancient mythologies, and freemasonry—all of which are not mere citations but are interlaced within the story by being of relevance for its characters and setting.

The 3 x 3 arrangement of panels persists through most of the comic. This simplicity of the layout contrasts with the plot's complex structure, which develops the lives of several characters and only gradually unveils their relationship to one another. While each chapter in the comic and its interlacing is complex on its own, it is more useful to concentrate on the second of the book's two metafictional appendices—which simultaneously clarify and mystify the story—to construe the collaboration of words and images in forming a multilayered but complete whole.

Although the first appendix relies heavily on words, the second appendix narrates through panels, most of which are superseded by narrative captions. Continuing from the background information provided in the first appendix, the second appendix concentrates on the piecing together of the story and its more universal significance. While the tone of this section is more humorous, it ends with a serious remark on the contemporary dismal situation in London's poorer parts. It is here that gull-catching becomes an allegory for trying to solve the Ripper case. This is explained later on by citing a Shakespearean quote that opens Stephen King's *Jack the Ripper: The Final Solution*: "Here comes my noble gull-catcher"; Moore adds that "[g]ull means fool, as in gullible, while gull-catcher means trickster."[47] Noteworthy is the unusual transition on the first page, where the text follows the vertical path of a falling feather at the end of the second tier and simultaneously continues from the tier's beginning, tracing two possible reading paths for the page.[48] Considering that solving the case is likened to catching an indefinable gull, this figurative, productive layout expresses the irresolvable, open end of the case and the comic based on it.

In beginning the string of possible suspects with Walter Sickert, meta-art musings are also incorporated, such as the comment in a panel showing Sickert's portrait of *Mrs Barrett*: "Perhaps this is the purpose of all art, all writing, on the murders, fiction and non-fiction: simply to participate."[49] The discussion of various Ripper stories by famous authors, such as Aleister Crowley, also highlights the dubious aspects of these stories, bringing in metafictionality while also creating doubt and ambiguity. The images accompanying Moore's words are more frequently metaphorical in the second appendix than elsewhere in the book, as with the string of cut-up paper dolls appearing during the narration of the increasingly colorful accentuation of the Ripper tales after the Second World War.[50] Both the writer and the artist are shown in the last eight pages as they explain how they created the novel and underscore the impossibility of solving the case: "Quantum uncertainty, unable to determine both a particle's location and its nature, necessitates that we map every possible state of the particle: its super-position. Jack's not Gull, or Druitt. Jack is a super-position."[51]

Another figurative visual element is the fragment from the main page of the *Illustrated Police News* of 8 September 1888 with Annie Chapman's murder making headlines. Torn at its edges, its miniscule particles metamorphose into leaves floating through the blank space at the lower right end. This not only refers to the prevailing autumn but also Abberline's sentiments as he becomes increasingly attached to a Whitechapel prostitute.

One of the most prominent visual intermedial references is Blake's painting, *The Ghost of a Flea* (1819), which appears at the end of Gull and W. B. Yeat's fictional meeting in the British Museum.[52] This panel portends a later occurrence when—in an anachronistic instant—after seeing Gull's spirit,

Blake sketches the monster in the painting, who represents the soul of a murderous man inhabiting a flea.[53] However, since the amorphous and mutating panels tracing Gull's spiritual flight are steadily drawn from his perspective, his appearance, and his possible identity as the Ripper, is left to conjecture.[54] The page after the meeting in the museum contains another artwork in its panels, this time focusing on a print hanging in Gull's hallway: William Hogarth's *The Reward of Cruelty*, the last of the *Four Stages of Cruelty* (1751) series, which is often seen as symbolizing ritual Masonic murder techniques.

While the comparably esoteric but more unrealistic universe of *Arkham Asylum* is rendered in full color, *From Hell*'s harsh, black-and-white realism, with the recurrent portrayal of blood as black fluid, is far more powerful than a colored version could have been. Aptly enough, this visual style recalls the sketches produced in lieu of photographs in nineteenth-century newspapers and advertisements, which persist in today's court drawings. Other visual motifs include the transformation of stills from the story into metaphorical images, as in the case of a panel showing a cricket ball hitting the wickets as John Druitt, another Ripper suspect and an avid cricket player, loses his job.[55]

Visual prominence and elaborate ideological significance is ascribed to London's architecture, particularly its churches, which in the story concretize the inexplicable and symbolize the conception of a nonlinear constant time that forms an unperceivable fourth dimension, consequently functioning as a chronotope. The link between the churches and nonlinear time is made during the discussion between Gull and fellow surgeon James Hinton in Hawksmoor's Christ Church Spitalfields, where they talk about time as an illusion, with eternity present in each instant, which Hinton's son, the mathematician, C. Howard Hinton, had argued for.[56] Moreover, among the eight disconnected scraps of information opening the second chapter is Guy's question, regarding the possible architecture of history, with both elements, corresponding to the possible facts and Hawksmoor's baroque churches, being variegated in the comic.[57]

Correspondingly, Moore refuses to explain the final portion of Gull's flight and his cryptic last words that appear on a white page: "God . . . and then I."[58] Again, obscurities are left for the reader to resolve but the story maintains a structure of possibilities—such as the possible suspects—that guides the interpretations and renders the work open. One could interpret Gull's last words as expressing the belief that the human mind has the capacity to near the divine, which in turn could function as a meta-reference to imagination and creativity. Yet the answer is far from clear or one-sided, and the ending is consequently open without being inconclusive. While the next comic also has an open ending, it is of a more playful nature.

POIGNANCY AND BLACK COMEDY IN *KUOLEMA KULKEE KINTEREILLÄ*

Born in 1973, Marko Turunen belongs to the contemporary generation of Finnish artists whose comics are attracting international attention. His case also confirms the claim in the *Jahaa!* catalogue on Nordic comics that many Finnish comics artists have been trained in the fine arts:[59] Turunen had obtained a degree in sculpture before focusing on comics. Although he has already published several books on his own, *Kuolema Kulkee Kintereillä* (*Death Lurks Here* or *Death Walks on Its Hind Legs*, 2004) was realized with his companion and fellow artist, Annemari Hietanen (1973–2010).[60] Their publishing house, Daada, has also issued other works that overturn science fiction and superhero clichés, such as the short stories in the magazine *Ufoja Lahdessa* (*UFO Bay*), where *Kuolema*'s protagonists made their first appearance. *Kuolema*'s layout of two equal-sized panels per page and the humanoid—but not completely human—protagonists echo *Pohja* (*Rock-Bottom*, 2003), where Muukalainen recounts his childhood. However, the bright colors in *Pohja*, which correspond to its theme of childhood, are substituted by dark brown and cream in *Kuolema*. These two colors, combined with the thin sharp lines, generate a dramatic chiaroscuro, which, while recalling woodcuts, remains distinct due to its simultaneous allusion to film negatives. This allusion to negatives connects with the protagonist and his friend J-cat, who had set up a photo studio at one point in the past.[61] Aptly enough, the lighting of this two-colored palette is as dramatic as that of many superhero and adventure comics and noir films. However, instead of the trade paperback or the *bande dessinée* format, *Kuolema* has a distinct format—slightly larger than the usual pocket book, and extending over ninety pages.

The distanced narration of facts, with repeated references to the slow passage of time and the nonchalant account of an unusual couple's banal existence, is enhanced through the employment of a typewriter font. The two protagonists only start speaking on the tenth page. The narrative voice, which sticks to plain facts, is accompanied by aspect-to-aspect panel transitions. This avoidance of creating the usual direct contact with the reader is further enhanced by the fact that none of the characters' eyes are shown; extraterrestrial glowing holes in Muukalainen's case, and hidden behind goggles in R-Rautanainen's, they emphasize the characters difference from humans. However, the repeated focus on Muukalainen both visually and through the sharing of his thoughts—particularly after his childhood friend's death, when the narrative voice often merges with Muukalainen's—is a way of creating a rapport between him and the reader. Another way of establishing rapport occurs on the few occasions when his eyes look directly at the reader.[62] Muukalainen's solitary moments are automatically shared by the reader.

The superheroine R-Rautanainen (literally, iron woman) and Muukalainen who, like his name (outsider or foreigner), resembles an alien-embryo hybrid, are not only mismatched in appearance but also by the fact that while R-Rautanainen ages, Muukalainen only grows younger. This runs parallel to the lives of the two artists behind the book; Hietanen died early from a brain tumor.[63] Exaggerating superhero conventions to a ridiculous extent, R-Rautanainen is perpetually dressed in a spandex outfit complete with a gas mask that covers her face, giving the impression of manufactured humanity.

Indeed, regular humans are nonexistent in the book, and the other anthropoid creatures are also mixed, beginning with the concierge or Death who appears in the very first panel and personifies the comic's title. Other strange creatures—including the doctor with a scarecrow's carrot nose and the penguin-headed pair representing R-Rautanainen's parents—underscore the uncertainty and fluidity between real and imaginary events. The beings that are closest to humans in appearance are also the most monstrous in their actions and exist only in Muukalainen's nightmare. Towards the end, however, Muukalainen transforms himself into a similarly monstrous superhuman being in order to change the tires of R-Rautanainen's car, a very ordinary Opel Corsa hand-me-down from her father.[64] Forming an anonymous horde, the men in Muukalainen's dream are the only villains in the book and their act of stuffing R-Rautanainen into a box can be interpreted as victimization, highlighting the situation of the two protagonists as outsiders.[65] However, since R-Rautainen's imprisonment leads to the disappearance of sound from the world, she is eventually released.

Other than the romanticized heroic element, superheroes also incorporate unusualness and abnormality; it is this facet that *Kuolema* focuses on. Equating heroism to dealing with life's basic issues, such as sickness and money, it also stresses the alienation and loneliness of anomalous beings.[66] And although the baby R-Rautanainen dreams of having is a superbaby, complete with mask and cape, the child seems to be inviable, even within a dream, because it almost drowns in its bath.[67]

The use of anthropoid figures renders the representations metaphorical, which is further underscored by the mélange of imagination and reality throughout the book. Since the story is largely focalized through Muukalainen, the absurd visual portrayals of the other figures can also be read as reflections of his opinions regarding himself and others. His alien-like appearance could likewise be a visualization of his internal difference from others. Similarly, the strange appearances of the other characters could express his distance from their world and the inability to connect with them. That Muukalainen's mother is not shown during the couple's visit to her—which is narrated, like several other events in the book, through shots of various pertinent objects, such as her walker—seems to underscore the emotional distance between the son and his aged mother, as well as their loneliness. Isolation remains a glaring element since Muukalainen is frequently depicted alone or with imaginary or inanimate objects, like the stuffed squirrel won through collecting toilet rolls.[68] The final panel in the story shows him with two tiny identical creatures with jack-o'-lantern heads, which—by appearing after a life-sized Lego mechanic confronts R-Rautanainen with his drill—increment the uncertainty of the book's darkly playful ending.

Muukalainen's imagination dominates the entire book, accounting for the fantastic twist given to the real, with the most visually evocative scenes occurring during his moments of suffering, particularly during the heatwave and after his friend's death. Science fiction and superhero genres are therefore not undone through their reversal but through their juxtaposition to everyday material and psychological concerns—all of which probably unfolds in Muukalainen's active imagination. Contrary to the immediate expectations fostered by the visual style, the book's atmosphere is persistently surreal or, given the emphasis on everyday aspects, magically real.[69] This is accompanied by a parodic strain persisting to the very last page, which lists the specifications of Rautanainen's old Opel, the complete opposite of the high-tech automobiles and other gadgets used by superheroes.[70]

Lightheartedness and seriousness therefore coexist in the book: the visual style's mimicking of film negatives bestows a darker quality to the events, which is balanced by the humor of the words and some of the images. A melancholic, poetic tone often creeps in, as in the description of the return journey from the hospital: "17.7 Muukalainen, R-Rautanainen, Raakajätti sekä Kalmankukka ajavat Vääksyyn uimaan" (17:7 Muukalainen, R-Rautanainen, Raakajätti, as well as Kalmankukka drove down to Vääksy to swim).[71] The next page reveals Kalmankukka (dead flower) to be a mutant like Raakajätti (vicious giant), whose skin is prone to dehydration by the lake's water. Both of these acquaintances, who are only fleetingly mentioned, nonetheless allude to the story's main themes through the reference to death in Kalmankukka's name and the allusion to the imperfection and fragility of living beings through Raakajätti's dehydrated skin.

It is the first set of hospital visits and the heatwave that act as a prelude for the news of J-cat's death. Correspondingly, the symbols of death increase, ranging from the skull sitting on the doctor's desk to J-cat's coffin, with which Muukalainen interacts as if it were his childhood friend, reminiscing about their past.[72] The panels therefore do not merely represent a reality infused with fantasy but succumb to Muukalainen's attempt to process the news. The six-page description of their close relationship, which is focalized through Muukalainen, even though it continues to refer to him in the third person, is accompanied by a one-on-one football match where the coffin successfully thwarts all of Muukalainen's attempts to score a goal.[73] While the football-match sequence avoids complete correspondence between the words and the images, the content of the two channels of expression remains connected. In other cases where words and images have no direct correspondence, the images are imbued with connotations that guide the search for possible connections. The sequence narrating the couple's visit to Muukulainen's mother, for instance, begins with two panels showing massive mythical beings watching the tiny car speed by.[74] While one of these beings alludes to the heat wave, since he is surrounded by jagged lines resembling flames, the other points towards the couple's later visit to the aquarium through his amphibious features and water-like habitat.

Dark humor, which is also a part of Muukalainen's character, prevails in the parallels drawn between Muukalainen's struggle to accept the death of his friend and a football match that is, ultimately, lost. Moreover, the entire story allows itself to be extrapolated to existential concerns regarding the human condition and the struggle involved in living and coming to terms with loss, all of which is filtered through wild imagination and grim humor. Much like the superhero comics in the previous section, openness is generated through the subversion of basic genre codes and expectations, which in *Kuolema*'s case include superhero comics and noir popular culture. Furthermore, like the stories and characters themselves, the indirect relationships between words and images, as well as between panels, reject comics conventions and offer considerable room for interpretation. Interpretational possibilities are also increased by the distinctive visual style that is rich in intermedial connotations and relevance for the story.

While the next comic, *Tohtori Futuro*, also focuses on a superhero reduced to ordinariness who faces far more desperate and impossible situations than those encountered by Muukalainen and R-Rautanainen, the comic is less dark and more humorous. Corresponding to this tone, complex devices such as tropes are absent. Nonetheless, by reflecting its stance, the caricaturizing style remains highly relevant for the story.

NOIR ABSURDITY: *TOHTORI FUTURO*

Born in 1958, the artist Jyrki Heikkinen is also a poet. *Tohtori Futuro* (2007) is his third comic book and, like most of his other comics, it was published by Asema. Like many other independent publishers, Asema issues a limited number of copies but publishes a variety of formats. *Tohtori Futuro*'s smaller, landscape format (similar to the one used for *Garfield* and *Peanuts* collections) is common, not only for Asema's publications, but also for Finnish comics in general, particularly the *Moomin* books. Unnumbered, *Tohtori Futuro*'s fifty-eight pages are divided into three sections or chapters of increasing size, with the first page of each chapter bearing an image as well as a summary of its contents.[75] This summary of the events to come can be seen as a travesty of the grand characters and happenings in both literature and superhero comics, the latter being, as Eco points out, heavily influenced by the culture of the novel.[76] While the chapter-like division has affiliations with literature, the division into three parts and the constraining of the narrative voice to the subtitles appearing before each part recalls both films with subtitles and plays, in which the action is classically divided into three acts.

Although the layout itself is fairly steady—varying between one long or two squarish panels in each of the two tiers, with splashes only appearing at the end of the first and last sections—the frame lines are deliberately wobbly. The free-hand drawn impression of the frames complements the drawing style with its shaky lines. The fluid, unflattering rendition of the figures is similar to the work of Heikkinen's contemporary, Ville Ranta. Significantly, this drawing style also makes most of the characters, as well as their surroundings, appear decrepit. Both Heikkinen and Ranta incorporate blatant watercolor washes enhancing the informal, unfinished aspect of their drawings. In accordance with its noir affiliations, colors in *Tohtori Futuro* are limited to the grey scale. Nonetheless, like the drawing itself, which both de-aestheticizes and exaggerates while remaining distinctively individual, the main characters do not merely reproduce stereotypes but play with them, simultaneously shattering the boundaries between the superhuman and the human.

The covers of both *Kuolema* and *Tohtori Futuro* bear an image extending from the front to the back, with Tohtori Futuro appearing on the front and a collapsed Muukalainen at the back of their respective books. While these images do not recur as panels in the book, as is frequently the case in other comics, they aptly condense the comparable, darkly surreal conditions of the two protagonists: Muukalainen lies flat in an unnaturally glowing forest where the thorny, bare trees grow like wires, while Tohtori Futuro is uncomfortably frozen in a transparent sack caught between bulbous tree roots. His raccoon mask, which he wears in the first and last chapters, alludes to the vigilantes superheroes are related to.

Tohtori Futuro's first page introduces the setting as "New Bombay" and depicts an exotic but unromanticized city, the drab surroundings of which are highlighted by the superficially careless quick lines and washes.[77] Futuro is shown in the last long panel of the second page in a decrepit interior matching the external surroundings (which are often indistinguishable in the comic). His only connection to superheroes is the thin raccoon mask he wears across his eyes. It is soon made evident that the alcoholic Futuro has not only lost his power to see into the future but is also confined to a wheelchair.

Futuro's mortality is emphasized not only by his physical weakness but also by his repeated crying out for more time. This weakness is the outcome of an accident that took place in a fertilizer plant in Madras, regarding which Futuro is suspected to know more than he reveals. His moral standing, which is already questioned by the authorities, is rendered more questionable by the end of the first chapter, when he has convinced Morton, one of the few people with inside information about the accident, to place a bomb in the office of the police commissioner, Rawala. Futuro makes sure that Rawala is not in the office by setting up a meeting with him in the mall; it turns out that the bomb, hidden in a dog paperweight, was supposed to kill Morton. This gives the police an excuse to raid Futuro's place. Upon learning of the raid, Futuro, with the help of his assistant Hudson, has no other option but to transform himself; shrinking, Futuro floats away in a capsule before the police can reach him. This extraordinary, absurd event sets the tone for the rest of the book.

The second chapter opens in the Romanian countryside near the Black Sea, thirty kilometers away from Constanța. Hudson has prematurely aged, whereas Futuro remains shrunk. They seek the help of a new character, the shady Publius, who has the technology to reverse Futuro's metamorphosis. Retaining the notion of mortality, it is now Hudson who is told by Publius that he does not have time. Publius's plan of eliminating Hudson is reversed by Futuro's climbing inside Hudson, because of which instead of dying, the two turn into a rat mutant.

In the third and final chapter, the miniscule Futuro is extracted with the help of a New Bombay surgeon, but Hudson ends up confined to the wheelchair after the operation. Although Futuro returns to his normal size, his power of clairvoyance remains lost. It is only when the police, in an attempt to lure Futuro, use electricity to light up the trees outside the city, and inadvertently set fire to the transformer, that Futuro's power is replenished. The same power also leads him to see something he cannot explain—an indefinable, life-giving entity linked to the shrine that he had wanted to visit since his adventure in Romania. Correspondingly, in this last chapter the conversations between Hudson and Futuro have a more philosophical and poetic tone, imbuing the violent mutations undergone by both with metaphorical value. The openly absurd events, such as Futuro's many metamorphoses seem to suggest his progress towards self-understanding.

As in several comics discussed above, such as the *Adèle* volumes, subversion is discernible in the mocking of authorities. The séance through which the police officers seek advice regarding Futuro's whereabouts by questioning a spirit is a jab at the police. Other systems such as science and religion are also mocked, albeit not so directly: a mystical power plays a role in Futuro's recovery and is merged with technological tools, just like Publius's "mega ray," which was responsible for the first metamorphosis and which sat at the site of a holy grave.

In spite of impossible events that are comparable to the *Adèle* adventures, *Tohtori Futuro* is a more self-contained story, since the whimsical, inexplicable twists converge into a conclusion. Instead of the feuilletons that the *Adèle* adventures sought to parody via their form, *Tohtori Futuro* parodies the superhero genre through taking up the human fallibility of the ex-superhero, while retaining, in contrast to such revisionist works as *Watchmen*, an atmosphere of light, albeit bitter humor. In spite of its understated, careless sheen, the visual style remains relevant for the content and suitable for the story's tone, while also, like *Kuolema*, paying homage to comics' inclination towards caricature and the disregard for logic.

Despite their diversity, all four books share noir aspects in both form and content, including dramatic lighting and the emphasis on flawed protagonists, the latter of which is recurrent in noir fiction. While *Adèle*'s seriality, leading to its stories' formulaic nature and loose structure (which remains incomplete without being suggestive) and the limited subversion of conventions and figuration, makes the series a closed work, the other three books, with their non-formulaic stories and the maintenance of a layered structure with interconnected tropes to guide the interpretations, incorporate several features that contribute towards openness in comics. Besides their individualistic styles, the unusual narratives are not only unusual on their own but are also complemented by pertinent techniques. These include the aspect-to-aspect transitions in *Kuolema*, with their deliberately banal foci for twisting the actual nature of the events,[78] the violence of the chiaroscuro, and the bloodiness of the shaky, fluid lines in Campbell's panels, as well as the casual fluidity of both words and drawings in *Tohtori Futuro* disregarding both logic and reality. Although many of the comics discussed here and in other sections contain unreal elements—and indeed, as already indicated, a degree of unreality and fantasy inevitably pervades comics, the ambiguity of which can generate openness as in *Le Voyage*—the following section looks at comics where fantasy and science fiction are the dominant elements and acquire vivid degrees of visuality.

CHAPTER FOUR

Fantasy and Science Fiction

Acknowledging the difficulty of defining the genre of fantasy, even for comic strips, comics scholar Pascal Lefèvre resorts to the broader Anglo-Saxon term of "fantasy" instead of the French "le fantastique."[1] Specifically, Lefèvre turns to the literary scholar William Coyle's description of fantasy as a deeply "subjective world of distortion and illusion," "a mode, a way of perceiving human experience," emerging from the writer's psyche.[2] Of the comics that will be discussed in this section, the *XXe Ciel* series and *Taxi van Goghin Korvaan* best exemplify the conception of fantasy as a mode of perception, while also highlighting the genre's affiliation to Surrealism and the trend of magic realism in Europe from the interwar period (Coyle himself had interpreted the departure from realism as an outcome of uncertainty caused by the perennial threats of disaster).[3] As elaborated later in this section, *XXe Ciel*, like *Arzach* and the *La Trilogie Nikopol*, also incorporates aspects from science fiction.

The comics scholar Jean-Paul Gabilliet points out that while fantasy is often more subtle in European comic strips than in their American counterparts, common aspects prevail that are germane to the nature of comics themselves.[4] For him, the very medium of comics inclines towards "la subversion, l'indicible, l'instable, l'hétérogène, l'hybride, la rupture" (subversion, the unspeakable, the unstable, the heterogeneous, the hybrid, the rupture). These features are particularly suited to comics because "la mixité semble être le principe premier de la bande dessinée: entre écrit et image, rationnel et affectif, réalisme et fantastique" (mixing seems to be the primary principle of comics: between the word and the image, rational and emotional, realism and fantasy).[5] He goes on to link the combination of words and images to the liberation of the signifying system of comics, which generates "des vertus phantasmatiques intenses" (intense fantastic characteristics) since "l'image apparaît entièrement libre de représenter sans signifier, alors que l'écrit l'est moins, la bande dessinée incarne cet hiatus, ce déséquilibre de l'expression, et se tourne comme par magie vers des images et des récits à strictement parler 'non-référentiels'" (the image seems completely free to represent without signifying, which holds less for the text; comics incarnate this rupture, this disequilibrium of expression and turn, as if by magic, towards images and narratives that are strictly speaking "non-referential").[6]

Lefèvre adds that brilliant graphics—and the reader involvement encouraged by them—are defining features of comics in general.[7] Baetens also affirms the bond between fantasy and comics by underscoring their visuality, since the tension in fantasy rests on "[r]efuser de nommer, être obligé de montrer" (refusing to name, being obliged to show).[8] In illustrating these conceptions of fantasy, the comics analyzed in this section often foreground the engagement with reality and its unsteady filtering through various media. Besides the aesthetic appeal of the detailed portrayal of fantasies, it is through the connections with reality and diverse media, ranging from painting to digital technology, that additional levels of significance are inserted in the stories, with some of the comics going so far as to appropriate the structures of certain media in their panels (newspapers, photographs, and the Internet in XXe *Ciel*; and newspapers and film in the *Nikopol* trilogy).

Compared to fantasy, science fiction is a newer, easily recognizable (if also heterogeneous) genre which, like the other genres brought up here, has the tendency to merge with additional, usually popular, genres. Simply put, science fiction is fiction that is heavily influenced by scientific and technological advancements, often unfolding in different eras or dimensions. While having predecessors going as far back as Lucian of Samosata's *True Story* from the second century, the genre's roots are often traced to the novels of Jules Verne and H. G. Wells from the turn of the nineteenth century. "Science fiction" as a term was popularized during the 1920s by Hugo Gernsback's pulp magazine, *Amazing Stories*.[9] Echoing the interpretations of fantasy in comics mentioned above, Paul L. Thomas notes that comics "have embraced science fiction" and that "the medium lends itself to the futuristic and surrealistic nature of the genre."[10] The first three of the four titles in this section contain several science fictional elements, particularly the confounding of space and time, which is shared by all four titles, but which in the first three is coupled with references to technological advancements.

Adhering to a chronological order, this section begins with Moebius's *Arzach, l'Album Mythique*, Bilal's *Nikopol*, and Yslaire's XXe *Ciel* and goes on to compare these works with other popular examples of fantasy in comics to show how the analyzed comics create greater openness. The section ends with Jarmo Mäkilä's *Taxi van Goghin Korvaan*, which blends reality and fantasy to narrate a story about coming to terms with the past and oneself. Mäkilä's comic is rendered open through suggestive images, as well as the narrative's autofictional and allegorical nature, which offers several, interconnected paths of interpretation. Once again, the generation of openness involves undoing some comics conventions, including figurative images and self-reflexivity (primarily through autofictional and media-based concerns).

EARLY FANTASTIC VISIONS, ABSENT NARRATIVES: *L'ALBUM MYTHIQUE*

Prolific and successful since the mid-1950s, Jean Giraud or Moebius (1938–2012) was one of the founders, in 1975, of the publishing house Les Humanoïdes Associés, which is famous for its pioneering adult comics and science fiction journal *Métal Hurlant* (which inspired an American counterpart, *Heavy Metal*). Primarily a fantasy artist, Moebius emphasizes the broad dimensions of his oeuvre; seeking to go beyond the limits ascribed to comics, he calls his works "pantomimes," which was also how William Hogarth described his print series, *A Harlot's Progress* (1732).[11]

Moebius's uniqueness lies in the fact that his works belong to vastly different genres, such as Westerns and science fiction. Suggesting multiple personalities, a theme that he often takes up in his comics, he signed his Westerns as Giraud (or its abbreviation Gir), while using Moebius for his science fiction and fantasy comics. Although his Westerns are extremely successful in France, the artist is renowned for his science fiction works in America.[12] His inspirations include the Westerns from the 1950s, the realistically rendered American comic strips from the same era, along with the classic science fiction of Isaac Asimov, Ray Bradbury, Robert Heinlein, and, most importantly, A. E. Vogt. For Moebius, masters of the art of comics include the playful, polemical Jean-Marc Reiser, the minimalist Copi (Raúl Damonte), and the unscrupulously graphic Willem.[13] Moreover, Moebius's mentor was *Spirou*'s editor, Jijé (Joseph Gillain), who played a vital role in transforming the field of francophone comics by encouraging artistic freedom.

The acclaim accorded to Moebius is essentially for his visual art and most of his renowned series are collaborations with writers such as Alexandro Jodorowsky for *L'Incal* and Jean-Michel Charlier for *Blueberry*. Comprising of science fiction sketches but also including an autofictional episode, *L'Album Mythique* (2006) is highly suitable for revealing Moebius's contributions to alternative science fiction and fantasy comics since it collects the title, *Arzach*, which stemmed from Moebius's "need to breathe new life into mid-1970s science fiction."[14]

The *Arzach* episodes collected in *L'Album Mythique* differ from typical comics due to their avoidance of emblematic features such as word balloons, as well as their reliance on a highly fragmented structure, which renders the stories comparable to postmodern literature and art. Moebius considers each panel to be a work of fine art and ascribes a Surrealist, redeeming relevance to his work by declaring that it allows him to tap into the unconscious. Like

Moebius's other pieces, "La Déviation" (1973) is supposed to be an outcome of his hallucinatory, out-of-body experiences when "[i]nconsciemment, le thème s'est imposé, les images se succédant et s'organisant l'une par rapport à l'autre" (unconsciously the theme asserted itself, the images following and organizing themselves, each one in relation to the other).[15] Through such statements, Moebius not only emphasizes the role of artistic inspiration for comics but also elevates the significance of his comics' images by regarding them as a supernatural mode of communication. In the same vein, he calls his comics apprenticeship an "initiation," invoking Carlos Castaneda's pupilage with the shaman Don Juan.[16] Castaneda's writings also had an influence on a more material, visual level since the aesthetic symbolism of Castaneda's deserts, pervades Moebius's comics, irrespective of their genre.[17]

The *Album Mythique* covers fifty-six pages and is published in the typical *bande dessinée* size. Apart from "La Déviation," it contains the five *Arzach* episodes interspersed with diverse *Arzach* posters. Mostly published within the first year of *Métal Hurlant*'s inception in 1975, the five episodes are loosely connected, usually only by the presence of Arzach, a humanoid alien with a tall pointed hat and unnaturally colored skin, who travels across strange, desert landscapes, often with his two *ptéroïdes* or mechanical pterodactyls.

Already the seven-page "La Déviation," the longest episode in the book,[18] is a sketch rather than a story, and only one *Arzach* episode vaguely builds upon it, while the rest recount isolated incidents, often solely through pictures.[19] This weakly associated content has been clothed in a varied, detailed, and attention-grabbing visual style.[20] Moebius categorizes *Arzach* as a space opera, which for him is not merely a genre "mais une posture mentale où le trait—voisin des gravures du symboliste Max Klinger—est indemné des contraintes qui enfermèrent" (but a mental attitude where the line—close to the etchings by the symbolist Max Klinger—is free from the constraints that cage it).[21] Fantasy in *Arzach* is openly founded on distortions of the known and combines conceptualizations of prehistoric planets with those of mutation propelled by biotechnological advances.

Incorporating the clash between fantasy and an uncomfortably possible reality, "La Déviation" relates the wacky events that befell the Girauds when the author chose to take a different route to their habitual holiday spot of the Île de Ré. According to Moebius, "La Déviation" is a parable for digressing from the norms of society.[22] Being both narrator and protagonist, he dominates the pages, verbally and visually. Even the first page, which is also the title page, toys with reality through its subtitles and footnotes, which paradoxically emphasize and deny the veracity of the narrative by, for instance, describing it as a "documentaire romance" or documentary romance.[23]

The first adventure is an encounter with an earth giant crouching around the artist's car as it hesitates towards the bottom right edge of the page.[24] This leads to an anticlimax on the following page, where Moebius is shown peacefully recounting a distorted episode from *Alice in Wonderland*.[25] The second climax, where the family is confronted by a horde of mutants, is ruptured by an extra-diegetic intervention in which, frameless, Moebius is shown at his drawing board.[26] Massive word balloons on both sides contain informal, retrospective commentary on the incident (combined with references to Moebius's other works, such as *Blueberry*), during which, as Moebius reminds the reader, the interrupted story progresses three minutes, allowing the family to take defensive measures.

The black-and-white drawings are detailed, the figures are portrayed with a considerable degree of realism, and stylization is absent.[27] Confirming Peeters's remark that the productive layout has yet to dominate an entire narrative, only the second page has a productive layout which embodies the narrative by whimsically following the traveling car as it is obstructed by the earth giant.[28] Arranged in fairly regular panels after the third page, the transitions are mostly large action-to-action leaps. The subjectivity of the narrative is indicated not only by the unreal surroundings and the dominance of Moebius's surprised face, but also through the intuitive transformation of images, which unfold like a visual stream-of-consciousness. Where a more regular division of panels persists, some of the panels, by lacking frames and blending into the background, engender tension between the narration and its visual organization through the layout.

Although the sequence of events is a string of action-packed occurrences with limited additional significance, it is accompanied by ironic, critical verbal commentary. Viewed as a whole and in spite of the monologues, the relationship between pictures and words in the sketch is balanced and symbiotic. The excess of dramatic events and the absence of logical links between them due to sheer exaggeration is not merely an indulgence in sensationalism but can also be seen as a parody of conventional formulae, much like the *Adèle* comics.

Although the sketch is too brief to develop the characters, the series of implausible adventures, by virtue of their unreality, highlights the autofictional essence—the mélange of personal facts and fiction—in autobiography. While Moebius does include himself and his family in the story, the verity of the implausible events (the earth giant, the mutant attack) is as dubious as foreshadowed by the story's label of a documentary romance. The only way of nearing the truth is to interpret the story metaphorically. Autofiction also ushers in a metafictional perspective when Moebius is shown in the act of creating, directing, adjusting, or commenting on the narrative. However, in contrast to the visual and verbal references to contemporary reality, the only discernible reference in the sketch to another work is a distorted version of the Cheshire cat episode from *Alice in Wonderland*.[29]

The back cover of the *Album Mythique* contains a recipe for *Arzach* listing the ingredients involved in Moebius's works:

> Un dessinateur humanoïde à pseudonyme,
> quelques ouvrages sur la peinture
> une caisse de romans de science-fiction
> un traité sur la gravure de bois
> un bon kilogramme du champignons du Mèxique
> [...] plusieurs numéros du [...] Métal Hurlant [...] Pilote.[30]
> (A humanoid cartoonist with a pseudonym,
> some works on painting
> a crate of science fiction novels
> a treatise on wood engraving
> a good kilogram of Mexican mushrooms
> [...] several issues of [...] Heavy Metal [...] Pilote.)

The recipe's last sentence declares the main aim behind the series' creation as "chasser les bulles" (banishing speech bubbles).[31] Consequently, most of the *Arzach* episodes are without word balloons and words; their stories unfold through pictures alone. These fantastic, vivid images, however, often remain superficial since their allusions are unguided. Even though the themes of subversion and rebellion persist—which call for a departure from conventions, a move away from the normative mode of thinking—the narratives are too brief and vague to provide a suitable structure filtering and interlinking the channels through which the self-reflexivity of the subversion or the significance of the images could unfold.

Like the phallic forms dominating the structures, the landscapes, and even the protagonist's head, the predilection for contrasting, fantastic colors prevails over all the *Arzach* adventures, although the palette itself varies.[32] Inspired by Jijé's use of subjective coloring for his otherwise realistic Western *Jerry Spring*,[33] Moebius used a similarly subjective palette for his science fiction and fantasy comics, to suggest moods but also to structure the narrative.[34] As with the balancing of black-and-white in "La Déviation," colors are employed in a manner that binds the different panels into a single cohesive whole.[35] Since the majority of the adventures are mute, their visual richness is the chief carrier of the narrative. Besides being attention-grabbing, the exclusive dependence on pictures generates ambiguity regarding the latent content. Nonetheless, this ambiguity is not channeled into possible avenues of interpretation, as it would be in an open work.

Arzach also has an autofictional element appearing in the fifth episode of the *Album Mythique*. Created in 1987, this five-page episode begins with a prologue introducing such visual motifs as a large scarlet block and the complementary color of green for the surroundings, which are repeated on the next page.[36] The V-form is also recurrent, especially in the first two pages, echoing the arrangement of a congregation of *pteroguerriers* like Arzach, which is shown summoning Arzach, or more accurately, Harzach, one of the several homophonic versions of his name. This congregation, however, does not reappear. The V-form is echoed by the pterodactyl's wings appearing on both pages, as well as by Arzach's flapping cloak. This decorative arrangement of the images, interspersed by some text, persists through the next few pages.[37] In this fifth episode, Arzach is the narrator and his words, which appear without word balloons, are linearly arranged and interspersed in the pictures to clarify the story. Disregarding another comics convention, most of the pages are not divided into panels. Moreover, each page is an independent entity; in spite of the words, the connection between the pages is often weak since each page introduces a new character and aspects that have little to do with the previous pages, being only linked to the extent that they are part of the quest for the powerful scarlet stone possessed by the evil sorcerer who had imprisoned Arzach. Though formally and content-wise completely different from "La Déviation," the episode reveals itself as its sequel on a page in the middle of the story, where its sole panel shows the Girauds talking to Arzach.[38]

The last page is comprised of two half-page compositions, both of which are comparable to the static images of illustrated novels.[39] This time, Moebius makes an appearance in his story with the partially Americanized name, John Gérard. The link between the creator and his creation is evident in Arzach's promise to provide the Gérards magical protection, which personifies the function of art as sanctuary. The implied parallel between artistic creation and the bestowal of life—the Pygmalion myth—is embodied by the Charadines, "maîtres-créateurs de vie et de mort" (the master-creators of life and death), whose name evokes "charade," implying the improvisational game as well as enigma, and who put together *ptéroïdes*, like the two often ridden by Arzach.[40] Such comments on the importance of art and the workings of comics as art combine self-reflexivity, which occurs only intermittently, with the more prominent feature of rebellion.

Revealingly, Earth is the place where the tyrant warlock exiles undesired beings like the magician Blanc Char-Limpota who was also trying to liberate the scarlet stone kept in the warlock, Sarukin's castle. And it is on Earth—a "monde sans magie, où il fut forcé de vivre de petits bouts de papiers coloriés" (world without magic, where he was forced to live off scraps of colored papers)—that Char-Limpota discovers Moebius "un humain doué de grands pouvoirs magiques" (a human gifted with great magical powers), whose daughter succeeds in freeing the scarlet stone.[41] This description of Moebius as a magician has more than pure narcissistic connotations: it points towards the aforementioned ability of an artist to generate worlds that in turn can offer escape routes for the artist and other readers or viewers. That nearly fifteen years have elapsed between "La Déviation" and the Arzach episode introduces uncertainty regarding the whereabouts of the Gérards during that period; the possibility that they may have abandoned their known world further underscores Arzach's escapist significance. The visual differences between the strips exemplify Giraud's cultivation of multiple artistic identities. Though monochrome, "La Déviation" is more elaborate with its complex page layout, detailed images, and dramatic lighting. In contrast, the fifth *Arzach* episode has a simpler layout with its rich, colored images composed in a more static, non-sequential manner.

The persistence of the desert-like landscape throughout the *Album Mythique* reflects Moebius's personal affiliation with the Mexican desert and its shamanic associations. According to Moebius, the main theme in *Arzach* is death. Since death is not blatantly portrayed, his remark, "[l]a mort est très présente" (death is very present) could refer to the barrenness of the desert landscapes.[42] Death also permeates the mechanical essence of Arzach's pterodactyls since the *pteroïde* is "un bon exemple de ces symboles morbides: il ressemble à un saurien préhistorique, espèce éteinte, et paraît fait de béton" (a good example of these morbid symbols: it resembles a prehistoric, extinct reptile and seems to be made of concrete).[43] Yet, like Arzach, the pterodactyls are also unusual, almost savage, emblems of freedom.

Fresnault-Deruelle extols the symbolism of Moebius's use of color, exemplifying "la capacité des artistes de savoir inventer des dispositifs aptes à laisser remonter des images premières—des imagines principes" (the capacity of artists for knowing how to invent the appropriate devices for resurrecting the primary images—the fundamental imagos).[44] The significance of Moebius's works for illustrating openness in comics lies in their visual experimentation with layouts and the rich images harboring numerous allusions, even though the potential of those allusions and ambiguities for openness is not harnessed. Similarly, while the visual technique is in itself an intermedial reference to painting, these references are not further developed or interwoven in the stories. This contributes to the relative closedness of the *Arzach* episodes, even though the striking images generate reader involvement—which remains limited to voyeuristic fascination—as well as some ambiguity. Since these aspects do not contribute towards the narrative, the possible story structures are too vague and not sufficiently closed for an open work.

The autofictional element already present in the *Album Mythique* acquires more concrete and complex dimensions in two of the works analyzed a little later in this section: the XXe *Ciel* series and *Taxi van Goghin Korvaan*. Besides highlighting the self-reflexivity of autofiction and visual techniques imitating the fine arts and other media, these comics also engender openness through the use of visual metaphors and intermedial references, all of which are interwoven in a story structure that is flexible without allowing for every possible interpretation. Visually intense, fantastic worlds are likewise incorporated in a solid storyline using intermedial references that are more inherently relevant for the story in the *Nikopol* trilogy. Layers of significance and interpretational scope are consequently created while including vibrantly imaginative, suggestive images similar to those discernible in Moebius's works.

POST-APOCALYPTIC DYSTOPIAS AND BAUDELAIRE: *LA TRILOGIE NIKOPOL*

Enki Bilal (born in 1951, in Belgrade) is renowned for his vivid images in direct color, which incorporate charcoal, chalk, crayon, and washes. His original panels are larger than their printed versions, which enhances the quality of the images and entails that the layout of each page is assembled on the floor. Similar to many artists working with comics, his stories take root in specific images, with the text being added later.

Like Moebius, Bilal has also worked as a film director, which corresponds to the visual intensity and fluid transitions in his works. Although he began drawing for *Pilote* in the early 1970s, his first movie, *Bunker Palace Hotel*, appeared in 1989, followed by *Tykho Moon* in 1996, both of which project futuristic totalitarian dystopias. His third and most recent movie, *Immortel, Ad Vitam* (2004), is a film version of the *Nikopol* trilogy, where the cinematic transposition has resulted in an extreme purification of the comics' visually dominant sordidness. Although inspired to draw because of films,[45] Bilal finds that the more introverted activity of making comics allows him greater freedom in contrast to the collaborative effort involved in making films.[46] Begun in 1980 in *Pilote, La Foire aux Immortels* (*The Carnival of Immortals*) is the first of the *Nikopol* albums, followed by *La Femme Piège* (*The Woman Trap*, 1986) and concluded by *Froid Équateur* (*Cold Equator*, 1993). As is the case with most of his books, these comics also adhere to the *bande dessi-*

née format with respect to the size but not necessarily the number of pages, which suggests greater flexibility for the narration of the stories.

Dystopias portraying the near future are a recurrent theme in Bilal's oeuvre. The intensity of their grotesqueness becomes evident through a comparison with *Watchmen*. While both books follow the *1984* paradigm of a totalitarian, oppressive state set in the near future, *Watchmen*'s adherence to a fairly realistic, pictorially sober mode has a more insidious, gradually accelerating impact. In contrast, Bilal's images with their glaring colors and impossible monstrosities that merge the organic and the inorganic create immediate sensorial repulsion. Underscoring the presence of several possible levels of interpretations, Bilal claims that although his dystopias were engendered by childhood memories of the war-torn, communist Yugoslavia of the 1950s, they remain rich in criticism against current sociopolitical conditions.[47]

As a strange but gripping story combining the various familiar features of popular fiction without adhering to genre-specific formulas, the post-apocalyptic world of the *Nikopol* trilogy unfolds on multiple levels. The overlapping of ancient religion, futuristic dystopia, and science fiction produces an eclectic collection of characters, among them gods, humans, mutants, and aliens. The unexpected yet apposite inclusion of Baudelaire provides additional levels to the story. This blend of different frames of reference unsettles temporality and creates confusion on par with the atmosphere of the story world itself. Chaos already impermeates the layout of the first page, which contains a list of facts slightly off-center, with extracts of panels from the next few pages forming a thick border around the page and depicting the conditions of the city, the pyramid, and the Palais de l'Élysée, the official residence of the French president. In the story, the residence is occupied by the dictator Choublanc.[48] The reader's simultaneous estrangement and familiarity with this world is exacerbated on the next page, which depicts the flying pyramid of the Egyptian gods. Devoid of splendor, with its pitted surface and cement grey color, the pyramid concretizes the depreciating tone dominating the *Nikopol* universe.

The authoritarian government combines all the horrors of improper ruling: inequality, nepotism, suppression through military control, and violence. Thus, similarities with the historical experiences of totalitarianism are inescapable. Waking up after thirty years of hibernation, the protagonist Alcide Nikopol, who had written a high school graduation paper in 1980 on Italian fascism, instantly recognizes Mussolini's slogans, which have been appropriated by Choublanc's government: "Tout est dans l'État. Rien d'humain ou de spirituel n'est en dehors de l'État" (Everything is in the State. Nothing human or spiritual is beyond the State).[49]

Figurative hints are also discernible in the trilogy, as in the opening of the underground station scene in which Horus accosts Nikopol. The former's scream of pain at the loss of his foreleg echoes the expulsion from a womb to which the subway had been likened in the narrative caption.[50] Such allusions towards complementary or alternative meanings are recurrent throughout the comic. In the above scene, Nikopol is in fact reborn into a new world: after being frozen for thirty years as punishment for not participating in an ongoing war, his capsule had been released from the sky by a freak accident, resulting in the loss of his right foreleg. Although Horus fixes the leg, he also takes over Nikopol's body and causes further psychological anguish.

Newspaper clippings are once again recurrent, serving as intermedial references, which appropriate an important medium and channel of communication. Since the backgrounds are panels that have already appeared, the recapitulative function of these articles is highlighted: time is frozen and recounted from the official propagandist perspective. As in Tardi's and Eisner's comics, newspapers play a significant role in *Nikopol* in conveying detailed contextual information, to such an extent that the basic story of *La Foire* can be constructed through the newspaper excerpts alone. Moreover, the supplementary handwritten commentary generates an awareness of the various discourses operating within and beyond the diegesis. Asserting the importance of newspapers for his creative process, Bilal declares that "news is the raw material for any projection into the future. I soak up news, and my story, which is set in the future, is packed with events from the present."[51] Underscoring the contemporary relevance of his stories, he adds that "if my readers don't follow current political events, they are sometimes likely to get lost."[52] This is especially evident in *Froid Équateur*, with its several jibes at the United Nations which tries in vain to curtail the activities of the powerful, multinational cooperation K.K.D.Z.O.

The sordidness in Bilal's world is complemented by the inclusion of verses from Baudelaire's *Les Fleurs du Mal* (*Flowers of Evil*). Significantly, it is Nikopol, someone stemming from another time, who quotes Baudelaire. As the story progresses, the frequency of the quotes increases, mirroring the protagonist's despair and growing derangement. For Mikkonen, such apposite intertextual references, which in *La Foire* recontextualize and reinterpret Baudelaire's poetry, exemplify "intersemiotic translation."[53] The first verse that Nikopol recites is the opening of "Une Charogne" (A Carcass) that is a spontaneous cover for explaining away Horus's voice as his own to the guard barging in his room:

> Rappelez-vous l'objet que nous vîmes, mon âme [. . .]
> Au détour d'un sentier une charogne infâme

Sur un lit semé de cailloux⁵⁴
(Remember, my love, the object we saw [...]
By a bend in the path a carcass reclined
On a bed sown with pebbles and stones)⁵⁵

Transposed to the story world, the recitation of this verse is followed by a panel showing Nikopol's son, who is also called Alcide (but often referred to as Niko), unexpectedly coming across his mother's grave, thus repeating the act Nikopol had performed only a day before. The poem is continued as Nikopol is flown to meet the president, who Horus will brainwash into resigning in favor of Nikopol.⁵⁶ Since the word balloons containing these verses are placed in external views of the vessel traveling over the devastated city, descriptions such as "brûlante et suant les poisons [...] son ventre plein d'exhalaisons" ("[s]weating out poisonous fumes [... h]er stinking and festering womb") complement the macabre cityscape with its bulbous structures.⁵⁷ The next panel skips several lines to reach the third last verse of the poem as the vessel transporting Nikopol hovers above L'Élysée and Nikopol faces the reader. Once again, the quoted words comment on the events taking place in the story:

> ... Et pourtant vous serez semblable à cette ordure
> À cette horrible infection,
> Étoile de mes yeux, soleil de ma nature,
> Vous, mon ange et ma passion⁵⁸
> (And you, in your turn, will be rotten as this:
> Horrible, filthy, undone,
> O sun of my nature and star of my eyes,
> My passion, my angel in one)⁵⁹

When, towards the end of *La Foire*, Horus becomes a falcon to avenge himself on his fellow gods, Nikopol sinks into delirium and recites "Le Revenant" (The Ghost) instead of answering him.⁶⁰ Quoted in entirety but leaving out the last line, this poem provides room for alternative readings of the events occurring around the oblivious Nikopol. As a killer insect edges closer to him, the animal versions of the Egyptian gods appear outside L'Élysée, including Bastet, Anubis, and Thoth, as well as the snake goddess Amaunet, whose form alludes to "Le Revenant's" last line, which is left out because Nikopol is struck by the mutant insect: "Et des caresses de serpent/Autour d'une fosse rampant" ("[a]nd I'll caress you like a snake/That slides and writhes around a tomb").⁶¹

Adhering to one of the common tendencies in popular fiction, a series of events congest the end of *La Foire*. Within one page, as the gods gather around the unconscious Nikopol, Aurélien, Choublanc's confidant and guardian of the telepathic cat, Gogol, who is the only being that is able to counter Horus's mental manipulation, is killed by Horus.[62] The other election candidate competing against Nikopol is likewise found dead in his bed.[63] When the gods revive a deranged Nikopol and grant him control over the city, he recites the first verse of "La Fontaine de Sang" (The Fountain of Blood) in reply with blood flowing from his nose and erupting from his heart:

> Il me semble parfois que mon sang coule à flots [. . .]
> Je l'entends bien qui coule avec un long murmure,
> Mais je me tâte en vain pour trouver la blessure[64]
> (Sometimes it seems my blood spurts out in gobs [. . .]
> I clearly hear it mutter as it goes,
> Yet cannot find the wound from which it flows)[65]

In the comic's context, these verses harbor an additional reference to the atrocities committed by irresponsible authorities. Once again, although Nikopol does not recite the entire poem, the second verse is also significant because it foreshadows the next few pages, which show a new revolutionary government that only increments destruction and degradation:

> À travers la cité, comme dans un champ clos,
> Il s'en va, transformant les pavés en îlots,
> Désaltérant la soif de chaque créature,
> Et partout colorant en rouge la nature.[66]
> (Then through the city, coursing in the lists,
> It travels, forming islands in its midst,
> Seeing that every creature will be fed
> And staining nature its flamboyant red.)[67]

Likewise, the omitted final line of "Le Revenant"—"[m]oi, je veux régner par l'effroi" ("I, I want to rule by fear")—applies to all the despots in the story, including Choublanc, the revolutionaries, and Anubis, the head of the gods.[68] That these excluded lines are also significant contributes towards the story's openness by encouraging the reader to seek and apply further meanings.

Disturbingly enough, when Niko reappears in the story to meet his father and tries to explain who he is, the older Nikopol, caught up in the words of *Fleurs du Mal* and his madness, begins reciting "Les Litanies de Satan."

The blue and yellow stripes of the chair on which Nikopol sits, and which also form the background for his profile, hint towards his distance from reality and the extent of his insanity. The juxtaposition of two look-alikes in one panel illustrates the fall of the hero, from depression and hopelessness to exuberant madness.[69] On the next page, after Nikopol calls out to the "[g]uérisseur familier des angoisses humaines" ([i]ntimate healer of our agitated hearts) and raves the refrain while drooling, "Satan, prends pitié de ma longue misère" (Satan, take pity on my misery), he indirectly expresses the hopelessness of the new generation and their inability to bring positive change.[70]

A major thematic relevance of the Baudelaire quotes, as pointed out by Mikkonen, is the dominance of the Romantic *quiproquo* trope of identity confusion and interchangeability that is both inter- and extra-diegetically relevant:[71] the identity confusion applies not only to the protagonist displaced from known time and space but can also be extrapolated to the reader, because Nikopol, by being an outsider stemming from the same time as the reader, functions as his double in the nightmarish environment; it is through Nikopol that the reader experiences a large part of the story and is able to comprehend the events.[72] Consolidating the concern with identity, two of the Baudelaire recitations begin while or soon after Nikopol looks in the mirror. Already during his first day in the new Paris, Horus had forced Nikopol to switch clothes—and by extension, identities—with three different people. The Baudelairian self-doubt and identity crisis persists to the end of the trilogy, with the younger Niko's self-loathing and confused relationship with his father, and further, their relationships with each other's love interests playing a more central role in *Froid Équateur*.

At the end of this final book, taking over the function of the narrator who uncharacteristically disappears in the last few pages, Jill (Nikopol's former lover), Yéléna (Niko's love interest), and Nikopol sum up their remaining lives, with the women being complacently realistic about the children they intend on having and their age at the time of death. Only Nikopol has an indefinite, eternal end: "c'est un cauchemar [. . .] ma vie est un puits sans fond, sans fin" (For the rest, it's a nightmare [. . .] my life is a well without a base, without an end).[73] Therefore, his destiny can only be expressed through Baudelaire's words, and more precisely, the last verse from "*L'Héautontimorouménos*" (*The Self-Tormentor*):

Je suis dans mon cœur le vampire,
un de ces grands abandonnés
au rire éternel condamnés

et qui ne peuvent plus sourire!⁷⁴
(I am my own blood's epicure
—One of those great abandoned men
Who are eternally condemned
To laugh, but can smile no more!)⁷⁵

Les Fleurs du Mal projects a cyclical concept of decomposition that is also manifest in the developments in *La Foire*.⁷⁶ The reference consequently merges temporalities while also expanding the poems' original, more personal scope to a more sociopolitical one.

The second volume, *La Femme Piège*, recounts Nikopol's romance with the journalist Jill Bioskop. "Bioskop" means "cinema" in Serbian and points to Nikopol and Jill's eventual roles in the incomplete film on their romance in the trilogy's final volume. Haunted by the conscience of having inadvertently killed three men, which she drowns through amnesia-inducing medications, Jill is, as the title makes obvious, the femme fatale evoked by Baudelaire's verses in *Foire*. Bilal describes the boldly colored rendition of his female characters as allusions to Warhol's images of iconic women. Amongst these, Jill stands out with her blue hair and pale skin.⁷⁷ Additionally, it is the women who are frequently depicted in the film reels, thereby recalling the series that Warhol made of excessively photographed, iconic female figures such as Marilyn Monroe and Jackie Kennedy. The newspaper persists as an important medium in *La Femme Piège*, which actually begins with a note to the reader promising an extract of the *Libération* at the end of the book for aiding the comprehension of the story (a promise that is not kept in several editions of the trilogy). However, the story itself is largely narrated through Jill, unfolding as her diary, with her typed or handwritten words taking over most of the narrative captions.

In the trilogy's final volume, Nikopol's own loss of comprehensible language in the chaos caused by Horus and Anubis's confrontation ties up with the identity issues prevailing over the trilogy: the absence of comprehensible words can be interpreted as indicators of erasure from the world. Nikopol's loss of words (albeit temporary) ties up with the confusion of identities pursuing him since the trilogy's beginning and his status as a displaced being.

In a final instance of metafiction, Jill Bioskop, who becomes the director of the film in *Froid Équateur* after the original director, Donadoni's disappearance, also steps into the role of comic book creator for the comic in which she finds herself. Donadoni's inability to complete a film resonates in *Froid*'s open end. Upon recognizing the small point below Yéléna and Nikopol's departing plane as Niko's satellite, Jill, with some irony, hints towards the reader's task by musing how Donadoni would have loved the ending and that "il aurait été foutu d'y trouver un symbole" (he would have screwed himself to find a symbol there).[78] The comic ends on an inconclusive note, with Jill ordering the cameraman: "Tu coupes pas! On laisse filer jusqu'au bout, jusqu'au noir, jusqu'à la FIN" (Do not cut! Let it run through, till the darkness, till the END).[79] Correspondingly, the stills in the film reel follow the plane and the satellite's tiny, bright dot until they are completely engulfed by the darkness of the storm in the reel's last frame, which, by being half the width of the previous scenes, suggests the story's continuity beyond the confines of the comic, which is also indicated by the words. The conventional happy ending is attacked in the trilogy since this ending is not really happy: one of the heroes is banished and the other succumbs to a state of semi-madness while remaining aware of a life in eternal despair. A positive end being impossible in the trilogy's hopeless milieu, it is appropriate that the characters visually fade away on a film reel portraying a growing storm.

Even though they form a trilogy, the comics are self-contained stories based in the same world introduced in the first book. Their mélange of popular literature and canonical works illustrates Bilal's belief that "the boundaries between genres are fading away."[80] Yet, in the same interview, Bilal also calls *La Foire* "a completely way-out comic book" in which he wanted to poke fun at the desire for immortality through, for instance, the depiction of the Egyptian gods as skeletons after their pyramid's crash, even though they form the storm engulfing the film reel at the end.[81] As shown in the course of the analyses, such rebellious humor is recurrent in comics across genres and can contribute towards opening up a work through the very element of subversion when it entails taking a new perspective departing from established values.

Although the *Nikopol* trilogy forms a cohesive story, several similarities with *Arzach* are also discernible. Both indulge in anachronism by painting worlds that are partially futuristic while also embracing ancient worlds. This juxtaposition of disparate realms generates unsteadiness in the story, leaving the reader unsure of what to expect, as well as offering multiple sets of codes to choose from. Another similarity is the glorification of the rebel. More important is the overlap between reality and fantasy, which has already been interpreted as a subversive instrument of underground comix.[82] The sardonic tone resounding through the works of both artists is also a legacy of underground comix that Fresnault-Deruelle sees permeating recent, more experimental comics.[83] In the next series, bitterness is cloaked in aestheticism, while the story world is placed uncomfortably close to reality and its molding through different media.

FANTASY AND ITS MEDIALITY: XXE CIEL[84]

Like the other artists discussed in this section, Yslaire (born in 1957, in Brussels) also lets his stories emerge from images. Proceeding from the notion that images abstract time while words generate temporality, Yslaire accords symbolic values to his colors, thus highlighting the interpretational potential of the images. The XXe Ciel comics, along with the more streamlined Sambre books, manifest a drastic change in Yslaire's visual style: the brightly colored, carefree stylization of his series from the early 1980s, Bidouille et Violette, has been exchanged for a more complex visual vocabulary, nuanced by a distinctive brand of magical realism. Using direct color and mixed media, his images come across as atmospheric compositions merging drawings and paintings.

Accompanied by an Internet project, the first, introductory album, L'Introduction au XXe Ciel, was published in 1997. Four additional albums followed: Mémoires du XXe Ciel 98 (1999), http://www.xxeciel.com/mémoires99 (2001), http://www.xxeciel.com/mémoires19<00> (2004), and http://www.xxeciel.com/mémoires20<00> (2004).[85] Each of the five volumes refer to a year or two before the actual date of publication, and the last two sister volumes were shaped by the 9/11 events. As an intermediary between ciel (heaven, sky) and siècle (century), the series' title triggers multiple associations. Allusions to cyberspace are also evoked through the web addresses in the titles of the Mémoires, which in turn point towards the media-dependency of the current collective consciousness.

Aiming to be an alternative history of the twentieth century—a "portrait partiel et subjectif, 'psychographique,' de ce siècle prométhéen" (a partial and subjective, "psychographic," portrait of this promethean century)[86]—the series was to unfold between the Russian Revolution of 1917 and the fall of the Berlin Wall in 1989, two turning points of Western history. The shock of an unexpected, large-scale attack, as well as its mediatization through images devoid of people, marks the last two books, with the parallel stories of the twin protagonists reflecting the image of the falling twin towers. The stories' publication in two separate volumes was, however, contrary to Yslaire's wishes because he wanted to emphasize the different endings of the same event.

Through incorporating contemporaneous changes the series became "avant tout une BD d'Auteur, dont l'infinie prétention est d'oser dire 'LE me souviens' en parlant de ces cent ans que je n'ai vécu qu'à moitié et dont j'ai imaginé le reste" (before all else an auteur comic, the infinite claim of which is daring to say 'IT reminds me' in talking of these hundred years from which I have only lived through half and have imagined the rest).[87] While the several possible endings (instead of a single, lucid conclusion) convey the uncertainty unleashed by 9/11, the role of the imagination in making memory and history is a more central concern.

In terms of format, all of the albums conform to the page number and size of the average *bande desinée*. However, as the psychoanalyst Laurence Erlich (who is also Yslaire's wife) writes in the last chapter, *Introduction* is a "roman dessinée" (illustrated novel).[88] This is appropriate given the absence of word balloons and panels. Instead, images are juxtaposed to blocks of text or other images. Consequently, it is the large body of text packed in a few pages that clarifies (or further mystifies) the subject matter of the many pictures and their place in the story. Owing to its attempt to create an alternative history, with newspapers and photographs as proofs, *Introduction* also resembles a documentary in print. *Introduction* relies upon the covers of the fictional newspaper, *Le XXe Ciel* and the *Mémoires* supplement the characters' narratives with pictorial proof, using panels while remaining largely free of word balloons.[89] Some of the pictures themselves recur throughout the series with several interlinked stories being built around them.

Heralding its anomalism, the first four pages of the book are completely black, with two centered, small, square images appearing on alternating pages. These images depict the sky, darkened at first, with a hint of light emerging from the center and then a reddened glow captioned by the first words of the book, which are misleadingly attributed to the Apocalypse of John:

> Au troisième jour, Dieu créa la terre et les cieux.
> Et les anges, de leurs larmes, firent les océans.[90]
> (On the third day, God created the earth and the heavens.
> And the angels, with their tears, made the oceans.)

These words recall the description in the Book of Genesis, which also begins with an undefined source of light and where the oceans are created on the third day. The part played by the angels in engendering the waters through their tears is Yslaire's contribution.[91] This theatrical beginning sets the despairing tone of the series, which is further enhanced by the double-page splash—a composition in pastels, paint, and pencil—of a barren landscape, with a few distant angels on the single, massive cliff dominating the picture. An unsteady trench fence runs from the middle ground of the first page to the foreground of the second page. This image encapsulates the book's main themes of violence, expressed through scenes of destruction, and a dead hope for redemption, symbolized by the desolate poses of the human-like angels. While the background colors of red and black in *Introduction* carry strong connotations of death and gloom, the black also recalls the blank computer screen. In contrast, hyperreal blue and the brown shades of old photographs dominate *mémoires19<00>*, in keeping with the reconstruction of one of the main characters, Eva Stern's past through pictures.

Already *Introduction*'s opening quotation from the notebook of Eva's twin, Frank Stern—dedicating the material to his mother—hints at the fluidity of identities between the creator and his characters. Visually encapsulating fluidity, many images continue beyond the edge of one page to part of the other, making the act of reading from page to page or turning pages mimic webpage browsing or "les bégaiements d'Internet" (the stuttering of the Internet).[92] As already indicated by the subtitle "http://www.yslaire.be," several visual references to the series' development from the artist's homepage, such as screenshots, are included in the book. The creation of the web-based project is attributed to Eva, who with Erlich and Yslaire's aid, used the Internet to diffuse the mute, visual messages of the angel and her psychoanalytic interpretations of them. The collaboration of these three personages is also an unsettling manifestation of creator-character interaction. Tied to the twentieth century, the Internet project ended at the turn of the new millennium.

The first page of each section in *Introduction* contains an open program menu in the upper left corner, with a cursor highlighting the relevant chapter. Recalling hypertext, where one key word triggers a separate body of text, the second chapter of *Introduction* contains nonlinearly arranged biographies of the four main characters: the female pilot Fabienne Rouge-Dyeu or Farouge, the artist Werner Ysler, and the Stern twins.[93] Rejecting conventional layouts, the subtitles for the second chapter are placed both vertically and horizontally in varying fonts and sizes.

Other than its structural and visual presence, the Internet also plays an important role in the story itself by being the medium through which the events are triggered and the story is brought into being. Eva had begun receiving anonymous e-mails, the first one dated 31 February [sic], which made her computer turn on and display a series of images. This continued for four months as she realized that it was she, as a psychoanalyst, who the angel of the century, traumatized by the violence it had witnessed, was imploring.[94]

While the four *Mémoires* use panels like other comics, the role of the Internet and the computer persists to the extent that many of the panels represent computer screens. In *mémoires19<00>*, the initial splashes are screen shots, and it is a series of overlapping windows that lead to Eva's recollection of her birth in 1900.[95] Computer screens, photos, and photography itself have an emblematic status in the series particularly because of their misleading aura of objectivity and authenticity—notions that these comics challenge.

As is paradigmatic for the new millennium, analogue material succumbs to digital data in the series since all of Eva's records—both photographs and diary entries—are stored in her computer, which is attacked by the millennium bug.[96] Correspondingly, with the nearing of the new year, her memory begins to fade and, although her suicide attempt is thwarted, she sinks into a deep coma. It is the young psychology student, Lucienne Dezee, who tries to piece together Eva's memory by contacting her friends and restoring her computer. The comic traces the path through which Eva's diary—and by unsteady extension, her memory—is reconstructed or deconstructed (for it turns out that the notes and photos may have been fake props for her psychoanalytic method of establishing an empathic bond with her patients).

The Stern twins, Ysler, and Farouge irregularly issued a tabloid-sized newspaper, *Le XXᵉ Ciel*, also known as the newspaper of souls. Reflecting the trauma of the First World War, the newspaper was concerned with the loss of faith, often printing images of angels in mourning before some of the most iconic, violent scenes of the twentieth century. Running between 1917 and 1989 and always published on the 31ˢᵗ of each month, the newspaper aimed to cover the century's major events. *Introduction*'s opening text is accompanied by the title page of the first issue. Covering the upper two-thirds of the book's page and marked by brown smudges of age, it contains a large, poorly printed black-and-white photograph showing soldiers taking aim at a bound person with wings, which is followed by the question, "Dieu est-il mort?" (Is God dead?)[97] The distance and haziness of the picture allows for the inclusion of unrealistic details, enabling the transformation of a human into an angel. These grainy, ambiguous photographs, which are often montaged or retouched with crayon, persist throughout the book in a manner reminiscent of the Canadian artist Martin Vaughn-James's reworking and imitations of photographs.[98] Relatively clear, colored photographs, conforming to a reality that is closest to the reader, only appear in the last chapter which elaborates on the book's creation.

Inevitably reflecting upon the known past, the *XXᵉ Ciel* newspapers depict an alternative twentieth century through their texts and images. Dated 31 February 1989, the last cover in *Introduction* follows the newspaper's formula of a representative image in the background with a mourning angel placed closer to the viewer; of the same color and material as the Berlin Wall, a desolate angel with a downturned face sits on it. A dim shadow of the Brandenburg Gate looms in the background. The subtitle has been changed to "Périodique Métaphysique" (Metaphysical Journal), and a conclusive remark by Eva Stern appears in bold on the side: "L'ange du XXᵉ siècle n'a pas de mots pour raconter son siècle car il s'est libéré du verbe" (The angel of the twentieth century does not have the words for narrating its century because it has freed itself from the verb).[99] This explains the angel's later communication through images, which recur throughout the series and sometimes also capture key moments in the lives of the four characters, showing them implicated in historical events, such as the photograph with Frank Stern amongst the prisoners in the Buchenwald camp. In contrast to the other three characters, Frank Stern never ages through the decades of the twentieth century; his life remains elusive, even for his twin.

Besides the manipulated photographs, another means of unsettling the relationship between reality and unreality is the juxtaposition of real quotes to those invented by the artist, as exemplified by the opening pseudo-biblical citation. In an imaginary interview recorded in the book, Yslaire declares that he wanted to give "un choc brutal entre quelque chose de terriblement réaliste et quelque chose de mythique" (a brutal shock between something terribly realistic and something mythical).[100] Consequently, the partially ethereal, immortal characters' lives are clearly situated in the twentieth century's context by referring to key happenings and personalities. Farouge, who brought the group together and financed the paper, owned the first plane made by Morane-Saulnier, christening it *L'Ange Rouge*. Ysler contributed to the *Blaue Reiter*, as well as the leftist *L'Éclaireur*. Having befriended George Grosz and Frans Masereel, he also participated in the 1955 Mannheim *Neue Sachlichkeit* exhibition. Similarly, Eva was a disciple of Freud and was strongly influenced by Jungian ideas, especially the notion of a collective or transpersonal unconscious, which is one of the concepts the series bases itself on, personifying it through the figure of the angel. After publishing her 1923 study, "Der Himmel über Krieg," on war's trauma and other psychological consequences,[101] she was forced to flee the continent due to her Jewish roots and ended up as a professor of psychology at Berkeley, developing close ties to Leary and the Beat generation.[102] Confusion regarding reality is thus generated by references to the real world, which is reinforced through the combination of photography and drawing. Correspondingly, Eva writes in *mémoires19<00>*, "tout le monde le sait, la photographie, ce n'est pas comme le dessin, c'est la réalité. La vérité" (everyone knows, photography is not like drawing, it is reality. The truth). She adds that "[t]oute ma vie est en photos et les photos sont toute ma vie" (all my life is in photos and the photos are my life).[103] As an additional twist, images in *mémoires19<00>*, though captioned as photographs, resemble animation stills and are vibrant drawings instead of photorealistic images.

In lieu of speaking through word balloons, the characters exist essentially through their own writings in the newspaper and the third-person narrator.

Since all the characters exist through both drawings and photographs, the fluctuation between reality and unreality is also captured. In accordance with the suggestive ambiguity of the pictures—including sketches by Ysler and photographs by Frank—the biographies also relate multiple, parallel possibilities, particularly in the lives of Ysler and Frank Stern.[104]

The third chapter of *Introduction* recounts Eva's encounter with the angel via cyberspace. Yslaire reveals that he replaced the original title of the webpage, "Psychographie d'un Ange," with "Psychoanalyse d'un Ange," thus switching the emphasis from psychosociological to psychoanalytical aspects. The next eighteen pages are dominated by large images, often in several versions, forming a haphazardly arranged photo album, often with generous black spaces. Eva's corresponding journal entries, inserted after each set of photos, echo the possible questions evoked by the narrative. One of the most significant, metafictional questions asks:

> Quel sens donner aux messages de l'Ange? Autoportrait, autobiographie ou effet de miroir? Miroir d'un siècle ou d'un Ange qui se meurt?[105]
> (What meaning is to be given to the Angel's messages? Self-portrait, autobiography or mirror effect? Mirror of a century or an Angel who is dying?)

While Eva's journal entries only express her ruminations regarding the relevance of the images, it is through Erlich's interview of Yslaire in the "Histoire de l'Histoire" section of *Introduction* that the mute angel's plea and the raison d'être of the images are elucidated. This section opens with a colored photograph of the same study that had been sketched in the previous chapter where the red sofa—Freud's proverbial couch—had been the only colored object.[106] A footnote informs the reader that Erlich had conducted psychoanalytic sessions with Yslaire from February 1997 to December 1999, with the aim of exploring the process of creation.[107] In her journal entries, she explains that Yslaire had been obsessed with angels and that it was one of these angels who, like a muse, led to *XXe Ciel*.

The interview concretizes metafictional commentary in a question and answer format. The first double spread of the interview is accompanied by a photograph of the artist with horn-rimmed glasses as well as its retouched version with a star-shaped wound sprawling across his temple, which highlights his resemblance to Frank. The next double spread contains colored but blurred photographs showing a gilded clock and mirror, each time reflecting different, unidentifiable persons. Besides representing the themes of illusion and temporality underlying the series, this photograph also illustrates Yslaire's linking of creation and illusion: "la creation est un peu la recherche de la vérité; d'un autre, si la verité n'est jamais que soit dans le miroir, c'est un peu triste" (creation is partially the search for truth; on the other hand, if the truth is only in the mirror, it is a bit sad).[108]

Yslaire's Jungian notions—a commonality with Eva—become apparent in the course of the interview, especially the belief in a timeless, universal unconscious. He also reveals a conceptual similarity with Surrealism by attributing a psychoanalytic function to the arts and considering artistic creation as a means of performing an internal quest for the self, just like someone trying to attain self-understanding through psychoanalysis. This leads to a discussion on art itself—another instance of "autoréflexion sur le médium"[109]—where Yslaire likens creativity to violence with the need to express being the driving force behind art. Declaring that psychoanalysts have taken the place of priests and that their sessions are like confessions, Yslaire explains that Eva's psychoanalytic method for self-understanding was the projection of her own history on the images sent from the angel. This method is more transparent in *mémoires19<00>*, where Eva forces Nathan to confront his past through photographs of her own past, one of which shows her father with Nathan's father at Auschwitz.[110] Echoing the entire series' manner of telling stories, she encourages him to look in the shadows of the photos, at what is not shown and thus move from the specific to the general. Consequently, the content of the series, while recalling cyberspace, also resembles a stream of consciousness, manifested by both words and images and inevitably filtered through the collective unconscious. Eva's Jungian beliefs, which persisted despite her discipleship under Freud, can also be interpreted as a self-reflexive comment, this time on word-image narratives themselves because, while Jung believed in the primacy of images in the consciousness, Freud believed in the supremacy of words; just like Eva hovered between the two thinkers, the medium of comics itself oscillates between word-dependence and image-dependence.

In addition to the identities construed or revealed through ambiguous images and psychoanalysis, the issue of identity is brought to the forefront by Yslaire's remark that the goal of the psychoanalyst is to recognize himself in others to the extent of acquiring a fluid identity for "le psychanalyste ne sait pas qu'il est et qu'il va essayer de se trouver à travers les autres" (the psychoanalyst does not know who he is and who he will try to find through others).[111] Identity also plays a significant role at the autofictional level of creator-character fusion in *XXe Ciel*, with the transition from autofiction to metafiction being stressed by the interview transcripts in *Introduction*: while talking to Erlich, Yslaire voices opinions identical to Frank's, such as that "une photo, c'est une volonté de se réincarner" (a photo is a desire to reincarnate oneself),[112] which is comparable to Frank's remark, "[l]es meilleurs photographes tuent les anges puisqu'ils leur donnent l'éternité" (the best photographers kill angels because they give them eternity).[113] Yslaire adds that the mediated similarity between himself and other characters, especially Frank Stern, is multiplied since Frank, Eva, and their stillborn brother, Erwin, were triplets. As confirmed by the later volumes, the story of the XXe *Ciel* has the structure of an unending spiral because of its recurring characters.

Drawing an analogy with Rembrandt, who had also searched for the immortal image, Yslaire points out that in spite of his numerous self-portraits, Rembrandt himself remains unknown, whereas his works harbor a universal, human relevance. He grounds this claim by adding that the self-portrait is the ultimate end of the creative process, aiming "de chercher l'universel en soi, de créer l'image immortelle" (to search the universal in oneself, to create the immortal image), and in the process, the artist's identity is effaced.[114] In the same vein, *Introduction* ends with the following words by Eva, appearing under a small, colored sketch from the beginning of the book showing Ysler or Frank or the artist himself rescuing Farouge or an angel: "au-delà de la personne il y a l'humain universel" (beyond the individual, there is the universal human).[115] While illustrating the Jungian philosophy impregnating the book, this remark brings out the confusion and interchangeability of identities in the series. It also ties up with the conception of the photo as a possibility for immortality, a view that goes back to the bestowal of immortality to the image in many cultures.

Yslaire's interest in angels is inherited by Frank. In a remark scribbled in Ysler's notebook, Frank declares that photographers, instead of being soul snatchers as the Red Indians conceived them, are "avant tout des chasseurs d'Anges (d'instants d'années, meme si tous ne cherchent pas l'éternel)" (primarily hunters of Angels [of moments, even if all are not seeking the eternal]).[116] This hints towards the significance of the angel as a personification of temporality, and even of the collective spirit of the times. It also connects with the comparison made in the 1972 issue by Jules-Dyeu (Farouge's nephew or son) between the computer and the angel as parallels of speed and light respectively and his question, "[l]'ange, l'esprit messager, est-il une métaphore du Personal Computer?" (the angel, the messenger spirit, is he a metaphor for the Personal Computer?)[117] Furthermore, as visualized by the hazy photographs adding vague wings behind her figure and her vocation as a pilot, Farouge also merges the earthly with the immortal. In the course of the series, it also seems as if Frank is the angel trying to contact Eva through the Internet. In addition, by sharing man's suffering and having lost its creator, the angel is both witness to the twentieth century and representative of a past when God was still alive. It thus also symbolizes loss of faith. However, even though these multiple associations overload the symbol of the angel, they remain interconnected and block the possibility of allowing every possible interpretation as would be the case in a closed work.

That Yslaire is one of those artists who has a predilection for aspect-to-aspect transitions, particularly for introducing a scene, is likely to have contributed to the suggestively disjointed arrangement of words and images, particularly in *Introduction*. The series, and especially *Introduction*, stands apart with its mixed media images, the employment of varied word-image relationships, as well as an open, malleable narrative that is "in movement."[118] Given the hypertextual structure and several narrative modes of the books, the reader is forced to piece together the stories on his own, just like the characters are forced to construe their worlds through photographs, and thus create multiple stories from the same text.

INTERLUDE: COMPARISONS

While *Introduction au XXe Ciel* does have affiliations with illustrated books, the factors that contribute towards its openness can be highlighted through a comparison with Jean-Claude Mézières and Pierre Christin's *Lady Polaris*, which also goes beyond directly illustrating the narrative.[119] Not only does it incorporate an autofictional aspect—since the artist-writer duo are simultaneously the protagonists of the story—but it also includes real-life documents, such as photographs and letters collected by the creators-protagonists in their quest to uncover the truth behind the destruction of the vessel, Lady Polaris.[120]

Another unusual feature is the appearance, on several occasions, of full-colored, drawn panels, lacking word balloons but containing the narrators' words running in between the tiers, which manifests the interaction between different kinds of word-image narration, particularly comics, illustrated novels, and picture books. Nonetheless, the dominant word-image relationship is that of an illustrated novel: the story is told through the words, and the pictures essentially reinforce them. In contrast, the images in *Introduction* are not only illustrations of the text but also contain additional, often indispensable clues regarding the story. This is linked to the visual essence of *Introduction*, based as it is on the newspaper issues and photographs through which the characters convey their personas. Moreover, the omniscience of words is undermined as the anonymous narrator remains uncertain about the facts, and the narration is intermittently transferred to the characters' writings and art.

Hence, apart from the multifaceted artwork and its apposite collaboration with the text, it is the very disjointedness of the narrative, unfolding across a flexible—but not loose—structure and compelling the reader to reconstrue the text, which contributes towards the openness of *Introduction* and the other *XXe Ciel* volumes. Further comparisons amongst the comics analyzed in this section along the dimensions of word-image narration, intermediality, visual style, and story are equally helpful for gauging how openness is generated in comics.

Although influenced by Bilal's stories and visual style, especially his use of direct color and the rendition of the characters, Yslaire's stills stand apart from Bilal's "paused" panels by having a more photographic quality. In addition, Bilal's works are impregnated with bitter irony, whereas cruel sarcasm is almost absent in Yslaire's works. Significantly, both Bilal and Yslaire chose an open ending comprising of several panels of sky in the last books of the titles discussed above.[121] The objectifying, ubiquitously observing, and preserving gaze of photography or film that has been clearly thematized by Bilal and Yslaire is also part of Arzach's world, where another power controlling the actual events is often shown. It is the inclusion and handling of self-reflexive themes such as mediatization that contributes towards the openness of Bilal's and Yslaire's comics. The interaction and formation of history and memory is another common concern in *Nikopol* and *XXe Ciel*. While this is most apparent in Yslaire's psychoanalytic sessions in *Introduction*, Bilal too believes that "[t]he creative process is based on memory."[122] As shown by Bilal's and Yslaire's comics, the inclusion of imaginary newspapers and other documentary material accentuates the themes of memory and alternative realities due to their function of creating and documenting collective history. Notably, all three artists emphasize the need to create and the relevance of images for engendering their stories. Moreover, Yslaire's and Moebius's descriptions of their art as a means of tapping into the unconscious brings out the expressive, interactive aspect of comics, which goes beyond one-way communication and storytelling.

A comparison between the fantastic worlds of Moebius, Bilal, and Yslaire reveals that it is through self-reflexivity, suggestive stories and images, and the presence of a solid narrative structure that openness is generated. Furthermore, formal, visual aspects of world-building, especially the use of direct color and mixed techniques, are brought into play to insert detail and also create layered and suggestive images, such as the retouched photographs in *XXe Ciel* or the destroyed landscapes in *Nikopol*, which reflect the characters' conditions while alluding to various other contexts and media. The suggestive potential of images using unusual, verisimilitudinous drawing styles, through the combination of photorealism and painting, for instance, is also evident in the last book analyzed in this section.

FANTASY TAKING OVER REALITY: *TAXI VAN GOGHIN KORVAAN*[123]

In contrast to the other artists in this section, Jarmo Mäkilä (b. 1952) is a painter and has so far produced only two comics for the *Day Dreamer* trilogy that was started in 2002. While creating interest in the sphere of visual arts, the artist is rarely mentioned in catalogues showcasing Scandinavian or Finnish comics.[124] His only other book was a visualization of the Finnish writer Arto Melleri's *Aavekaupunki* (*Ghost Town*, from 1995) in 1998. While the *Day Dreamer* books are both written and drawn by Mäkilä, they share many aspects with *Aavekaupunki*, which is set in a dystopic Helsinki caught between the warring European Union and Russia and incorporates varying self-portraits.

Published in 2008, *Taxi Van Goghin Korvaan* (*Taxi Ride through Van Gogh's Ear*) is the second book of the trilogy and, at forty-two pages, has the size of a *bande dessinée*. Not only does the title engender an association with painting, which is congruent with the comic's visual style, but it also foreshadows the story's fantasy world. Mäkilä's paintings frequently depict him in partially or completely unreal settings and, indicating their inclination towards sequential narratives, most of his paintings form series of eight or more pieces.[125] While remaining the protagonist of the *Day Dreamer* stories, Mäkilä in an autofictional mode created an alter ego named "P. Itikka," which means both "mosquito" and "midget." Another major similarity between Mäkilä's paintings and the *Day Dreamer* books lies in their themes: like most of his paintings, the trilogy, also based on his memories, serves as a means of coming to terms with his present. While art historian Mika Hannula interprets Mäkilä's concern with the past in terms of Paul Gilroy's postcoloniality—which contextualizes the past through the present in order to attain some kind of resolution—the psychoanalytic facet of the works (which is also mentioned by Hannula but not accorded as much importance) is even more prominent due to the comic's intensely subjective and introspective nature.[126] What adds to the vividness of the images in Mäkilä's comics is his construction of installations of several scenes from *Taxi*, revealing the very real sense of space in those fantasy scenes.

Beginning with a splash showing Itikka as a child falling through space next to an insert containing the owl—who had been Itikka's companion in the first book, *Day Dreamer*—allusions to the unconscious are made via the rich red and black hues and abstract spaces. Already the second page, taking an unexplained leap of time and space characteristic for the story, shows the boy opening a door that is cut into the universe, with its red glowing stars and dark planet. Such *trompe-l'œil* elements of quiet surprise are present in many of Mäkilä's panels, where realism is subverted on closer observation and additional avenues of interpretation are offered.[127]

As indicated by the descriptions above, the notion of being lost, both physically and psychologically, is emphasized from the very beginning of the comic. The story's attempt to resolve this state of being lost involves the middle-aged Itikka voyaging back into the past represented by his childhood home, which is usually rundown and abandoned. While the first sequence ends with the young Itikka stranded on an asteroid in space, the older Itikka/Mäkilä is shown in Helsinki, where he randomly hails a taxi in order to avoid a conversation with an acquaintance and orders the driver to go to Van Gogh's ear.[128] It is this Helsinki, and the indefinite woodland through which the taxi travels and with which Itikka's mental journeys are intertwined, that becomes a chronotope reflecting the importance given to home and place in the story. Place itself is metaphorical—symbolizing the unconscious and providing a means of coming to terms with the self, as concretized, for instance, by the multiple depictions of the house in flames from which Itikka emerges with skeletal wings of wood at the end.

The sudden transition from the younger to the older Itikka occurs without warning while his thoughts continue without interruption in the narrative captions. Correspondingly, the young Itikka already displays signs of aging through the bags under his eyes and the serious expressions.[129] As the story progresses, with the older Itikka attempting to understand the void inside him, the juxtaposition of times and places—the young and old Itikka/Mäkilä, outer space or the universe and Helsinki—gives way to overlapping or, like the form of an ear, spiraling towards an idiosyncratically fantastic climax. The introspection begun in the wood, triggered by a photograph of his childhood home, leads to Itikka dressed as a clown rowing through space where toys float with asteroids.[130] He finds his younger self and carries him in his boat as the asteroids and toys burn up. This burning seems to signal a purging of the past and reoccurs in the image of his rundown childhood home in flames, which is then resurrected in its original, pristine condition on the last page.[131]

Besides the house, the owl appearing throughout the book is another symbol, alluding to its shamanic significance as a watching, guiding companion. A symbol of wisdom, the owl in this comic is an indicator of the escape of the young and old Itikkas from the material world in order to come to terms with themselves. On the other hand, the penguins, which only appear during the older Itikka's hallucinations and visit to his burning house, can be seen as a whimsical factor highlighting the absurd nature of the situation by subverting the norms associated with reality. The symbolic role accorded to many of the images is complemented by visual sophistication, which often enters into a dialectic with (psychological) realism. Such a visual style deserves further consideration due to its symbiotic pertinence for the story and the consequent contribution towards openness. The verisimilitude and improbable juxtapositions correspond to what artist and art historian Michael Casey called the New Image, while describing Mäkilä's paintings, in which

> the essence of two apparently contradictory states—the dream and reality—have merged into the reality of the New Image and Neo-Surrealist state. A state that draws attention to those strangely suggestive coincidences and resemblances which stimulate the mysterious workings of the subconscious and give us a glimpse of a world beyond our ken.[132]

Wavering between photorealism and its dissolution through hyperreal colors, Mäkilä's visual style often reflects the nature of the event being narrated, as is the case with the transition from the almost realistic rendition of the stream to shaky hyperrealism during Itikka's climactic self-realization.[133] The surreal tone in *Taxi* builds an apposite intermedial connection with the Surrealist movement when one considers the relevance accorded by the Surrealists to art, which, for them, was a means of tapping into the creative energy propelling life in order to attain a deeper understanding of the universe and themselves.

Corresponding to the painterly appearance and construction of the panels, the frames and interstices are always straight and geometrical. Besides being conventional, this also gives the impression of logical clarity that contrasts with the content. Dynamism is introduced with the thin, page-wide panels. Yet, aside from the subtle changes in the degree of realism, the artistic techniques employed remain consistent, especially in comparison to the other comics discussed in this section.

Moderately varied layouts comprising of large panels complement the rich images. Since full-page panels or splashes are limited, they acquire both visual and narrative monumentality.[134] The effect of these splashes is comparable to that of Mäkilä's paintings, which often have large dimensions and cover an entire wall. Moreover, the depiction of landscapes from an elevated perspective evokes Romantic renditions of the sublime in nature.[135] Describing this tendency in Mäkilä's works as "postmodernist interpretations of the Romantic sublime landscape," art historian Kimmo Sarje also sees it as a fusion of science fiction and realism.[136] Beyond its link to art movements, the contrast created between reality and unreality in Mäkilä's panels imbues the everyday with a psychological, subjective quality.

The switching between third- and first-person pronouns in the narrative captions creates several subtle effects. While the narrative captions at the beginning are in the first person (which persists when the focus shifts to the older Itikka),[137] a metafictional moment is created when the protagonist refers to himself in the third person, thereby repeating Mäkilä's action of giving himself another name and constructing his story around it.[138] Moreover, the third-person pronoun is used when Itikka is alone in the wood, indicating the protagonist's stepping aside from himself in order to achieve a better understanding. In the same sequence, the pronouns also change to first and second person, thus forming a part of the protagonist's conversation with himself while also referring to the reader.[139] The first-person perspective steps in once again as Itikka rows through space to rescue his younger self.[140] For the remaining portion of the book, however, as Itikka visits the inferno that contains his father and his house, the third person is used. The visit is followed by a bizarre climax where Itikka/Mäkilä appears as a transvestite, with Itikka watching the transexual version of himself levitating and leading the four ghosts of his aged father in a song on death and heartlessness.[141] Here, Itikka reveals himself as both age- and genderless.[142] In combining the aspect of self-portraiture with autofiction, which is enhanced by the unsteadiness between reality and fantasy, *Taxi* generates several interpretational possibilities.

Comparable to the other works discussed in this section, *Taxi* has an elaborate visual style rooted in painting. Furthermore, all the primary cases analyzed in this section use detailed, suggestive images. While Moebius carves a niche through the vivid images and the absence of a clear narrative, Bilal and Yslaire have created coherent stories that are both aesthetically striking and imbued with different, interlinked levels of meaning. Although this also applies to Mäkilä's comic, *Taxi* stands apart due to its close relationship to the artist's oeuvre, as well as its intensely personal content. Although the comics by Mäkilä, Bilal, and Yslaire indicate the ways in which conventional comics have been altered, it is noteworthy that Mäkilä's and Bilal's comics open up diverse paths of interpretation—particularly through intertextual and intermedial references—in adhering to the basic tools of comics.

The tendency of transforming existing techniques in comics and combining them with those from literature and the visual arts through references to content—as well as the appropriation of literary and artistic techniques—is recurrent in the more open comics from all of the genres discussed above. It is therefore time to explore comics' interaction with other forms of word-image narration, as well as literature and artists' books.

C'était la Guerre des Tranchées, Jacques Tardi, © Casterman. Reproduced with kind permission from the artist and Éditions Casterman.

Salut, Deleuze!, © Martin tom Dieck. Reproduced with kind permission from the artist.

Lovecraft, © Reinhard von Kleist. Reproduced with kind permission from the artist.

Mariko Parade, © Frédéric Boilet, Kan Takahama, and Ponent Mon. Reproduced with kind permission from the artists and publisher.

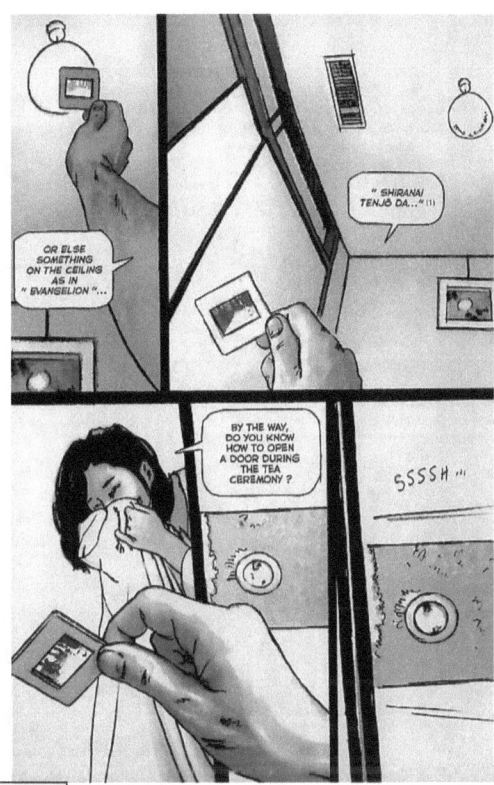

Mariko Parade, © Frédéric Boilet, Kan Takahama, and Ponent Mon. Reproduced with kind permission from the artists and publisher.

Le Voyage, © Edmond Baudoin. Reproduced with kind permission from the publisher.

Adèle Blanc-Sec, Le Labyrinthe Infernal, No. 1, Jacques Tardi, © Casterman. Reproduced with kind permission from the artist and Éditions Casterman.

Kuolema Kulkee Kintereillä, © Marko Turunen. Reproduced with kind permission from the artist.

Tohtori Futuro, © Jyrki Heikkinen. Reproduced with kind permission from the artist.

Introduction au XXe Ciel. http://www.yslaire.be, © Yslaire. Reproduced with kind permission from the artist.

XXe ciel.com. http://www.xxeciel.com/mémoires‹19›00, © Yslaire. Reproduced with kind permission from the artist.

Taxi Van Goghin Korvaan, © Jarmo Mäkilä. Reproduced with kind permission from the artist.

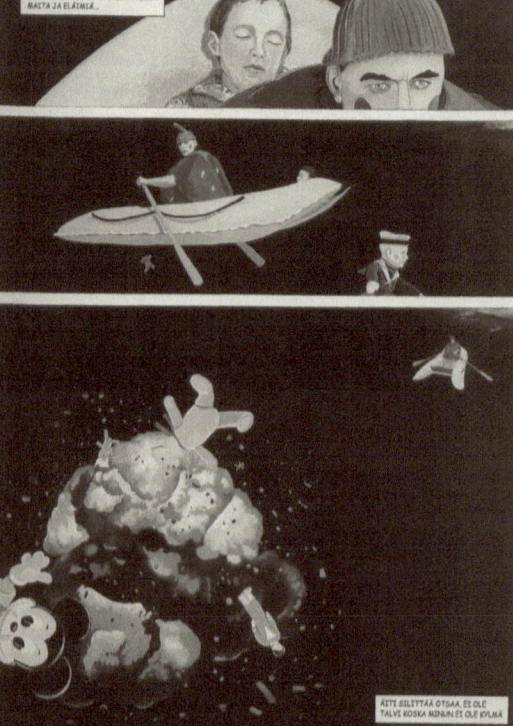

Taxi Van Goghin Korvaan, © Jarmo Mäkilä. Reproduced with kind permission from the artist.

Le Château, © Olivier Deprez.
Reproduced with kind permission
from the artist.

CHAPTER FIVE

Comparisons between Forms of Visual Narration

This section compares comics with other forms of visual narration, such as illustrated novels and artists' books, in order to trace comics' employment of tools from other, related forms for aesthetic rejuvenation (which can acquire additional significance through the subversion of conventions and functioning as intermedial references), as well as meaning-making. Using the illustrated novel—one of the most traditional word-image narratives—as a comparison, this section begins with two graphic novel versions of literary texts: *Dr. Jekyll & Mr. Hyde* and *City of Glass*. Although there are numerous illustrated versions of *Dr. Jekyll and Mr. Hyde*, the complex structure and content of *City of Glass* make it an unlikely candidate for an illustrated novel but not, as Mazzucchelli and Karasik's visualization proves, for a comic. Both create openness through experimentation with the original narrative, inclusion of additional figuration, and the employment of visual styles that are rich in connotations. By contrast, *Introducing Kafka*, in spite of its intertextual connections, adopts a more conservative approach; its omniscient narrator and episodic scraps of Kafka's works offer only limited interpretational possibilities.

Picture books for adults, where the stories are based exclusively on images, are also worth considering for establishing links with the more abstract interaction between pictures in several open comics. After discussing the visual experimentation discernible in wordless woodcut novels since the earliest decades of the twentieth century, a recent woodcut adaptation of Kafka's *The Castle* is analyzed to show how visual ambiguity and motifs are used to create a narrative offering several possible readings that can even transform the original work. To conclude, the visual techniques of creating openness, as well as the meaningful interaction with the book form itself, are discussed by distilling some of the techniques used in artists' books and other works relying on the visual materiality of the page and the word (word iconicity), such as Stéphane Mallarmé's *Un Coup de Dés*.

VISUALIZATIONS OF LITERATURE[1]
City of Glass[2]

Born in 1947, Paul Auster is primarily known for his postmodernist novels and his French-English translations and screenplays. *The City of Glass* is the first of three short stories making up *The New York Trilogy* (1987). *City of Glass: The Graphic Novel* (1994) is the collaborative effort of two artists, David Mazzucchelli (b. 1960) and Paul Karasik (b. 1956), with the latter joining because Mazzucchelli felt that he was unable to capture "the inner rhythms and *real* mysteries that made the story worth telling."[3] Karasik's solution for transposing Auster's multilayered story to comics was to include visual symbols capturing the characters' words and thoughts. This highlights the difference between merely narrating events and presenting its latent content, and thus moving towards more open works.

Before *City of Glass*, Mazzucchelli was renowned for his superhero comics, including the cliché-destroying *Batman Year One* (1997), with Frank Miller, and his self-published magazine, *Rubber Blanket* (1991). While Mazzucchelli cites Chester Gould, Hergé, and Alex Toth as influences, Karasik had studied under comics artists such as Will Eisner, Harvey Kurtzman, and Art Spiegelman, with Spiegelman being the one who attuned Karasik to the psychological potential of comics.[4] Though the final drawings have been made by Mazzucchelli, they remain a blend of Karasik's and Mazzucchelli's styles, not merely on the level of content but also with the drawings owing to the dominance of minimalism.

The comic carries an introduction from 2003 by Art Spiegelman, who describes it "as a strange doppelgänger of the original book."[5] He calls the transformation of literary novels into comics "visual 'translations' actually worthy of adult attention" in contrast to the "dumbed-down 'Classics Illustrated' versions"—that is, comics versions of literary novels published since the 1940s which often used conventional layouts with extensive dialogue and captions relying mostly on direct word-image relationships and panel transitions.[6]

Covering 138 pages, *City of Glass* has the format of a regular paperback. Opening like any detective novel, the genre's conventions are gradually dismantled in the course of the story through a metafictional twist simultaneously showing the creation of the story and undoing it. Already the title of the original novel, by evoking a milieu made of glass, visualizes the self-reflexivity that pervades the story's form and content.[7] The story is layered with several narrative levels, the interaction of which is left to the reader's discretion. This is augured by the declaration on the first page that "[t]he question is the story itself [...] and whether or not it means something is not for the story to tell."[8]

The comic's multilayered structure is also emphasized by the rare reappearances of the authorial voice with its typewriter-like font from the first page.[9]

One of the earliest self-reflexive, metafictional moments in the comic shows the protagonist, Daniel Quinn, writing run-of-the-mill but successful mystery novels under the pseudonym of William Wilson, with the protagonist of these novels, Max Work, directing Quinn. Quinn, being mistaken for the detective Paul Auster by a caller, is then roped into a case of his own. This involves following and preventing Peter Stillman from reaching his son, who is also called Peter. A brilliant scholar, Stillman had imprisoned his child for nine years in hopes of making him speak the original language of man in which the word and the thing were indistinguishable. An old man after having completed his jail sentence, he collects fragments and gives them new names in order to reconstruct the prelapsarian language. Quinn—who is hired by Virginia Stillman, the younger Peter Stillman's therapist and wife, as a private detective for following the older Stillman and preventing him from reaching his son—eventually absorbs Stillman's habits and gradually disappears, leaving behind only his red notebook.

The layering of stories within stories makes the structure resemble a Chinese-box world that willfully collapses from the inside in the end.[10] As with Cervantes (whose *Don Quixote* revealingly crops up in Quinn and Auster's conversation when the latter explains his latest writing project), the main, nameless narrator justifies his knowledge of the story at the end of the comic by claiming to be a former friend of Auster who gave him Quinn's red notebook.[11] During the story itself, the narrative voice is at times dangerously close to Quinn's.[12] This uncertainty regarding the layers of narrators augments the comic's complexity, and is reaffirmed at its end when the narrator's words first appear on typewritten paper and then on a leaf from Quinn's notebook.[13]

The fluctuation of identity and narrative voices augments the comic's openness by offering fluid characters who likewise increase interpretational possibilities. Indicating the fluidity of his identity early in the novel, Quinn begins shuffling like Stillman soon after Stillman's disappearance. A similar confluence of identities exists between Quinn, William Wilson, and Max Work. This triad thematizes the notion of autofiction, which is further consolidated by the appearance of Auster himself. Besides the aspect of authorship, another self-reflexive concern persists through Stillman's obsession with language and the relationship between the signifier and signified. This is visually corroborated by the very first panels that engender ambiguity between representation and the actual object, which is ultimately also a drawing: beginning with a zero on the dial, the panels shift to a telephone and then show the picture of a telephone on the directory.[14] The comic, therefore, not only preserves the original novel's movement and openness but also provides additional interpretational room through its visual symbols urging the reader to reconstrue the story. As McCloud, grouping symbols under the broader category of icons or representative images, points out, they "demand our participation to make them work. There is no life here except that which you give to it."[15]

Taken directly from the novel, the text remains deceptively simple, and the visual style is correspondingly minimalist. Black and white are kept flat, the lines are equally severe, and all the characters are either expressionless or depict typified emotions. This stylistic economy imbues every technical aspect of the comic with considerable relevance, especially the typeface and word balloons. In spite of its superficial simplicity, however, variations in the visual style do occur, particularly when other media are referred to, such as painting, drawing, or books. Thus, during Quinn's perusal of Stillman's book, *The Garden and the Tower*, geometric silhouettes, recalling silhouette animation, illustrate the book's description of Henry Dark's puritan upbringing.[16] In contrast, the book's biblical references appear predominantly in white, abstract spaces suggesting primordial conditions.[17] By not merely referring to *Paradise Lost*, but also manipulating John Milton's story through introducing his fictional secretary, Henry Dark, Stillman's book engenders an alternative history and thus strengthens the links between the fictional and nonfictional worlds, which widens the scope of the events and their construals.

Confirming the proximity between comics and cinema, Karasik likens the beginning of the book to Alfred Hitchcock's films that open by introducing the setting.[18] He also mentions using the "triptych" developed by Harvey Kurtzman to show different aspects of the same object in a manner comparable to camera shots with changing perspectives or aspect-to-aspect transitions. Karasik, however, not only portrays varying states of an object or setting but also accentuates its connections with other objects and aspects of the story.

Objects are also established as symbols during the monologues. This technique is especially potent in the young Peter's narration of his past, which begins with the gradual zooming from his face to his mouth.[19] In contrast to the other characters (and word balloon conventions), Peter's unnatural manner of speaking is indicated by a speech balloon tail uncannily slithering into his mouth. This unusual speech balloon recalls the banners and dialogues in medieval manuscripts serving to identify and give a voice to the figures.[20] On the next page, the word bubbles continue to emerge from a white pool, from which an expressionless statue of Charon with his boat surfaces. The same pattern of zooming in continues and picks up pace, making the speech balloons emerge from different objects, including a shamanic cave painting, a gutter, a gramophone horn, a well, an ink pot, a guitar, a teddy, a jail, and eventually a broken marionette resembling Peter. By contrast, Virginia's narration of Peter's past intersperses the scene of her ongoing conversation with panels portraying the drastic events through impersonal, stylized icons.[21]

One of the most prominent visual motifs introduced by the comic to capture the novel's abstract subject matter is the grid. The first of these is the labyrinth derived from the increasing abstraction of the neoclassical buildings visible from Quinn's apartment.[22] This recurrence of the grid in different objects within the panels extends its metaphorical scope.[23] In its most abstracted form, the grid also symbolizes Peter's childhood confinement at the hands of his father.[24] Quinn too is shown trapped by it since his first act of writing in the red notebook is a full-page splash superimposed by the grid.[25] Hence, the grid's disintegration during the last few pages, to the extent of completely emancipating the frames, also signals Quinn's disappearance. Since it is only at the end of the novel, while recounting Quinn's last activities recorded in the notebook, that the grid collapses altogether,[26] the rhetorical layout becomes productive, playing a figurative role by auguring the final collapse of the story and the protagonist's disappearance from the world. Trying to protect Peter from his father, Quinn kept a manic vigil outside the Stillman apartment house until he ran out of money, only to find out that Virginia's check had bounced, that the older Stillman had killed himself, and that the younger Stillman's apartment was empty, while Quinn's own apartment was inhabited by a stranger. Staying in the younger Stillman's apartment, Quinn records disjointed thoughts in his notebook until he runs out of paper and the light fades out.

As Groensteen observes, in contrast to the 1950s, when a rigid rectangular grid was highly common in comics, the use of this classic form today, in the absence of all restrictions, is often significant in itself.[27] Becoming a polyvalent motif in the story, the grid incarnates the self-reflexive structure of the book. Though the motif of the ventriloquist's doll—unlike the grid—is mentioned in the original novel, it evolves into a visual motif for the comic drawing a link between Peter and Quinn far earlier than was possible in the original text, silently reinforcing that link while underscoring its scope for figuration throughout the comic: first, Quinn appears as William Wilson's dummy, with Wilson himself as a two-dimensional, faceless figure in the background;[28] a broken marionette resembling Peter then appears at the end of his monologue and also lies at the heart of the fire concluding the novel.[29]

Hence, although the narrative burden still lies principally on the words, the pictures bind the story together by capturing situational changes or currents of thought as well as augmenting the figuration in the story. The visual motifs and symbols in *City of Glass* generate an unusual, intense relationship between words and pictures for which none of McCloud's categories for word-picture combinations really fit.[30] Morever, the visual representation of abstract concepts engenders both aspect-to-aspect and subject-to-subject transitions because, in capturing a story within a story or symbolizing a character's—usually Quinn's—thoughts, such panels often traverse ideas instead of scenes.[31] Generally, however, the transitions are often moment-to-moment or action-to-action.

Besides the many symbols, various references to religion, popular culture, and art are dispersed throughout the book. Like the conversation on Cervantes, many of these intertextual references are involved in a symbiotic relationship with the novel's central ideas. For instance, the visual citation of the comic strip *Henry* during Peter's monologue, which zooms in on the mouthless, mute boy in the famous Hamlet-pose with a skull, depicts the existential ambiguity of Peter's situation.[32] Similarly, Stillman's allusions to Humpty Dumpty as a symbol for man who, like an egg, is yet to develop his full potential, also confirm the theme of existentialism.[33] Lastly, though never directly cited, Quinn's wanderings around New York echo James Joyce's *Ulysses*.[34] Such compulsive, aimless drifting through the city can in turn be metaphorically interpreted as the search for oneself. Like the references to media, intertextual references also engender variations in the visual style that complement the novel's layers of meaning. The biblical section of Stillman's book, for instance, is illustrated in a manner reminiscent of the medieval, Christian predecessors to the comic strip. Monochrome imitations of canonical paintings, such as Peter Brueghel the Elder's *Tower of Babel* (1563) and Albrecht Dürer's engraving of *Adam and Eve before the Tree of Knowledge* (1504), also appear in the book within the comic, and are imbued with several possibilities of signification tied to the story's main themes.[35]

Longer, more radical changes in the visual vocabulary accompany major changes in the story, such as the transitional period between Stillman's suicide and Quinn's disappearance.[36] Punctuated by the click of Quinn's pen at both ends and captioned for the only time by his handwriting (which is usually reserved for his notebook), the images narrating this period are reminiscent of expressionist woodcuts: the splintered space in a medium shot with a backdrop of city buildings echoes Ernst Kirchner's *Nollendorfplatz* (1912) or *Potsdamer Platz* (1914).[37] More playful expressionist strains, recalling the bold strokes favored by the Fauves, appear later during Quinn's walk through

Central Park.³⁸ A final marked change in the pictorial style occurs in the last three pages, when the main narrator of the story steps forward. Headed by a typewriter typing out the first words of each page, the images are freely arranged over captions in a manner reminiscent of children's books. The lines are thicker and filled by washes. Frameless, these pictures are devoid of people.

While the aforementioned expressionistically realized episodes also emphasize the subjectivity of all that is shown, their broken lines enhance the decrepitude of the lives described—their fragmentation and that of the city. Due to its extreme deindividualization, Quinn's story is the contemporary Everyman's story, and this is further emphasized by Quinn's portrayal as the suffering Christ during his last known days. The theme of erasure also appears early in the book through the increasingly faded versions of the photograph of Quinn's family.³⁹ Moreover, a child's crayon drawing of an anguished young boy becomes synonymous with Quinn's self.⁴⁰ This implosive structure of the story, where identities are interchanged and consumed visually, surfaces at the end when the loose panels morph into torn leaves from Quinn's notebook.⁴¹ The disintegration that Quinn's personality undergoes is also indicated by depictions of cracked earth and Stillman's remark, "You can't make an omelet without breaking the egg," which is echoed by Quinn.⁴² This motif of fissures recurs in Stillman's collection of broken, discarded objects; it is connected to other signs of fragmentation, such as the disintegrating grid that ultimately gives in to a—possibly figurative—fire as Quinn is swallowed by the void.⁴³

A comparison with the original novel is useful for exploring the facet of *transmédiatisation* or the transposition of material from one medium to another, since the changes are indicative of the relationship between comics and literary novels, particularly comics' means of inserting comparable layers of meaning.⁴⁴ *City of Glass* depicts the transposition of expression from the singular channel of words to a hybrid one of words and pictures. The difference between the novel and its graphic counterpart consequently lies in the varying signifying powers of words and pictures because words are abstract, comparatively distinct icons with specific meanings, whereas "meaning is fluid and variable according to appearance" in pictures.⁴⁵ Consequently, the *confrontation transsémiotique* or the problems raised during transpositions between media lies in transferring the multilayered content of words into pictures. Through its many visual motifs and figurative style, the visualization of *City of Glass* succeeds in preserving most of the original novel's undertones while contributing additional ones.

Both comic and novel have a similar length: 133 pages for the former and

129 for the latter in trade paperback format. Paul Auster's novel twists the popular genre of a detective story with noir elements into a highly self-reflexive novel, where the abstract concepts introduced acquire precedence over the story, which, like its characters, fades away. In a comparable vein, the comic's suggestive but conventional layout and visual symbols, instead of directly illustrating the narrative, render it open to several possible interpretations. One such instance occurs during the disintegration of the grid at the end of the comic: the middle tier begins with a long shot of Quinn at his desk, followed by a panel with Max Work's grave and another with William Wilson's books burning, where the words in the captions have no direct link with the pictures.[46] While the words describe the dissolution of Quinn's memory, the pictures allude to the increasing distance and eventual elimination of specific elements of his past. The connection between the two channels of expression is consequently figurative, allowing for several interlinked interpretations building on the consequences of his memory loss.

Notably, the most visual aspect of the original novel, Quinn's drawing of the paths taken by Stillman across New York, is maintained in the comic.[47] Here, however, the very process of drawing is shown, with the diagrammatic mapping from the original book acquiring a more personal appearance in its comics version.[48] A more blatant visual motif that has no direct precedents in the original text is the windup mechanical toy.[49] While directly linked to Stillman by the caption, the toys symbolize many of the novel's characters and connect with the motif of marionettes associated with Quinn and Peter and their essence as characters conjured by the authorial mind.

In comparison to illustrated books and other comics versions of novels, the most revealing difference in *City of Glass* lies in the greater use of allusive pictures, which visually sustain and enhance the themes via the figurative scope of the depictions and their broad connections. In addition, the style itself often uses the emotional power of pictorial simplicity that, as mentioned above, has been used in some of the most widely acclaimed autobiographical comics of our times. The potency of this tool lies in its reversal of the stereotypes attached to comics, particularly the association of stylized art with superficial, frivolous content. When complementing the narration through functioning figuratively, as in *City of Glass*, the use of stylized images reflects the broad signifying spectrum of minimalist depictions. Nonetheless, as the next comic proves, minimalism is not the only way of visually enhancing the transposed stories and opening them.

Dr. Jekyll & Mr. Hyde

The Italian writer-artist duo Jerry Kramsky (Fabrizio Ontani, b. 1953) and Lorenzo Mattotti (b. 1954) have been creating books for more than two decades. Their earlier works include *Labyrinthes* (1988) and *Dr. Nefasto* (1989), as well as children's books such as *Un Soleil Lunatique* (*A Temperamental Sun*, 1994).[50] Recently, they also collaborated with several artists and writers in the animated film, *Peur(s) du Noir* (*Fear[s] of the Dark*, 2008). Working more frequently in collaboration with writers, Mattotti claims to always add the text of his own stories after the images and underscores the deeper, unsaid, emotional significance of images as opposed to words.[51] It is not merely the wide variety of visual narratives created by Mattotti that makes him stand apart but also his distinctive style of vividly colored, fluid compositions which reflect his affiliation to painting. Although he wrote several non-fiction works, Robert Louis Stevenson (1850–94) is best known for novels such as *Treasure Island*, *Kidnapped*, and *Dr. Jekyll & Mr. Hyde* (1896). Mattotti and Kramsky's comic from 2002 condenses the ninety-seven pages of the novella into sixty-four pages of panelled images and dialogue.

For most of the comic, the layout is relatively consistent. The panels are generally arranged in three equal tiers per page, and only the number of panels per tier varies from one to three. Kramsky's narrator begins by mentioning the inherent cruelty of mankind as Hyde's shadow slithers over the buildings, trams, and walls of a city by night.[52] This is followed by Hyde's senseless flogging of a little girl. Although this event conforms to the story that Richard Enfield tells the prosecutor John Utterson about seeing Hyde in Stevenson's text soon after the characters have been introduced, the expressive unreality of the panels more accurately illustrates Utterson's dream from the second chapter:

> Mr. Enfield's tale went by before his mind in a scroll of lighted pictures. He would be aware of the great field of lamps of a nocturnal city; then of the figure of a man walking swiftly; then of a child running from the doctor's; and then these met, and that human Juggernaut trod the child down and passed on regardless of her screams [...].[53]

Mattotti's labyrinthine, febrile, expressionist settings likewise capture the surreal visions of Hyde:

> The figure [...] haunted the lawyer all night; and if at any time he dozed over, it was but to see it glide more stealthily through sleeping houses, or move the more swiftly and still the more swiftly, even to dizziness, through wider labyrinths of lamplighted city ... And still the figure had no face by which he might know it; even in his dreams, it had no face, or one that baffled him and melted before his eyes [...].[54]

While Stevenson uses a steady extra-diegetic, third-person narrator, Kramsky's narrative captions belong to different characters from the story. Already on the third page, before Jekyll's butler, Poole's telephone call cuts through Utterson's disturbed night, the narrative caption contains a direct threat using the second-person pronoun, which, due to the absence of a clear addressee, could be both Utterson and the reader.[55] Although the original text is focalized through Utterson, it is only in the last panel of the comic, upon discovering the dead body, that the narrative caption adopts his viewpoint. The second event in the comic is parallel to Poole's visit to Utterson in the eighth chapter, suggesting that the comic has selected a later climax to hasten the pace and thrill of the story. As Utterson and Poole's conversation continues through narrative captions in alternating panels, Hyde is shown in Jekyll's laboratory.[56] On the next page, however, the captions use direct quotes from Jekyll's letter from the novel's sixth chapter, and halfway through the page, the panels flow into Jekyll's final letter from the tenth chapter, where he confesses on behalf of Hyde and himself for having used his scientific knowledge for bringing out his darker, bestial side.[57] From this point onwards, the letter forms the overarching, narrative frame for the comic.

Mattotti's transitions are frequently sharp but meaningful, juxtaposing events that are linked but do not always follow each other in the original novel, as is the case with Jekyll's two letters. This ties up with his claims of attempting "composer des B.D. à la manière d'un film" (to compose comics in the manner of a film) by concentrating on the narration through images and their interlinking.[58]

Correspondingly, however, Stevenson's descriptions are also visual and switch from aspect to aspect, as in the passage below:

> A great chocolate-coloured pall lowered over heaven [...] as the cab crawled from street to street, Mr. Utterson beheld a marvelous number of degrees and hues of twilight; for here it would be dark like the back-end of evening; and there would be a glow of a rich, lurid brown, like the light of some strange conflagration; and here, for a moment, the fog would be quite broken up, and a haggard shaft of daylight would glance in between the swirling wreaths. The dismal quarter of Soho seen under these changing glimpses [...] seemed, in the lawyer's eyes, like a district of some city in a nightmare.[59]

Imagery rich in colors and figuration recurs through Stevenson's text, as in the following description of London where "[t]he fog still slept on the wing above the drowned city, where the lamps glimmered like carbuncles."[60] It is also present in the narration of precise acts, such as Jekyll's friend Hastie Lanyon's description of the mixture Hyde created to turn himself back into Jekyll, which finds an echo in the comic's bold, contrasting colors:

> [Hyde] thanked me with a smiling nod, measured out a few minims of the red tincture and added one of the powders. The mixture, which was at first of a reddish hue, began, in proportion as the crystals melted, to brighten in colour, to effervesce audibly, and to throw off small fumes of vapour. Suddenly and at the same moment, the ebullition ceased and the compound changed to a dark purple, which faded again more slowly to a watery green.[61]

As already indicated, Mattotti and Kramsky have not settled for a direct, linear division of the original novel into words and pictures, and thus sentences from Jekyll's ending "Statement" flow into scenes described in Stevenson's earlier chapters. The unspeakable adventures and acts of depravity that Stevenson never elaborates upon are vividly sexual in Mattotti's depictions, albeit not in the words, which remain close to the original text, without directly quoting from it. Exemplifying the extent of interpretational variation offered by images, Hyde's gradual domination of Jekyll's being is visualized on the page relating Jekyll's refusal to see his friends, where the doctor appears as someone in between the two personalities.[62] Later, the one direct, albeit partial, portrayal on the page shows Jekyll's eyes narrowed and nested in a greenish complexion, close to Hyde's grey tone, with only his hands having yet to change color and turn into claws.

Like the violent murder of the prostitute, the meeting with the diplomat's wife, Lady Elda, and her subsequent murder are not from the original text. Elda's murder replaces the Carew murder in Stevenson's fourth chapter, which exacerbates the infamy surrounding Hyde, branding him as a criminal and forcing him to flee. It is precisely at this point in the comic, when both Hyde and Jekyll are driven to desperation by the external pressure to escape and the unpredictable effects of the medicine, that the narrative caption is also infiltrated by Hyde. Conversely, after leaving Lanyan gasping for his last breath, Hyde admits to a deep self-loathing, thereby proving Jekyll's powerless presence within Hyde.[63] This visual and textual juxtaposition of Jekyll's and Hyde's perspectives brings the conflict of split personalities to the forefront in the comic. Nonetheless, the roots of the nightmarish hallucinations, as well as the Jekyll-Hyde conflict exacerbated through Jekyll's description of himself and Hyde in the third person, can be traced to the original text, as is evident in the following extract:

> I became, in my own person, a creature eaten up and emptied by fever, languidly weak both in body and mind, and solely occupied by one thought: the horror of my other self [. . .] I would leap almost without transition (for the pangs of transformation grew daily less marked) into the possession of a fancy brimming with images of terror [. . .] The powers of Hyde seemed to have grown with the sickliness of Jekyll. And certainly the hate that now divided them was equal on each side [. . .] he (Jekyll) thought of Hyde, for all his energy of life, as of something not only hellish but inorganic.[64]

The elaborate haunting hallucinations towards the end of the comic unfold as a grotesque carnival, with the twisted, distorted bodies reflecting Jekyll's agony.[65] These nightmares then recede into the background with the illustration of Jekyll's boyhood memory of the goldfish that became the first victims of his experiments. These creatures recur as a visual trope in the remaining pages of Jekyll's uncontrollable metamorphosis in the terrifyingly fluid surroundings. Tellingly, the comic has devoted four pages to the incessant, final metamorphosis before Jekyll's death, where neither Jekyll nor Hyde remain distinguishable.[66] This sequence is comparable to the first depiction of Jekyll's metamorphosis into Hyde that unfolds across two pages in a much brighter milieu, where the organic elements remain distinct from their surroundings.[67] While being original visualizations, the later metamorphoses in the comic also appropriate instances from Stevenson's novella. The alternating embryo- and skull-like forms of the transforming Hyde-Jekyll illustrate "a grinding in the bones, deadly nausea, and a horror of the spirit that cannot be exceeded at the hour of birth or death."[68] Yet these exorbitant depictions are also rooted in Mattotti's personal interest in the formal potential of the line and its mutation.[69]

The thematic significance of mutation is visually prevalent from the very first page, affecting both the style and the composition of the panels. Each panel juxtaposes sinuous lines with geometrically rigid ones, and these sharp but unparallel lines create a warped space. Since the figures in this space are also curved and flow into each other, the deranged atmosphere is enhanced. Consequently, the similarities to early movements of modern art—which aimed at imbuing depictions of the external, predominantly urban world with individual feelings and moods—are impossible to overlook. This link is much more obvious in certain instances, such as the external views of the streets and houses,[70] as well as the bar scenes, where the grotesque figures resemble those made by George Grosz.[71] In addition, the splintered light and unsteady construction of houses, enhanced by the bright unnatural colors and confined to geometric shapes, are comparable to the work of Lyonel Feininger, whose comics have strongly influenced Mattotti.[72] In keeping with these artistic influences and similarities, the setting and costumes are also from the 1920s instead of the Victorian era.

The unnamable deformity characterizing Hyde in Stevenson's words is captured in the images by the expressionist distortion affecting all the figures, with darkness—an inhuman grey complexion and dark clothes—and repulsiveness remaining Hyde's distinctive attributes.[73] The deformation of the figures can be linked to Jekyll's realization of "the trembling immateriality, the mistlike transience, of this seemingly so solid body in which we walk attired."[74] Likewise, the vibrant colors and dynamic forms express Jekyll's early sensations as Hyde:

> I felt younger, lighter, happier in body; within I was conscious of a heady recklessness, a current of disordered sensual images running like a millrace in my fancy, a solution of the bonds of obligation, an unknown but not an innocent freedom of the soul.[75]

The cacophony of colors complementing the spatial distortion echoes the comic's structure where several climaxes of intense cruelty and their aftermath are juxtaposed. The congruence of the narrative structure with the palette is apparent in the contrast between the page concluding Hyde's sexual rampage and the opposite one beginning with a brooding Jekyll in his laboratory:[76] a screaming red dominates Hyde's scene, construing the background for the figures' naked flesh that is tinged green by the lighting. By contrast, Jekyll's laboratory is subdued by somber tones of blue and purple, with the red being only marginal and most apparent towards the end of the page when he opens the drawer with the injection for transforming into Hyde. The expressionistic style is also appropriate for the paradoxical collective consciousness of the characters in the Victorian novel, where the reliance on reason and logic coincides with a strong belief in supernatural forces, especially the devil. Most of all, however, the striking contrasts incorporated by the visual style express Jekyll's conviction that the good-evil split underlies all mankind, making a dual identity inevitable:

> With every day, and from both sides of my intelligence, the moral and the intellectual, I thus drew steadily nearer to that truth, by whose partial discovery I have been doomed to such a dreadful shipwreck: that man is

not truly one, but truly two [...] It was the curse of mankind that these incongruous faggots were thus bound together—that in the agonised womb of consciousness, these polar twins should be continuously struggling.⁷⁷

Despite differences in both source texts and styles of visualization, *City of Glass* and *Dr. Jekyll & Mr. Hyde* tackle the issues raised by the *transmédiatisation* of their respective original texts and even increment the openness of those texts through their visual figuration, which brings in complementary levels of interpretation within the story. On the other hand, the next comic, *Introducing Kafka*, contains only excerpts of Kafka's works; their narration through comics using direct, unambiguous illustrations is relatively one-dimensional, which can be attributed to the comic's aim of being an informal guide to Kafka's life and works.

DIDACTIC PICTORIAL NARRATION: *INTRODUCING KAFKA*

Comics are frequently used for educational purposes because of the effectiveness of their word-image narration. They are found not only in textbooks but also in supplements issued for public information. The directness of many of these educational comics, which aim to provide easy reading for the young, the semiliterate, or those reluctant to read lengthy texts, often leads to closedness.

Robert Crumb (b. 1943) is hailed as one of the pioneers of American underground comics, whereas David Zane Mairowitz (b. 1943) is best known for his radio plays. Being part of the "Introducing" series, *Introducing Kafka* (1993) condenses information about the author's life and works into roughly 175 A5 pages. Most of Kafka's biography is conveyed through blocks of text spoken by an omnipresent, frank narrator. Steadily accompanied by at least one or two illustrations taking up half of the page, a word-picture relationship common for simpler illustrated books is established since the pictures only corroborate the text.⁷⁸ Although Kafka's posthumously published novels appear as comics, their content is drastically truncated and ruptures are also frequent.

The comic begins with a sentence from Kafka's diary written in ink on a diagonally placed parchment, with the first letter bulging beyond the tattered fragment. The diary piece cuts through a visualization of the violent death described by it. The comic's opening words are, therefore, both part of the illustration and a description of it (much like the rainy opening of *Contract with God*, with the words describing the rain also being part of it).⁷⁹ This unusual word-picture relationship is maintained on the second page but appears rarely after that.⁸⁰ Different voices are distinguished through the lettering, with the typed style indicating the narrator and contrasting with Kafka's handwritten words, which are always part of the images.[81]

Kafka's Czech context is introduced above a cityscape of Prague and is followed by a description of the Jewish traditions in his ghetto.[82] Some undocumented Hassidic influences are also mentioned.[83] A brief, comics version of *The Castle* concentrates on Joseph K's interaction with the large cast of female characters. The narrator then discusses Kafka's fear of women and its reflection in the female types in his stories; this text is summarized by an illustration.[84] Another interlude describes the worsening times, as well as Kafka's closeness to his sister Ottla and his last girlfriend, Dora. Particularly vivid is the double-page spread visually summing up the interwar era with the rising influence of National Socialism and Communism.[85] Titled *Berlin 1923!* in Gothic letters and accompanied by commentary emerging from Dora's portrait, it depicts swirling masses of people and clashing armies meandering into a long line outside a shop, with a coughing Kafka at its tip. The afterword then describes what happened to Kafka's works, his letter to his father, and the subsequently socialist Prague. Before ending, the comic summarily recounts *Amerika*.[86] Although this section is named after the novel's eighth and last chapter, "The 'Nature' Theatre of Oklahoma," the subject matter of the original chapter is only covered by the last three pages. In contrast to the previous stories, Mairowitz's words dominate the entire story, with most of the panels merely illustrating the words and rendering it similar to his commentary throughout the book rather than the other comics stories.[87] In the course of the book, it is only occasionally that the narrator allows the images to do some of the talking, as with the illustration showing the sign change at Kafka's work place, which follows a description of the post-World War I situation and the establishment of Czechoslovakia.[88]

Crumb's trademark unflatteringly fleshy style appears in a more serious mode in this comic, without losing its self-deprecating trait. Some depictions remain blatantly caricaturizing, aiming at mild ridicule, which suits Mairowitz's colloquial and humorous language.[89] The most widely employed device from the conventional repertoire of comics is the stylized rendition of inner states, such as the spirals replacing eyes to indicate hypnosis,[90] or the stars, swirling lines, and bulging eyes representing hallucination.[91] Like the words, the images do not call for further interpretation.

On the other hand, the main intermedial references, which are visual, are pertinent for the subject matter. Confirming the aptness of George Grosz's disillusioned urban worlds as illustrations for Kafka's milieu, Crumb's flabbergasted Kafka—although more three-dimensional than the other figures crowding the drawing—appears in the corner of an illogical Groszian scene.[92] Some unaltered visual references are also present, all of which belong to the world of print: Rabbi Loew's book from 1578, *Gur Ayeh*, as a background sprawling across two pages,[93] the original cover of Kafka's *Die Verwandlung* (*Metamorphosis*),[94] and Kafka's technical drawings for the Worker's Accident Insurance Institute provide some visual variety in the comic.[95] Subjectively altering a real-life reference in accordance with Kafka's description, a belligerent Statue of Liberty, with sword and shield, marks New York's skyline when Karl Rossman, the protagonist of *Amerika*, sees it for the first time.[96] Yet, once again, further interpretation is not called for, nor is it steered in a particular direction, like the undeveloped references mentioned above. The model reader is consequently one for closed texts.

The visualizations of Kafka's stories are too condensed, rendering their sequence of events and structure patchy. While the sordidness and despair persisting through Kafka's books is preserved, mostly due to Crumb's style, a relative lack of experimentation with the techniques persists, especially on the verbal level. Altering between simple word-image relationships and complete word dominance, the mode of communication remains direct and avoids recoursing to additional levels of meaning. Since it aims at imparting factual information, the comic cannot afford ambiguities and does not desire extra exertion from the reader.

Having looked at different kinds of visualizations of literature, it is now time to turn to other modes of narration through pictures.

WOODCUT AND WORDLESS NOVELS

Like illustrated novels, mute or wordless books can also be seen as distant relatives of comics, relying this time exclusively on visual narration. Such books are not limited to picture books for children and also include works for adults, which can reveal links with some of the visual experimentation unfolding in comics that leads to openness. The most popular of these books from the early twentieth century used the woodcut technique, and their creators regarded themselves as artists (rather than cartoonists) narrating through sequences of images. The discussion of woodcut novels here is followed by an analysis of a contemporary woodcut novel, *Le Château*, by Olivier Deprez, where the narrative is imbued with multiple, allusive reading possibilities. These features push *Le Château* closer to artists' books, where narration is rarely a main concern and more abstract notions accompany the work's formal aestheticism and conceptual play. Artists' books will thus also be discussed in order to highlight the potential of abstract, disparate visuals, which, through their ambiguity and the preservation of connections—however weak—with each other, result in works allowing for diverse interpretations.

Wordless or mute narratives were apparently a German invention that became popular at the end of the nineteenth century with, among others, the "pantomimes" of Caran d'Ache.[97] At the beginning of the twentieth century, expressionist mute narratives made up of woodcuts and published as books appeared in Germany and Holland, as well as America, encouraged by immigration from Europe to the New World.[98]

Though starting out in the broadsheets catering to the masses, the production of prints—usually as a series rather than a continuing story—has been associated with the realm of fine arts, especially since Hogarth (1697–1764). Comics and prints have occupied, and continue to occupy, opposite ends of the cultural hierarchy, with the latter coming under fine art and the former under popular culture. This also corresponded with the activities of the artists since those producing prints frequently indulged in other fine art techniques, such as painting (Frans Masereel and Otto Nückel), whereas those making comics generally did not venture beyond illustration. As shown by the comics analyzed here, this has changed in recent decades to reveal greater interaction between the different arts and comics, which is most blatantly mirrored in the comics' visual styles. Artists such as Moebius, Bilal, and Yslaire exhibit and sell their panels and preparatory drawings as individual works, and others, such as Lorenzo Mattotti and Jarmo Mäkilä, are more active as painters than as comics artists.

Indicative of the current interest in graphic narratives, the wordless novels of Frans Masereel (1889–1972), Giacomo Patri (1898–1978), Lynd Ward (1905–85), and Laurence Hyde (1914–87) have only recently been reissued after decades of neglect. Collected in a volume titled *Graphic Witnesses* (2007), the book bears the subtitle, "Four Wordless Graphic Novels." This hardbound, glossy edition is the opposite of the original cheap paperback format, intended to be accessible for the masses, which persists in the 1957 German edition of Masereel's *Mon Livre d'Heures, Mein Stundenbuch*.[99] According to *Graphic Witnesses*' afterword by comics artist Seth, the only commonality between these works and graphic novels is the aim of "producing a serious sequential novel for an adult audience."[100] Like Seth, the woodcut novel historian David Beronä maintains that instead of comics, woodcut novels, with their avoidance of several panels and word balloons, are more similar to cinema, particularly the early silent films.[101]

A striking commonality amongst these woodcut novels is that they have clear rebellious messages that echo the tradition of using prints for sociocritical and political purposes. By virtue of being issued as multiple, affordable copies, prints were the first forms of popular visual art. Conveying religious or political propaganda, these early prints aimed to influence the public through exploiting the power of images to concisely and effectively convey general ideas. In addition, since the major woodcut novels appeared in the first half of the twentieth century between the two world wars, their wordlessness also imbibes the trauma and the censorial practices of the times. Furthermore, the sheer quantity of prints in most woodcut novels serves to distinguish them from the print series from the same era that averaged between twenty to forty prints: Masereel's *Mon Livre d'Heures* is comprised of 165, Ward's *Wild Pilgrimage* of 96, Patri's *White Collar* of 124, and Hyde's *Southern Cross, A Novel of the South Seas* of 119 woodcuts.

Notably, *Wild Pilgrimage, White Collar*, as well as Masereel's twenty-five-print sequence, *La Passion du'n Homme*, revolve around the same theme of a man struggling to survive in the industrial, capitalist world. However, Masereel's *Mon Livre d'Heures*—as suggested by the title and confirmed by Mann's preface—is simultaneously more personal and distanced than the other works, since the woodcuts are more autofictional than autobiographical. Given Masereel's social concerns, the protagonist in these drawings typifies the average modern man. In the process of rendering the story relatable to the male readers of the time, the artist has been effaced, letting his concerns become one with those of the common man. The subjectivity of the content is complemented by Masereel's trademark style, which is evident in the soft edges prevailing over his woodcuts and confirming his affiliation to painting. Before *Mon Livre d'Heures*, he had illustrated literary works, including novels by Tolstoy and poems by Blaise Cendrars.

While Patri's *White Collar* was also influenced by actual experiences, the story is not completely his own, but mixed with those of the people he knew. This distance from the protagonist is evident in the objective style of the images. Furthermore, Patri has a tendency to simplify and deindividualize certain scenes and figures, imbuing them with universal significance. In the new edition, these stylized images are highlighted through the replacement of the black used for the other woodcuts with brown. Since the other linocuts remain in black and unmistakably depict the protagonist, the insertion of brown plates, with their stylized objects and people, underscores how the heavily stylized images punctuate the story, condense its main ideas, and in the process create distinctive motifs, such as the opening image of a gigantic white collar. Recurrent in woodcuts due to their lack of words and compact size, such motifs concretize the main themes while retaining the ability to spark multiple interpretations.

Amongst the woodcut novels collected in *Graphic Witnesses*, it is in

Ward's *Wild Pilgrimage* that harsh reality is monumentalized to nightmarish proportions with Ward's images being the most violent in the collection. In contrast to Masereel's subjective tone, Patri's, Ward's, and Hyde's novels are more blatant protests, against capitalism in the case of Patri and Ward, and against the 1945 atomic bombing in the case of Hyde's *Southern Cross*.

Hyde also stylizes to the extent that he transforms certain objects by zooming in on them. It is in Hyde's woodcuts that the affiliation to cinema is most evident and can be linked to his employment at the National Film Board of Canada. His prints are not only lighted in a cinematically specific, controlled manner—as opposed to expressionistic chiaroscuro—but the transitions between the images occur in a way that accentuates the momentum of the narrative, varying from very slow changes, gradual zooming in on certain details, to aspect-to-aspect transitions. Moreover, both Hyde and Masereel adhere to a single size for each image, which functions essentially as a unifying factor. It is Patri whose prints vary dramatically in size and shape and are often limited to the outlines of single objects or people.

To a certain extent, these books also recall what was known as the poor man's cinema—books which carried an image per page. The impression of movement was created by rapidly flipping through the pages, with the individual image being often highly similar to its neighbors and having limited autonomy. Yet the images of woodcut novels, by limiting repetitions to certain motifs, have greater autonomy and are often able to stand on their own. Comparable autonomy of the image is noticeable in many open comics where, despite being part of a sequence, an individual panel already offers additional interpretational possibilities through the use of figuration or intermedial references.

While acknowledging the limited influence of wordless novels on cartoonists, Seth does note a change in the attitude of contemporary artists. As a possible offshoot of the increased interest in comics, the woodcut novel has been marginally revived in the new millennium, as exemplified by Eric Drooker's *Flood! A Novel in Pictures* or the more sociopolitical *Blood Song: A Silent Ballad*. Besides picture books that target both children and adults, other books for adults have also been published, such as Peter Kuper's detailed 192-page *The System*, which Groensteen considers a laudable example of how a story may be directed without words.[102] Given its appropriation of mechanical, industrial techniques, and graffiti, the book's use of stencils and spray paint is not only unusual but also apposite for its anticapitalist concerns.

Generally, picture books are regarded as part of children's literature. However, the woodcut novels described above, which usually do not have any words, are for adults. Groensteen points out that the basic difference between picture books for children and adults lies in the simplification of the syntagmatic relationship in the former to make the happenings on each page significant and lucid. Yet it is not necessary to have clear relationships between each panel even in children's literature.[103] The incorporation of sophisticated variations in wordless narratives does not render them ineligible for children; indeed, Maria Nikolajeva and Carole Scott regard the counterpoint or disjunction between words and pictures that allows for multiple readings in picture books for children as an indicator of the book's creativity.[104] Such a disjunction between words and pictures is also discernible in some of the more experimental comics analyzed above, such as *Kuolema* or *City of Glass*.

By using woodcuts in an abstracting literary adaptation, where the materiality of the images functions as one of the levels of signification in the story, Deprez's *Le Château* highlights the overlap between comics, woodcut novels, and artists' books.

WOODCUT VISUALIZATION: *LE CHÂTEAU*

Born in 1966, Olivier Deprez is active in printmaking and visual narratives. He is one of the founding artists of the publishing house Fréon, which distinguishes itself from other independent publishers of comics through its aims to publish *livre-objets* or artists' books, collaborating closely with the artist in the creation of the book and offering flexible format and binding options.[105] An intermediate object exemplifying the open work's "contravention of conventions"[106] through its form as well as its free, allusive adaptation of Kafka's *Das Schloss*, *Le Château* (2003) is more of a woodcut novel or an artists' book rather than a comic, although it shows, especially through its limited dialogues, how close the two can be. Its intermediate position is underscored by its marginality in the market due to the higher costs incurred by the special production techniques, along with the restricted number of copies.

With an almost square format, *Le Château* encompasses 222 pages. All of the images are woodcuts, but the technique's clarity has been rejected in favor of expressionistic ambiguity, generated by crude lines and heavy forms. The lines vary from thick, powdery lines imitating blurred crayon marks to the sharp lines mostly used in the depiction of structures, such as the canted streets and houses.[107] The irregularity of the lines and the alternation between black and white also imitates the texture of wood while incrementing the obscurity of the forms and figures: the technique thus accentuates the abstract and allusive nature of the story being told.[108]

The flatness of the objects and the background captures the claustrophobic atmosphere of Kafka's novel. The background, pitted by either white or black, resembles the static on malfunctioning television screens. Likewise, the white faces with hollow eyes and the similarly contrasted appearance of the objects recall overexposed negatives. Certain panels, with their barely discernible content, accentuate the nightmarish atmosphere of Kafka's story where, proportional to K.'s mounting despair, the weather is persistently harsh. The heavy streaks of white in the first images, where only K.'s torso is discernible, echo the opening lines of Kafka's original *Der Schloß*, which was published posthumously in 1926:

> It was late evening when K. arrived. The village lay deep in snow. There was nothing to be seen of Castle Mount, for mist and darkness surrounded it, and not the faintest glimmer of light showed where the castle lay.[109]

Obscurity, especially due to snow, recurs throughout Kafka's story and is expressed in Deprez's woodcuts by the unclear images and the dominance of white.[110] As one of the many instances where the chronological order of the original novel is slightly shuffled in Deprez's adaptation, this opening episode is mixed with scenes of K.'s memories of his homeland, which appear later in Kafka's story.[111]

The original, unfinished, novel tells the story of K., a land surveyor summoned to a village, where everything is controlled by the bureaucracy housed in a castle that is impossible to reach. Told at first that he is not wanted, K. is then informed that a certain Klamm is the official responsible for him. Finding Klamm becomes a never-ending quest, in the course of which he falls in love with Frieda, a barmaid at the Gentleman's Inn and also Klamm's mistress. For Frieda, K. eventually accepts a janitorial position in the local school but their relationship remains strained because of K.'s obsession with the castle and his refusal to emigrate from the village. In need of more attention, Frieda ends up running away with one of the two assistants assigned to K. by the castle, who follow him and are more annoying than helpful. Most of the villagers are distrustful of K., the outsider, and it is this aspect that is foregrounded in Deprez's adaptation. Notably, without the foreknowledge of Kafka's novel, the events and the happenings in Deprez's adaptation "burn out" like Eco's joint by seeming to be little more than a strange, disjointed story about an outsider.[112] Consequently, it is Kafka's original novel that provides a structure for Deprez's adaptation.

Typical comics conventions—such as panels, interstices, and word balloons—are left out. Instead of standard lettering, the words have been carved into the images and are sometimes distorted according to their relevance in the story, as with the massive block letters used for the first mention of Klamm by Barnabé, the castle's messenger.[113] Such renderings of words as images recall the onomatopoeic elements in comics. Allusions to comics devices also persist through the splitting of most of the pages into two, usually equal, images per page, divided by black lines that serve to frame different scenes. It is during K.'s frantic search for Klamm's first secretary Erlanger's office in the Gentleman's Inn that the divisions between the panels—which are in themselves the clearest visual elements, despite paradoxically aiding the generation of ambiguities—are eliminated. In the top half, K.'s searching pose is mirrored so that he looks both left and right as a third K. extends his hand from the profiled shadows.[114]

Arrows are only rarely used to indicate the speaker.[115] In transposing the story, Deprez creates his own dialogue instead of directly incorporating Kafka's text. He also establishes the motifs of fading images, watching, and frequently threatening faces.[116] Both dialogue and images emphasize the aspect of persecution that was subliminal in the original story. Significantly, K.'s visual identity is already effaced on the third page when, facing the reader, his face melts in a flurry of lines similar to the background.[117] Persisting essentially as a shadow through most of the book, his attire—bowler hat, long coat—and sharp features recall Kafka's photos while still remaining anonymous. The issue of individual identity is already present in the original story since the protagonist has an initial instead of a name, an unclear past, an equally ambiguous present, and shuffles identities by changing personal facts about himself and his assistants.

Like the images, the dialogue is also fragmented, and the material is freely altered. While Kafka's novel does not concentrate on the man from the castle who finds and wakes up K. in the Bridge Inn, Deprez devotes two pages to showing the man walking into the village and asking the villagers about K. The repeated depictions of the bridge not only foreshadow K.'s stay at the Bridge Inn, but also make the bridge a trope indicating K.'s perpetual alienation and stagnation—a constant state of inbetweenness just like the recurrent, essentially unchanged bridge, which suggests the possibility of traversing both time and space without really fulfilling it.

Deprez often inserts panels focusing on specific, relevant objects from the original story and transforms them into tropes through visual abstraction. These objects include the keyhole in the Gentlemann's Inn with Klamm's name written across it,[118] suggesting his perpetual elusiveness, and the bridge leading to the village signaling its isolation. Notably, the panel following the mayor's announcement of K.'s job as janitor in the school shows K.'s face slashed by several streaks of white, hinting towards the position's demeaning nature and the difficulties that would follow, including Frieda's breaking up with him.[119] Only a close-up with canted edges of a suitcase indicates K. and Frieda's (and the two assistants') move to the schoolhouse.[120] Recalling the incident when the four had transformed a classroom into a bedroom and the assistants had overheated the place, the focus on wood and its burning for two pages also points towards K.'s dismissal.[121]

The horse is another visual symbol introduced by Deprez, functioning as a metaphor for the traveler, as well as escape and freedom. Furthermore, when K. goes looking for Frieda after she had returned to the Gentleman's Inn, the bare unending wooden interior becomes more prominent and claustrophobic, consequently establishing the everlasting, confined space as a metaphor for desertion and inescapable solitude.[122] Yet another instance of abstraction occurs during K.'s inconclusive telephone conversation with an employee of the castle represented by an angry theater mask.[123] The employee's loud "Non!" is followed by a splash showing buildings hovering in the darkness as frail white beings populating the foreground look up at it.[124] The ridiculous image of the castle's employee reflects the inanity of the bureaucratic system; the massive buildings in the other panel indicate its dominance. Such abstractions that make the images function on a metaphorical instead of purely representational plane, while adding to the story being told, contribute towards *Le Château*'s openness. Nevertheless, the open manipulation of Kafka's story to the extent of unrecognizability goes beyond what most comics adaptations attempt.

Yet another significant addition by Deprez is the use of portraiture as a motif in the background, as in the scene where K. asks the innkeeper whether he is a powerful man. Divided into four equal-sized panels per page, the double spread contains vague portraits and concludes with a negative answer from the innkeeper.[125] Each of the *en face* portraits occupying individual panels in this double spread makes references to modern portraiture through echoing styles, including Klee's geometric, infantile style, Georges Seurat's pointillism, and the upside-down portraits of Georg Baselitz. This juxtaposition of stylistic references expresses the varying conceptualizations of the self.

"[M]y position is extremely insecure," K. admits to Gardena, the landlady of the Bridge Inn, early in the original novel. Underscoring K.'s otherness, she immediately negates his claim that Frieda's situation is likewise uncertain.[126] This persistent feeling of alienation and uncertainty is expressed through the ambiguity of the depictions. In Kafka's novel, it is primarily during his conversations with Frieda that K. expresses his feelings of alienation,[127] which in *Le Château* are condensed into two words: "Ma situation."[128] In keeping with the hazy depictions, especially at the beginning of the book, the protagonist disappears at the end, following the anonymous messenger offering him work, which is a vague reference to the landlady interested in hiring K. in Kafka's novel. K. is shown gradually walking out of a panel where the horizontal lines, once again mimicking blurred television screens, distort the images.[129]

Even though the essence of the scenes in *Le Château* are from Kafka's story, specific images have been selected at the expense of others, and the extent of abstraction or directness of the novel's imagery is suggestively altered. *Le Château* is therefore not a direct illustration of Kafka's story but an unabashedly liberal interpretation of it. A reader unaware of the original story is not likely to construe Kafka's story by reading Deprez's book. Hence, the artist's disclaimer at the beginning of the book: "Ce livre faisant, je songeais moins au récit qu'a la phrase" (In making this book, I thought less about the story than about the phrase).[130] Nonetheless, Deprez's visualization reflects the gambit of meanings associated with the book by its translators: although Kafka's first English translators, Edwin and Willa Muir, saw it as a futile search for God, a more recent translator, Mark Harman, interprets the novel as a quest for meaning itself.[131] Moreover, the mood of the original story—the rejection K. experienced at the hands of the hostile locals and eventually Frieda, as well as the sense of futility in trying to change his situation—is ingrained in the images, in their content, and in the harsh materiality of the woodcut forms. By using the allusive potential of images, *Le Château* imbues the comics medium with features from artists' books to an unusual degree by foregrounding materiality and exploiting the openness of abstract images and highly allusive transitions.

ARTISTS' BOOKS

The rise of word-image interactions concentrating on the pictorial form or iconicity of words can be traced to the end of the nineteenth century and is thus contemporaneous to the inception of modernism. As Guy Schraenen points out, Stéphane Mallarmé, with his *Un Coup de Dés Jamais N'Abolira le Hazard* (published by Gallimard in 1897), played a major role in freeing the book form, emphasizing its spatial possibilities, while also bringing out the significance of the visual form of words.[132] For J. Hillis Miller, such words, where the visual aspect is as important or even overshadows the semantic content, incorporate the ur-conflict between words and images.[133] This can be traced back to the word "graphic," which is applicable to both words and images and which is etymologically linked to the notion of grafting.[134]

Eco saw *Un Coup de Dès* as an open work "where grammar, syntax, and typesetting introduced a plurality of elements, polymorphous in their indeterminate relation to each other."[135] The iconicity of words likewise plays an important role in comics. Mostly used for attracting attention and sound effects, iconicity occasionally also acquires a different kind of significance as with the words expressively chiseled in Deprez's panels capturing the emotion behind the letters. While statements such as "[j]e suis pour—aucune illustration" ([I] am for—no illustration) may seem contradictory to Mallarmé's role in emphasizing the visual aspect of words, they underscore the importance accorded to the word, page, and book's physical or material essence."[136]

The book as a compound of both literary text and fine art has far older roots but the bestowal of artistic value to illustrated novels occurred only gradually during and after Romanticism. It was from the Romantic era onwards that an increasing number of artists began producing lithographs for major literary works, with one of the well-known examples being Eugène Delacroix's lithographs for Goethe's *Faust* (1827). Compared with other printmaking techniques, lithographs allow for considerable stylistic freedom in reproducing the artists' strokes and limiting the constraints imposed by the plate's material. The art historian Riva Castleman points out that the allotment of a page to each lithograph, which was necessitated by the different print techniques required for images and texts (planographic instead of relief), bestowed greater importance to the illustrations, rendering them almost on par with the text itself and encouraging their treatment as compositions in their own right.[137] Another milestone for artists' books was the spread of color printing in the 1890s. This was accompanied by the revival of traditional techniques, especially woodcuts, as in Paul Gauguin's *Noa Noa: The Tahiti Journal* (1901), which, by sharing many similarities with Japanese prints, also highlighted the increase in transcultural exchange.[138]

Castleman describes artists' books as those "primarily known for artists' contributions."[139] The artists' books scholar Johanna Drucker has observed that artists' books are often sketchbooks, with the book form enhancing the private nature of the drawings.[140] The concept of artists' books originates from the French *livre d'artiste*, which was popularized by art dealers Ambroise Vollard and, later, Daniel-Henry Kahnweiler.[141] Published as limited luxury editions, such books were made by renowned writers and artists. Being the products of close collaborations between artist, writer, and editor, these early forms can be seen as predecessors of artists' books, even though Johanna Drucker distinguishes between the *livres d'artiste* and artists' books on the grounds of the predominance of conceptual and material concerns in the latter, both of which were arguably already present in the *livres d'artiste*.[142] Possible candidates for such early artists' books stem from the end of the nineteenth century and include Maurice Denis and André Gide's *Le Voyage d'Urien* (1893) and Pierre Bonnard's illustrations for Paul Verlaine's poems

Parallèlement (1900), which, as Drucker highlights, reveals a particularly holistic incorporation of image and text.

Contemporaneously, poets such as Guillaume Apollinaire fused word and image through their calligrams. Taking word iconicity further, Futurist and Dadaist typograms treated words as pictorial elements instead of signifiers in order to free them from the constraints of language. A little later, conceptual artists such as Marcel Duchamp and Jasper Johns built upon this plasticity, consequently highlighting the signifying potential of a book's material aspects. Many post-World War II artists created books, sometimes as objects rather than texts, such as Wolf Vostell's *Betonbuch* (1972), but more frequently in tandem with texts. In either case, interaction with the form or materiality of the book is unavoidable.[143] Certain comics, through their distinctive format and experiments with word iconicity, incorporate this materiality and imbue it with significance for the narrative. This is especially true for the square format of *Salut, Deleuze!* which echoes the shape of its repetitive panels.

The difference between the post-World War II artists' books and the earlier publications is that the latter had a much stronger affiliation to illustrated books because their purpose was to visually accompany a given text. Nonetheless, the nature of illustration had already undergone a change in the early twentieth century: the "high-tension" word-image relationship that Mitchell discerns in Blake's poems[144] is incremented in Picasso and Sonia Delaunay-Terk's abstract accompaniments to their respective friends' poems, with concerns of spatiality and form being magnified in Delaunay-Terk's massive rendition of Blaise Cendrars's *La Prose du Transsibérien et de la Petite Jehanne de France* (1913).

It was Duchamp who played a major role in undoing traditional notions of art, including the concept of artists' books, through his *Green Box*, which became the prototype of artists' books from the 1950s onwards.[145] In addition to highlighting the plasticity of the book form, Duchamp also legitimized the notion of issuing artworks as multiples or series, thus broadening the scope of art by making it reject the importance of the original and become more conceptual. Upholding the artistic tradition of self-made books, several artists—including Sol LeWitt and Dieter Roth—established their own publishing houses. Although the content of artists' books is not always conceptual, since artists' books are often only catalogues documenting an artist's works, the more conceptual artists' books share certain commonalities with comics, particularly those comics which manipulate the form and technique to make it significant and self-reflexive for the story being told, as is the case in *Le Château* and *Lovecraft*. These commonalities include an awareness of the materiality of the page and its contents, as well as the use of abstracted images and allusive image-image and word-image relationships.

While the conceptual and non-narrative aspect of many artists' books automatically distinguishes them from comics, works such as *Le Château*, which stretch the limits of storytelling to highly abstract levels, unsettle the boundaries between comics and artists' books. Moreover, like many artists' books, *Le Château* also ensconces its stories in the materiality of the images. However, even though many artists have created sequentially arranged works—such as Walker Evans's *American Photographs* (1938) or Anselm Kiefer's large, wordless collection of woodcuts, *Der Rhein* (1983)—the absence of a concrete narrative in most artists' publications remains a major factor that differentiates them from comics.

In contrast to the previous chapters on genres, this chapter has attempted to bring out the distinguishing features of comics adapting literary material, as well as their interaction with related print media such as novels, illustrated books, and artists' books. As *City of Glass* and *Dr. Jekyll & Mr. Hyde* show, further interpretation in comics adaptations is encouraged through the use of indirect word-image relationships, abstraction, or the foregrounding of the technique as being significant for the story. Although comics visualizations of novels can be reductive, this is avoided when images cease to merely illustrate and add further dimensions to the original stories, retaining or incrementing the openness of the original texts. It is here that certain techniques from artists' books—such as the infusion of broad links between images and words, abstraction, or the exploitation of the material properties of the supports (covers, pages, words)—bring in openness. As is already evident in *City of Glass*'s limited changes of visual style, stylistic diversification is also a useful tool for increasing the signifying scope of the picture through exploiting the figurative implications of different styles. This visual potential of opening up a text is successfully taken to its extreme in *Le Château*, where the images generate such an allusive interpretation of Kafka's novel that the original story cannot be fully reconstructed without prior knowledge of the novel; instead, several related, alternative stories are possible, which nonetheless remain contained within the overarching structure of the original text. Indeed, the challenge for open comics is to allow for several interpretations without dissolving the narrative.

The dialectic between the openness of a work and the closedness of its structure will be clarified in the next part, which condenses the findings of the readings conducted here. After mapping the openness of comics, the book ends with a discussion of comics' anchoring in the current multimedia environment.

CONCLUSION

Generating Openness in Comics

As indicated above, comics such as *La Ballade* pave the way for longer, more autonomous narratives, which are usually necessary for developing and reinforcing the structure of an open work. Length is a relevant factor because a certain amount of space is required to enable the telling of a story and to create a structure along which openness can unfold. Although shorter comics can also be open, longer works have the advantage of more space to play with and to connect the different devices. This notion of an overarching, essentially closed structure within which openness unfolds can be concretized through considering Gianni Colombo's 1960 *Strutturazione Fluida* (*Fluid Structuring*).[1] Comprising of a three-dimensional frame with glass panels containing a long, twisting band of aluminum that is driven by an electric motor, it changes shape while remaining contained within its iron frame. A non-serial narrative provides a comparable structural framework, serving as "an organizing rule which governs [. . .] relations" between the aspects while maintaining a broad spectrum of signification.[2] Flexibility and self-reflexivity unfold, and are indeed only effective, when contained within a structure guiding the narrative.

Less open works, such as *Contract with God*, *Introducing Kafka*, *Arzach*, and the *Adèle* adventures, help in tracing a development of sorts—a non-linear and unintentional development—towards more open works. *Contract with God* and *Introducing Kafka* do so with their literary inclinations, by being, respectively, a novel-like comic imbued with autobiographical elements and a comic interacting with a literary figure and the intertextual network of his works. Moreover, their experimentation with visual figuration, especially word iconicity, albeit limited, points towards the repertoire of possibilities for openness that is ensconced in comics. In a similar vein, the *Arzach* and *Adèle* comics hint towards openness through their experimentation with page layouts and their subversive, parodic strains.

The means of generating openness in comics can be grouped under four broad categories based on ambiguity, suggestiveness, and subversion, which will now be elaborated, starting with the technical aspects of the medium and progressing to the media references, characters, and themes.

Disjointedness

As mentioned at the beginning, fragmentation lies at the heart of comics because of their reliance on dividing space to create a continuous narrative. Furthermore, each division uses scraps of both words and images that are, to varying extents, dependent on each other for their meaning. One is dealing with two kinds of disjointedness: those between the words and images and those between panels. Openness often depends on the extent of the indirectness and allusive scope of relationships between and amongst words and images, as well as between and amongst panels.

On a more practical level, this disjointedly sequential nature of the comic strip renders it ideal for depicting morphologies, and by extension, hybrid figures and spaces, that can attain a degree of vastness through their incompleteness since the interstices have to be filled in by the reader's imagination.[3] Hence, Fresnault-Deruelle's conclusion that "[l]a capacité d'émerveillement du *cartoonist*, l'esprit de la *mirablia* sont à l'origine d'un art qui—bien que souvent galvaudé—produisit des chefs-d'œuvre que seule une science consommée de l'ellipse pouvait engendrer" (the *cartoonist*'s capacity for engendering wonder, the spirit of the *mirablia* are at the origin of an art which—even though often compromised—produced masterpieces that only a science consumed by the ellipse could engender).[4]

As pointed out by Lefèvre, a certain awareness of the constructed nature of the images in comics is always present:

> Ce qui est sûr, c'est que dans la bande dessinée, la matérialité et l'artifice des signes ne passent jamais vraiment à l'arrière-plan, contrairement à d'autres types de narration visuelle où l'illusion référentielle joue de façon plus massive: l'effet trompe-l'œil y est improbable, le lecteur de bande dessinée étant un lecteur bien conscient du caractère construit, artificiel, des êtres de papier dont il suit les aventures.[5]
> (What is certain is that in comics the materiality and artificiality of the signs is never really in the background, in contrast to other kinds of visual narration where the referential illusion plays a more important role: the trompe-l'œil effect is unlikely in such cases since the comics reader is conscious of the constructed, artificial nature of the paper beings whose adventures he follows.)

Hence, comics are imbued with a certain degree of unreality, which can also acquire self-reflexive dimensions, as discussed below in the section on themes. In the more open comics, the atmosphere fluctuating between reality and unreality is enhanced by the employment of unusual layouts and transitions that often occur between psychological realms instead of physical ones but maintain a flow of possible meanings rather than whimsical jumps. Examples for this include the fluid, subtle switches between memory, imagination, and reality as Saint-Exupéry reconstructs his life minutes before his disappearance, and the interlaced mental and physical worlds in *Le Voyage*—in both cases, the surreal moments reflect upon the characters and events in the story's reality.

Although from Töpffer on to Hergé, comics using a third-person perspective have presented mental activity through images,[6] what happens in more open comics—such as *Arkham, Saint-Exupéry, Le Voyage, Dr. Jekyll & Mr. Hyde*—is that the rendition of characters' mental landscapes molds the reality of the story, and the psychological states themselves become more allusive instead of being clearly outlined. In such cases, the disjointedness of comics ends up acquiring figurative relevance by reflecting the disjunctive yet interlinked transitions between psyche and material reality.

The external, formal disjointedness aside, the conventional flow in comics, which usually relies on common transitions, such as moment-to-moment and action-to-action transitions, is largely lucid and the sequence of happenings is simple and indubitable. Thus, Fresnault-Deruelle regards the rupture of the conventional flow, the use of indirect transitions, such as McCloud's aspect-to-aspect transitions, and unconventional layouts as an innovation.[7] This also holds for more unexpected word-image relationships. Such features that counter a smooth flow of reading, raise questions regarding the story, and force readers to choose from multiple possible interpretations are recurrent in most of the analyzed comics, such as *Arkham Asylum* and *Lovecraft*, where quick reading is often hindered through the additional interpretational levels opened up by collages. In semiotic terminology, these collages create breaks in the process of horizontal syntagmatic reading by extending the vertical paradigmatic axis of alternatives at several points.

For understanding the allusive scope of symbiotic word-image combinations, it is worthwhile turning to Varga's categories which place instances of word-image unification, such as calligraphy and calligram, opposite situations where words and images remain visually separate, as in comics: in the case of the former, the usual hierarchical relationship of word-image combinations is subverted and rendered more interactive, offering multiple interpretational paths to the reader.[8] While iconical words, which merge the word with the image by emphasizing its visual form, are less relevant for openness and appear only intermittently in the cases discussed, the variety of visual and typographic styles employed by comics such as *Arkham* provides examples of word iconicity that is imbued with connotations revealing the character's psychological dispositions: Batman's diary is filled out in a white typewriter font, the Joker's writing is bright red and uneven, and Two-Face uses two different kinds of fonts. While comics typically only alter the font of the onomatopoeic word and often three-dimensionalize it for sound effects, word iconicity has the potential to merge the physical appearance of the word—frequently not an onomatopoeic one—with its connotations. This device was used at the very opening of *Contract with God*, where the narrator's words trickle with the rain announced by them. As with Moebius's *Arzach*, where most of the innovation unfolds at the level of the image and the layout, Eisner also introduced visual techniques that were expanded by the subsequent generation. Thus, while Crumb also exploited the connotations of typefaces in *Introducing Kafka* for distinguishing between the several narrators, it is in stories like *City of Glass* and *Arkham Asylum* that the form of the word plays a more revealing role by visualizing the unsaid of the tales and reflecting the various levels in the narrative.

As pointed out in the previous section, imbuing the materiality of the page as well as the book form with significance for the narrative is a commonality between comics and artists' books. While the adjustment of the format to the advantage of the narrative is infrequent, it can add an additional layer of significance, as in *Salut, Deleuze!* where the square format echoes and repeats the shape of the panels inside and thus also alludes to Deleuze's conceptualization of difference and repetition.

Generally, clear page layouts go hand in hand with easy and quick reading. An unusual layout is a means of attracting attention to the images and the comic's construction, as well as slowing the pace of reading. Although in *Salut, Deleuze!* it is the rigidity of the layout that is significant—through the contrast between the fixed visual pacing and the complex verbal narration of the story, as well as its literalization of the concept of repetition—atypical and varied layouts can also accentuate the openness of a text when they carry relevance for the story being told. This is the case with the splashes incorporating word-image montages in *Arkham Asylum, Lovecraft, From Hell*, and *Introduction*.[9] Spreading over one or two pages, these splashes produce disorientation, forcing the reader to make sense of the material on his own, consequently rendering the precise construal of the events unique for each reading. Thus, while radical page layouts themselves are not a recent innovation—already many American superhero comics and the artists of *Métal Hurlant* took liberties with the underlying structure of a page—it is worthwhile to distinguish between sensational layouts and those that work figuratively for the story, as in the contrast between Moebius's decorative layouts for the *Arzach* episodes and the role of the regular grid in *City of Glass* or the crumbling grid in *Lovecraft*. Through their allusive scope, such significant, self-reflexive layouts mold the narration in ways words cannot.

Visualizing the very layering of meaning, collages require the reader to find his way by exploring the connections offered in the visual rendition of each narrative moment. Moreover, collages in some comics, such as *Arkham*, thrive on the ambiguity stemming from the vagueness of the images as well as on the vast range of intermedial references. While Fresnault-Deruelle likens the act of reading comics to a quest towards comprehending their meaning since "lire une BD, c'est s'«abîmer» dans ses vignettes, comme si ces dernières n'étaient que les étapes d'un long creusement et les *strips* autant de corridors menant au lieu enfoui de quelque révélation" (to read a comic is to "drown" oneself in its panels as if they were nothing but stages in a long excavation and the *strips* corridors leading to the hidden place of some revelation),[10] the difference in open comics lies in the presence of several interconnected options of interpretation or hidden places that weave in multiple perspectives to form the story.[11]

In contrast to word iconicity, the collage is a more powerful technique of combining words and images in an allusive manner. Like Varga, Foucault also believes that verbal signs and images are always subordinated to a certain order. Nonetheless, for Foucault, it was Paul Klee—and not calligraphers—who eliminated the hierarchy and created a new space "by showing the juxtaposition of shapes and the syntax of signs in an uncertain, reversible, floating space (simultaneously page and canvas, plane and volume, notebook graph and ground survey, map and chronicle)."[12] Interpreting a collage by Plantu for *Le Monde*, where figures are superimposed on a printed background, Fresnault-Deruelle's commentary on the dialectic of its form also underscores the relevance tied to mixed media techniques such as the collage for opening up the fields of signification (especially self-reflexivity regarding real and constructed worlds) and appreciation in comics:

> Sémiotiquement parlant, un collage (ou un montage?) de cette sorte fonctionne sans accroc pour un autre raison: hormis sa fonction instrumentale (ou monstrative), l'image a pour vocation de se constituer en «universe»; autrement dit en un lieu de convergence (uni-versus) où les frontières séparant le physique du méta-physique ont tendance à se neutraliser: le rêve et l'état de veille s'y compénètrent; le lunaire et le sublunaire travail-

lent à s'y mêler; le banal et le prodigieux cessent d'y être perçus contradictoirement.[13]
(Semiotically speaking, a collage [or a montage] of this kind functions smoothly for another reason: beyond its instrumental [or demonstrative] function, the image is intended for "forming a universe"; in other words as a place of convergence [uni-versus] where the borders separating the physical from the metaphysical have the tendency of neutralizing themselves: dream and reality penetrate one another there; the lunar and the sublunar try to merge there; the banal and the extraordinary are no longer perceived as contradictions.)

The visual style employed in many of the comics analyzed here also counters the philosopher Alain Cambier's claim regarding the reduced value of the image due to its mass production.[14] Frequently resembling fine art, despite remaining a mass-produced item, certain comics (sometimes carrying the graphic novel label) blur hierarchical distinctions between the higher and lower or more popular arts. In addition, while still being part of the comic's context, certain images, which are sometimes only slightly connected to the other images, do acquire a considerable degree of autonomy. This, for instance, is the case with the drawings and photo collages in Yslaire's *Introduction*, where the images themselves incorporate silent self-reflexive commentary that refers to the story world but also goes beyond it through its allusions to, and transformation of, the twentieth century's history.

Many of the open comics here use either direct color—as in the *Nikopol* and *XXe Ciel* volumes and *Dr. Jekyll & Mr. Hyde*—or mimic some other technique associated with the fine arts, such as the woodcut technique in *Salut, Deleuze!* and *Le Château*. Even though it is only mimicked in *Salut, Deleuze!*, the woodcut is significant for the story because it concretizes the dialectic engendered by the contrasts of black and white, which is a key concern in the comic.

Although the issue of the original is automatically rendered irrelevant in comics, some comics do accord importance to their images as bearers of artistic expression instead of mere transmitters of information, which contributes towards the status of comics images as autonomous works of art.[15] It is also noteworthy that many comics artists, such as Baudoin, Yslaire, and Mattotti, attach both figurative and emotional qualities to their art. This allows additional notions linked to the value of fine arts to be transferred to comics including the link drawn by Heidegger between the painting's ability to "speak" and the materiality of the medium involved, such as the visibility of paint.[16] Although an imprecise explanation of the connections between viewer and artwork, it does explain the bold step taken by direct color in allowing the materiality of artistic techniques to bring in another layer of significance and thus contribute towards the openness of comics. Stemming almost directly from the artist's hand (or at least giving the impression of doing so), the use of direct color in comics infuses similar qualities of the *Zug, trace*, or aura in works originally dismissed as mass-produced, popular products.

Many of the more open comics discussed above, such as *City of Glass* and *Lovecraft*, and to a lesser extent *Saint-Exupéry*, alter their visual style for bringing in another layer of significance to the narrative—to transmit, among other aspects, the nuances of character, mood, and setting in the story. In *Mariko Parade*, the stylistic difference is used to underscore the difference between the two collaborating artists and visualize their voices. Yet, as comics like *Salut, Deleuze!*, *Tohtori Futuro*, or *From Hell* show, variations in visual style are not essential for creating openness. Nevertheless, the insertion and variation of visual styles in figurative and self-reflexive ways accentuate the dimensions of the narrative and its openness.[17] Moreover, as shown by the diversity of visual styles involved—ranging from the extreme reduction in *City of Glass* and *Salut, Deleuze!* to the photorealistic panels in *Mariko Parade* and *Taxi*—verisimilitude, or its absence, can enhance a comic's field of signification when it is of relevance to the subject matter.

Besides the allusions ensconced in different styles, the ambiguity of both detailed and abstract images also opens up avenues of interpretation in a manner that echoes J. Hillis Miller's description of illustrations as "falsifying abstractions from the ungraspable idea they never adequately bring in the open. What they bring to light they also hide [...] they leave the idea still out of sight, grimly reposing in the dark."[18] As Fresnault-Deruelle observes, abstract images, by lacking references to their surroundings or any clear external relationship, "se situent [...] dans l'absolu" (situate themselves [...] in the absolute).[19] In turn, abstract images can often serve as symbols or motifs, such as the bridge in *Le Château*. Such figurative elements are recurrent in open comics, and provide additional interpretational scope, as with the metaphor of the open head in *Le Voyage* and the motif of the crucified Christ in the second part of *La Guerre*. The ensuing ambiguity not only arouses curiosity or suspense but also offers several possibilities of construing the text. *Le Château* comes across as one of the boldest exemplifications of using pictorial indistinctness, which is also recurrent in *From Hell*, to offer multiple interpretations.

Media references

References to other media in comics range from their formal incorporation or imitation to their interweaving into the content of the story itself. That the comics analyzed above frequently employ varied and unconventional visual styles and techniques, such as collages,[20] is indicative of the medium's desire to explore and enhance the signifying potential of its hybrid essence. The stylistic variation in certain comics frequently makes express references to the fine arts. In *XXe Ciel*, for instance, elaborate paintings and drawings are combined with other artistic techniques, such as sketching and photography. Depending on their signifying scope and relationship to the rest of the work, references to literature (as well as the other arts and media) can also increment the openness of comics.

While elements of mass media are employed mainly for providing information about the story's situation and contextual factors in most comics, these references are imbued with self-reflexivity in more open works like the *Nikopol* trilogy: in contrast to the insertion of newspapers in the *Contract with God* stories or *Adèle et la Bête* that merely announce events, *La Foire aux Immortels* includes newspaper snippets bearing the narrator's annotations in red. Other references extend beyond the traditional newspapers by pointing towards newer visual media, including television, film, and the Internet. These references sometimes go so far as to take over the mode of narration, as is the case with digital technology in Yslaire's *Mémoires*.

Apart from its role in the *XXe Ciel* books, mediatization is also thematized in the *Nikopol* trilogy: the presence of the camera in the process of recording or in the form of film reels prevails over the trilogy's last book *Froid Équateur*, capturing the tumultuous lives of its characters. The variety of the media references in these comics highlights the specific attributes of each means of communication, ranging from the handwritten word in a diary to the image-dominated television advertisements. In doing so, the comics medium itself is elaborately flexed. This boundary-dissolving effect of intermedial references is noteworthy because, by taking up different media, the panel-photograph or panel-computer screen also highlights the comic's own machine-made or hand-drawn trace and thus works self-reflexively. As Samson points out, the very style of modern comics draws attention to the dialectic between the simulation of an objective, panoptic camera view and the essentially subjective nature of drawing in comics.[21]

The employment of cinematic techniques, particularly for narrative purposes, has the potential to insert additional layers of meaning through the very act of referencing another medium. Still, all comics use cinematic conventions to some extent,[22] and the styles of certain artists is frequently compared to films. The atmosphere of Eisner's comics often recalls film noir and related hardboiled fiction due to the mood generated by their dramatic lighting and the employment of certain character types. Openness is created not only by imbuing such technical borrowings with self-reflexivity but also by undoing genre expectations, which brings out additional perspectives, while maintaining a link with the traditional codes. Thus, *City of Glass* pretends to adopt the model of a detective story only to subvert it at the end through its metafictional layers. *From Hell* similarly undoes the notion of an easily resolved mystery told by an omniscient, barely perceptible narrator who casts increasing doubt over the story.

The techniques themselves can also acquire significance for the story being told, as with the mimicking of a distanced, recording camera by several panels in *La Guerre*, which complements its theme of deindividualization. Likewise, reflecting on the comic's story, Boilet's interaction with the *nouvelle vague*, which is already suggested by the *nouvelle manga* label, manifests itself in both the form and content of his work by revealing his (constructed) self and his creative process. Introducing the notion of auteurism, the *nouvelle vague* director became an auteur who made his presence felt in the film by treating the camera as if it were his pen.[23] Correspondingly, as pointed out by Baetens in his description of graphic novels, the auteur acquires prominence in such comics.[24]

Relevant intertextual references to canonical works of literature are also discernible in the open comics analyzed. The references to major literary works, specifically Coleridge's "Rime of the Ancient Mariner" and books by Melville in *La Ballade*, and the interweaving of Baudelaire's *Fleurs du Mal*, in *Nikopol* add further dimensions to the stories being told by establishing links with the referenced literary worlds. That these references form a more inherent part of the story in the *Nikopol* comics contributes towards their openness due to the multiple links discernible between the comics and their references. Although the references in the second section of *La Guerre* are not from literature but from Abbé Sertillanges and General Rebelliot's patriotic words during World War I, their inclusion furnishes the works with an ironic tone while illustrating the link between intertextuality and the layered rendition of reality that raises "la question du réel."[25] This quality can be extended to intertextual references in general, due to their inclusion of actual works (regardless of their degree of fictionality) beyond the story. Apart from the comics discussed as visualizations of literature or biographies of literary and philosophical figures, all of which inevitably incorporate references to other works, intertextual and intermedial references also play an important role in *Sandman*, *XXe Ciel*, *From Hell*, and *Arkham*.

"Contraventions of convention"[26] in characterization

The generalization that protagonists often reflect the target audience holds throughout the history of comics. While Töpffer narrated the doctor, scientist, and gentleman, his admirer Cham, a decade later, introduced a grocer as the protagonist of his album, *M. Lamélasse* (ca. 1840). Yet Marie Duval's Ally Sloper, arguably "the first comics superstar" because of the marketing campaigns attached to him, was essentially an antihero.[27] Using the type of the antihero was a means of securing popularity amongst readers, who would not only be amused by his stupidity but were also bound to feel better about themselves.

Going further along the same line, mock heroes or antiheroes evoking the contemporary Everyman are recurrent in comics. Such subversion of heroic stereotypes through, for instance, *Arkham*'s Batman, Nikopol and Niko, or R-Rautanainen and Muukalainen in *Kuolema*, can also contribute to the narrative's openness. This is especially the case when the character portrayals engage in a self-reflexive dialogue with stereotypes through rejecting the expectations attached to the figure of the hero, both in comics that are closer to the mainstream such as *Arkham* and the *Nikopol* trilogy, as well as comics that reference it, such as *Kuolema*. Mockery underlies the two Nikopols' fluctuation between almost-heros and antiheros, recalling both types but creating a new character combining Baudelairian disillusionism with psychosis provoked by a god's manipulation of Nikopol's body. While stereotypes, such as the rebellious, intelligent, and attractive youth, persist in protagonists like Frank Stern, even this type is tempered by other aspects, such as Frank's transitory identities. By offering several options for piecing together Frank's elusive identity in the course of the XXe *Ciel* series, different, but interlinked paths of interpretation are also opened up.

Thus, black-and-white characterization is tempered in the more open comics. Even unpardonably evil villains, such as William Gull and Hyde, are partially justified by the end of their respective comics. This graying of the differences between good and evil reflects a move towards psychological realism and the medium's increasing interest in focusing on the complexity of the characters, especially through the inclusion of suggestions that allow for several interpretations, as in the case of *Arkham*'s Batman and K. Consequently, a degree of incomprehensibility or ambiguity is discernible in the protagonists of open comics. This is already hinted at in *La Ballade* through references to Corto's past, but plays a more central role in such works as the XXe *Ciel* series or *Arkham*, where Batman is as disturbed as the criminals he sent to the asylum, and *Le Château*, where K.'s very being, like his situation, is steeped in uncertainty. In all three cases, the fluidity of the protagonists' identities reflects their comics' central concerns, namely, the fragmented, shattered world of the *XXe Ciel* books, the dissolution of boundaries between sanity and madness in *Arkham*, and the deindividualization enforced through bureaucratic structures in *Le Château*.

In contrast, a large number of the female characters in the analyzed works can be lumped under the category of the femme fatale—the dangerous, or at least problematic, seductress. However, already Adèle undoes the female stereotype in the course of the series through her unconventional behavior and transition to a more matronly, less seductive figure. Moreover, the very fact of her being the protagonist is also unusual since, with the exception of *Mariko* and *La Femme Piège*, the main character is consistently male in the other works and even in these two comics, the importance of the female characters is tied to the male protagonists, their lovers. While *La Femme Piège* blatantly links Jill Bioskop with the femme fatale, a similar move is made by Pratt in *La Ballade* through naming the beautiful, young heiress Pandora. Likewise, Léa (*Le Voyage*),[28] Farouge (*XXe Ciel*), Virginia (*City of Glass*), R-Rautanainen (*Kuolema*), along with Consuelo and Sonia Greene, the real-life love interests of Saint-Exupéry and Lovecraft, evoke the femme fatale. However, scrutiny proves this link to be superficial in most cases, with the exception of Consuelo and Sonia, since they only appear marginally. Delineated in greater detail, Léa and Jill Bioskop ultimately deviate from the type, even though they resemble the femme fatale at the beginning of their relationships with Simon and Nikopol. Starting already with her name, R-Rautanainen pokes fun at the notion of the femme fatale, and this is strengthened by her perennial costume, for while the bodysuit accentuates the sensuality of her figure, it simultaneously undoes it by covering every inch of her body. Dream's sister Death, who also evokes the femme fatale, also reverses the stereotype and acquires abstract, universalized proportions, like most aspects of *Sandman*.

The ambiguity of characters and their subversion of stereotypes contribute towards openness through their transformation of expectations. Subversion itself can be seen as an almost natural inclination of comics, owing to their affiliations with caricature, the presence of which can also work self-reflexively since it comments on the influences that have fed into comics. Open comics also incorporate other kinds of self-reflexive themes based on concepts of identity, as well as the making and telling of a story.

Subversion, autofiction, metafiction

A mentioned above, a background comparable to what Linda Hutcheon calls "the novel's parodic origins" is discernible in comics themselves through their affiliation to caricature and other popular practices of image-making, such as prints. Correspondingly, a subversive tone recurs in many of the comics analyzed here.[29] While rebelliousness against dominant powers already had a strong presence in Moebius's works, it is at its strongest in the *Nikopol* trilogy, where every aspect of the story—the rendition of its setting, the characterization, the narrative tone—mocks not only authoritarian figures but also notions of progress and the supernatural. Subversion also persists in a milder form in *La Ballade*'s disparagement of war and patriotism, which acquires a far more bitter tone in *La Guerre*. Likewise, *Sandman* mocks the pop culture clichés of omnipotent superheroes and happy endings.

In addition, as exemplified by the extensive intertextual references in comics like *Sandman*, *From Hell*, and *Arkham*, such incorporations of other texts are often not mere quotations but willed transformations, subordinating the displaced material to the specificities of the new medium, as exemplified to the extreme in *Le Château*'s adaptation of *Das Schloß*, which renders the latter almost unrecognizable. By pointing towards at least two different sets of codes—the ones they undo and the ones they create—these subversions have *per se* a self-reflexive element, which imbues the characters of many open comics, as mentioned above, as well as the treatment of certain themes, which will now be elaborated.

One of the most recurrent themes in comics is that of identity, of which autofiction is a self-reflexive version. Naturally, the mere presence of characters raises questions regarding their identity—about who they are and what their significance is. In addition, Murray points out that "the process of reading a comic becomes an extremely complex one, with the intersection of the visual message (with its competing impulses towards sequentiality and fragmentation), the textual message, and the role of the reader; resulting in a text that is very much a hall of mirrors, one that reflects, distorts and projects images of identity suggested by the text and brought by the reader."[30] This explains the success of comics characters that have long adhered to universal types. Thus, Antonio Altarriba sees *Little Nemo* as an archetypal character, adding that the protagonists of comic strips are usually types that are deliberately kept free of specificities so that they might fit into a wide range of narratives and enable the continuation of a series.[31]

Mikkonen regards the popularity of the theme of identity in comics or graphic narratives as an outcome of the reliance on the two expressive channels of words and pictures since "[t]he comic book [. . .] questions the distinction of signs that is a prerequisite for identity in translation."[32] This, along with the physical appropriateness of sequential panels for depicting morphological processes,[33] accounts for Mattotti and Kramsky's successful foregrounding of the conflict between Jekyll and Hyde, where the greatest emphasis is on the transitional stages between the two characters rather than any other element of the original novel. Such identity crises reflect the nature of comics themselves, since they are dependent on disjointedness and the intertwining of two very different modes of expression.

This self-reflexive relevance of the medium for the themes also holds for identity conflicts thrust into the foreground, as with the psychological turmoil of the main characters in *City of Glass* and *Arkham*. This tussle is linked with the characters' construction of identities for themselves and others, including Batman's persona as a fearless superhero with no other goal than to fight evil, or the several roles Quinn adopts, from the characters he creates through his writings to the people he meets, such as the older Stillman and his son Peter. Likewise, many other figures, such as K. in *Le Château*, the protagonists in *XXe Ciel*, and Kleist/Carter/Lovecraft in *Lovecraft*, incorporate obscure or disparate identities, often without being aware of it. Apart from ambiguity, this transition of identities is also a means of inserting movement into the comic and increasing its interpretational possibilities and openness.

Furthermore, the consciousness of a fractured, mediated reality is steadily conveyed in such comics as *La Guerre*, *XXe Ciel*, and *Taxi van Googhin Korvaan*, through the syncopated structure of the stories and the images accompanying them, which also underscores how openness is generated through the allusive interaction between verbal and visual channels. As already indicated, one of the most important themes tackled by comics is the nature of reality, regarding which Fresnault-Deruelle considers comics as being closer to magic lantern projections where "les niveaux de représentation (reel/allégorie et/ou songe/proche/lointain/présent/passé) se contaminaient les uns les autres" (the levels of representation [real/allegory and/or dream/near/far/present/past] contaminate each other).[34] While reflecting upon the nature of the medium, allusions to this reality-unreality dialectic also bring in ambiguity.

The symbolic significance of the unreal for reality lies in the fact that "[l]'imaginaire n'est pas un mode de irréalité, mais une manière de prendre en diagonale la présence pour en faire surgir les dimensions primitives" (the imaginary is not a mode of unreality but a way of measuring presence in order to suggest originary dimensions through it).[35] This is linked to fiction for "[t]he fictitious is never in things or in people but in the impossible verisimilitude of what lies between them [...] fiction consists not in showing the invisible, but in showing the extent to which the invisibility of the visible is invisible. Thus, it bears a profound relation to space [...] space is to fiction what the negative is to reflection."[36] That fantasy's distance from reality is a comment on it, is already apparent in Moebius's "La Déviation," and acquires even greater lucidity in *Nikopol's* dystopic realms which criticize the inhuman, power-hungry, and warring tendencies of despotic rulers. Comparable commentary through psychological, distorted realities is also discernible in other comics, encompassing the alternative worlds of *Sandman*, the cruel distortions in *Le Château* and *Arkham*, as well as *Salut, Delezue!*, with its cyclic limbo. These realities are not always limited to the individual's perspective but can unfold on a collective level, as in the *Nikopol* trilogy, *XXe Ciel*, and *From Hell*, where the extremity of the horrors that makes them infringe upon the unreal holds for the entire context and not just one character, as is the case in *Le Voyage* or *Taxi*.

Departing from Kant's conceptualization of human perception, Cambier underscores the significance of images for forming a reference frame for comprehending the world: "L'image est le presuppose incontournable de notre rapport au monde" (The image is the unavoidable precondition for our connection to the world).[37] This is where the self-reflexive potential of comics images comes in since they can highlight the very filtering of reality. As Gombrich points out, "[a]ll artistic discoveries are discoveries not of likenesses but of equivalences which enable us to see reality in terms of an image and an image in terms of reality."[38] The open comics here take a step further by thematizing the mediatization of reality via images through their incorporation of elements from the mass media, as is the case in *XXe Ciel* and *Nikopol*. Conveyed both verbally and visually, the thematic shift towards real life lies at the core of the increasingly popular comics (or graphic novel) genres of reportage and (auto-)biography but, to recall Lefèvre's quote from above,[39] this is never an unadulterated rendition of reality and the subjective sheen is likely to have contributed to the popularity of such narratives in comics.

Kunzle had already concluded that "the narrative structure seems to invite a documentary approach" because the representation through a sequence of events (which suggests rationality) in comics appears more objective than single-paneled allegories.[40] Through visual sophistication and narrative detail, the aspect of world-building is concretized by comics since they retain the polarity between the real and the unreal that is the essence of pictures.[41] This polarity was illustrated in René Magritte's famous *Ceci n'est pas une pipe* (1926), which also exemplifies the interactive tension between words and pictures, as well as the tendency of linking the two when they are juxtaposed, allowing for the inference of links between two completely unrelated objects through mere proximity.[42]

According to Fresnault-Deruelle, comics frequently portray "interférences entre l'animé et l'inerte" (interferences between the animated and the inert) because of their paradoxical essence as fixed images making a narrative undergo incessant transformation.⁴³ The interaction between the animate and inanimate is reflected by the recurrent motif of metamorphosis through which both the readers and the creators of comics end up in a dream world "dont le roi est Morphée, Morpheus, l'activateur [eus] des formes [morph-] et de leurs metamorphoses discontinues" (where the king is Morphea, Morpheus, the activator [eus] of forms [morph-] and their halted metamorphoses).⁴⁴ In the more self-reflexive comics discussed here, the pretense of this dream world is undone, and questions regarding the construction of the stories and their tellers are raised, with many works taking up the themes of autofiction and metafiction, frequently combining them with self-reflection on the narrative role played by words and images in comics and other media. This is especially prominent in *Saint-Exupéry, Mariko Parade, Lovecraft, From Hell, City of Glass*, and *XXᵉ Ciel*, and is also hinted at in other works, such as *La Guerre* and *Kuolema*. In interlinking different perspectives for viewing the same work and highlighting its multiple connections beyond the story, self-reflexivity also opens up several paths of interpretation.

The recurrence of autofiction, as well as the crumbling or fusion of identities, is associated with the postmodern tendency to deconstruct the subject, which is reflected in both contemporary life and the arts. Referring to the current situation of "un monde virtuel plus vrai que le réel, devant les milliards de pixels sur nos écrans" (a virtual world more true than the real one, before millions of pixels on our screens), Védrine declares that "[l]ibérée de son rôle de mixte, l'imagination, tout comme la subjectivité cherche d'autres voies [. . .] l'inquiétant étrangeté de l'histoire et de notre époque, implique qu'à la croisée de la réflexivité et de l'inconscient, l'imaginaire arrache le présent à l'effondrement" (liberated from its mixed role, imagination, just like subjectivity, seeks other ways [. . .] the unsettling strangeness of history and our era imply that, at the crossroads of reflexivity and the unconscious, the imaginary causes the present to collapse).⁴⁵ This is especially discernible in the settings fluctuating between reality and unreality, which contribute to the latter's symbolism.

In many comics, the presence of the artist becomes more tangible through his taking over the traditionally divided roles of inker, letterer, colorist, and sometimes writer. In turn, this emphasis on individuality reflects the modernist situation where the indexical is privileged over the iconical, or the desire for authenticity. However, the comics artist's presence is arguably still only discernible in the style's dialectic of presence-absence, as with Eddie Campbell's persistently bleeding, ominously messy, monochrome drawings for *From Hell*, which recur in many of his works, just like Baudoin's gestural lines or McKean's complex collages make them stand apart and contradict the mass-produced essence of the medium and bring in artist-specific elements to comics. Notably, while the artist's distinctive presence is not indispensable for many comics—a series is often made by several artists who maintain a similar visual style—it is usually an indispensable feature of artists' books. As shown by the comics analyzed above, artistic-authorial traces acquire relevance not only in autobiographies or through an individualistic style but also in the content itself, regardless of the degree of fiction involved (the resemblance between Pratt and Corto is frequently emphasized, to give only one example).[46] Sometimes, however, as in *La Déviation* and *From Hell*, the author's presence is more prominent and provides a metafictional perspective to the story.

While metafiction is a recurrent theme in contemporary literature,[47] its transposition to the visual arena implies, among other things, the thematization of the act of visualizing the narrative in book form. In addition to the incorporation of metafictional and autofictional themes in the stories themselves, as in *Lovecraft* and *City of Glass*, the potential for self-reflexivity in visual narratives is manifested through the self-conscious employment of visual elements on pages drawing attention to the conventions of art and image production (as in "Les Ampoules de Mariko" in *Mariko Parade*, or the "paused" panel at the beginning of *La Foire aux Immortels*).

The metafictional potential of the framing device has been highlighted in several comics as with the inclusion of background panels (embedded or multiple frames) in *Arkham Asylum* visualizing its different narrative strands, or the movement of frames in "Les Ampoules de Mariko." Many panels consequently come across as metapictures, commenting on the nature of pictures and their making.[48] While meta-reflections on the level of form and experimentation with visual styles are two of the commonalities between artists' books and comics, it is the verbal presence of metafiction that is more recurrent in comics, discernible to varying extents in most of the comics analyzed here, ranging from the writers' commentaries accompanying *Arkham* and *From Hell* to the elaborate interview between Yslaire and his psychoanalyst in *Introduction*.

To sum up, the characteristics contributing to openness in comics, within the given of a structured story, include significant visual styles and layouts, suggestive word-image relationships, intermedial references, figuration, and self-reflexivity. From these, suggestive word-image connections, tropes, intermedial interactions, and self-reflexive themes are the most recurrent features in the comics analyzed here. While these aspects are essentially possibilities rather than necessities, most open comics contain more than one of them. It is noteworthy that the very nature of the medium—with its reliance on disjunction, multiple modes of expression, as well as its subversive desire, in general and with regard to its own conventions and worlds—renders comics susceptible to openness. Having mapped out the features contributing towards openness in comics, their echoing of our era's predilections will now be considered, since aspects such as intermedial references and disjointedness bear the mark of the prevalent modes of multimedia communication.

COMICS AND CONTEMPORARY COMMUNICATION

In every century, the way that artistic forms are structured reflects the way in which science or contemporary culture views reality.[49]

Exploring the nature of openness also "underlines the crucial role aesthetics plays in defining what previous generations have called the 'spirit of the age,'" or the proclivities of the times for certain forms of communication and expression.[50] For the present era, these proclivities are for the multi-modal and mutating, even virtual and fleeting, which in turn is reflected by the newer kind of open work, the work in movement. On the other hand, some movement is always present in the open work thanks to the different interpretational paths offered. Comics panels can move in this sense through their technique (varied visual styles), page layout (productive and rhetorical, both of which entail word-image interaction), and stories (through incorporating figuration or self-reflexivity).

The visual nature of comics can be seen as mirroring a world that is dominated by images in varying forms and combinations to the extent that "[n]otre société est celle de l'image" (our society is that of the image).[51] Moreover, the conception of the image itself has gone beyond being fixed to a single image "to a nameless image, a discourse image."[52] The abundance, movement, and hybridity associated with visuals is reflected in the sequential images of comics, not only through their experimentation with visual techniques that mimic other visual media but also through their very dependence on images and varied relationships within and beyond each panel.

On the other hand, the high image-dependency of communication and information is accompanied by a decline in the number of readers. While today's fast-paced life can be blamed for allowing only limited time to read, reasons behind the thinning readership include the possibility of resorting to the most direct, quickest methods that usually communicate through adding pictures, animation, and sound to brief texts. Recently, however, comics (often under the more acceptable guise of graphic novels) have acquired institutional support in hopes of attracting teenagers, particularly boys, and convincing them to read.[53]

Ann Miller deliberates whether "words and images of popular culture and the mass media are constitutive of our culture or only mediate preexisting ideological formations."[54] The proliferation of comics and its aptness for their milieu suggest that the two aspects are reciprocal and in flux.[55] The increasing diversification in comics today reflects the image-dominated environment and is fostered by it, in a similar way as the comics published in the nineteenth century aimed at catering to the needs of the typical, rushed reader by providing brief and discardable easy reading for the length of a train trip—easy reading which incorporated the passengers' experience in its very form through mimicking the train's speed and the fleeting views offered by its windows.[56] Eco drew a similar parallel between the concept of the open work and the changing mindset of its times, which were marked by the acceptance of Einstein's relativities and Schrödinger's uncertainty principle. A similar parallel holds true for comics and their milieu, since the medium speaks to the inhabitants of a digitized, visually oriented world who are accustomed to seeing words and images together (indeed, many would not have it otherwise).

Like the *nouveau roman*, an increasing number of comics break away from conventional models, experimenting with the medium's hybridity. And—also arguably like the *nouveau roman*—these comics are not the outcome of a conscious movement but reflect the potential of a vehicle of expression that has been concurrently adopted and enriched by several artists the world over. Many of the comics discussed here experiment with the limits associated with the medium. Both *Salut, Deleuze!* and *City of Glass*, for instance, exploit conventional forms for complementing their loaded content, simultaneously making the reader aware of the complexity of the medium itself. Although one need only recall McCay's *Little Nemo* or George Herriman's *Krazy Kat* to prove that such self-reflexivity in the medium is nothing new,[57] the current popularity of comics tackling a wider range of themes than ever before,[58] as well as the nature of their experimentation—intermedial references, indirect relationships—can be linked to the prevalence of mixed media and digital technology, both of which function through the piecing together of diverse fragments.[59] Hence, open comics also serve as "epistemological metaphors"[60] for their times and highlight the modernity—and postmodernity—of comics.

NOTES

INTRODUCTION

1. Beginning with *Opera Aperta: Forma e Indeterminazione delle Poetiche Contemporanee* (Milan: Bompiani, 1962) and continuing, most notably, in his introduction to *The Role of the Reader* essay collection ("Introduction," *The Role of the Reader: Explorations in the Semiotics of Texts*, Bloomington: University of Indiana Press, 1984, 3–43).

2. Eco, *Role of the Reader*, 39.

3. The experimentation discernible in contemporary Finnish comics is sufficiently ardent to deserve inclusion in this transcultural exploration of the openness of comics. Although not well-known in the Anglophone world, some of the Finnish works discussed here have been translated into other languages, particularly French.

4. See, for instance, Thierry Groensteen's concept of *tressage* or braiding that unfolds between panels in *Système de la Bande Dessinée* (Paris: PUF, 2011).

5. Paul Atkinson, "Why Pause?: The Fine Line between Reading and Contemplation," *Studies in Comics* 3.1 (2012): 63–81, 66. Although Atkinson emphasizes the difference between paintings and their reproductions, he also states that "[t]he spatial structure of the graphic novel is important insofar as [it] renders some images 'aesthetic' through isolating them from the broader narrative and the succession of panels that comprise it."

6. David Robey, "Introduction," *The Open Work*, Umberto Eco, trans. Anna Cancogni (Cambridge: Harvard University Press, 1989), vii–xxxiii, viii.

7. Julia Round, *Gothic in Comics and Graphic Novels* (Jefferson: McFarland, 2014), 59. As mentioned a little later, Julia Round uses this "literalization of Iser's model of literary experience" in order to highlight the similarities between certain comics and gothic fiction.

8. Eco, *Role of the Reader*, 39.
9. Eco, *Open Work*, 12.
10. Ibid., 40.
11. Ibid., 115.
12. Ibid., 18.
13. Ibid., 19
14. Ibid., 64.
15. Ibid., 4.
16. Eco, *Role of the Reader*, 8.
17. Ibid.
18. Ibid., 9.
19. Ibid.
20. Ibid., 9–10.
21. Eco, *Open Work*, 40.
22. Ibid., 40–43.

23. See Hillary Chute and Patrick Jagoda, "Special Issue: Comics & Media," *Critical Inquiry* 40.3 (2014): 1–10, 3–5.

24. Eco, *Open Work*, 9.

25. Ibid., 32.

26. Ibid., 55.

27. Ibid., 60. Italics in original.

28. Groensteen, *Système de la Bande Dessinée*, 64.

29. Cf. André Gaudreault and Philippe Marion, "Transécriture and Narrative Mediatics," *Companion to Literature and Film*, ed. Robert Stam and Alessandra Raengo (Hoboken: Wiley-Blackwell, 2004), 58–70.

30. Pierre Fresnault-Deruelle, *La Bande Dessinée, Essai d'Analyse Sémiotique* (Paris: Hachette, 1972), 49. Unless otherwise indicated, all translations in the parentheses are my own.

31. Scott McCloud, *Understanding Comics: The Invisible Art* (New York: Harper, 2006), 9.

32. Fresnault-Deruelle, *La Bande Dessinée*, 74.

33. See, for instance, his article, "The Limits of Time and Transitions: Challenges to the Theories of Sequential Image Comprehension," *Studies in Comics* 1.1 (2010): 127–47. For an analysis of the reading paths offered by page layouts, see: "The Architecture of Visual Narrative Comprehension: The Interaction of Narrative Structure and Page Layout in Understanding Comics," *Frontiers in Psychology* 5 (2014), accessed 13 February 2015, http://journal.frontiersin.org/Journal/10.3389/fpsyg.2014.00680/full.

34. Karin Kukkonen, *Contemporary Comics Storytelling*, 6–7. Kukkonen takes up Eco's semiotic analysis of a Milton Caniff comic in "A Reading of *Steve Canyon*," as a starting point for developing her argument for an approach focusing on "more basic cognitive processes" rather than the code underlying a work (ibid., 18).

35. Eco, *Role of the Reader*, 3.

36. Fresnault-Deruelle, *La Bande Dessinée*, 49. The *bande dessinée* as "une succession d'hiatus" (a succession of pauses) contains four kinds of gaps: temporal, spatio-temporal, spatial, and technical. The technical hiatus is further divided into interior and exterior, and according to subjective and objective points of view (ibid., 52). Notably, the locational derangement or switches in points of view (aspect-to-aspect transitions in McCloud's terminology as discussed below) were absent in the earlier *ligne claire* comics but are especially popular in recent works.

37. Joseph Hillis Miller, *Illustration* (London: Reaktion, 1992), 66.

38. See Wolfgang Iser, *The Fictive and the Imaginary: Charting Literary Anthropology* (Baltimore: John Hopkins University Press, 1993).

39. Round, *Gothic in Comics*, 62.

40. McCloud, *Understanding Comics*, 63. See also Hans-Christian Christiansen and Anne Magnussen's introduction to the edited volume, *Comics Culture*: "Introduction," *Comics Culture: Analytical and Theoretical Approaches to Comics* (Copenhagen: Museum Tusulanum Press, 2000), 7–27, 14. However, Christiansen and Magnussen name only two studies that emphasize the reader's role in reading comics, namely, Richard J. Watts's 1989 article, "Comic Strips

and Theories of Communication," *Word and Image* 5.2: 173–80; and Marcel Bodmer's Licentiate paper, "Comics: Semiotics and Paralinguistic Approaches to a Mixed Medium" (University of Zürich, 1985).

41. Fresnault-Deruelle, *La Bande Dessinée*, 176.

42. Jan Baetens, "Graphic Novels," *The Cambridge History of the American Novel* (Cambridge: Cambridge University Press, 2011), 1137–53, 1145.

43. Ibid., 1138. Perloff coined the term for digital poetry.

44. Perloff cited by Baetens, "Graphic Novels," 1150.

45. Ibid.

46. Peter Bondanella, *Umberto Eco and the Open Text: Semiotics, Fiction and Popular Culture* (Cambridge: Cambridge University Press, 1997), 26.

47. For the purposes of this book, "self-reflexive" and "self-referential" are used interchangeably.

48. Peter Wagner, ed., *Icons—Texts—Iconotexts: Essays on Ekphrasis and Intermediality* (Berlin: Walter de Gruyter, 1996), 38.

49. Richard Reynolds, *Super Heroes: A Modern Mythology* (Jackson: University Press of Mississippi, 1994), 96–97.

50. Christopher Murray, "Holy Hypertexts!—The Pose of Post-modernity in Comics and Graphic Novels of the 1980s," *Reflections on Creativity*, ed. Hamid van Koten (Dundee: Duncan of Jordanstone College of Art and Design, 2007), accessed 13 February 2009, http://artanddesign.dundee.ac.uk/reflections/pdfs/ChrisMurray.pdf.

51. The popularity of using combinations of images and texts for playing with concepts of the self is apparent through the presence of labels like "autographics" (see Gillian Whitlock, "Autographics: The Seeing 'I' of Comics," *Modern Fiction Studies* 52.4 (2006): 965–79, where Whitlock transposes Leigh Gilmore's notion of "autobiographics" to describe autographics as "draw[ing] attention to the specific conjunctions of visual and verbal text in this genre of autobiography, and also to the subject positions that narrators negotiate in and through comics—features of discursive frameworks" (ibid., 967).

52. Ivan Farron, "Die Fallen der Vorstellungskraft. Autofiktion—ein Begriff und seine Zweideutigkeit(en)," trans. Barbara Villiger Heilig, *Neue Zürcher Zeitung*, 31 May 2003, accessed 20 June 2014, http://www.nzz.ch/aktuell/startseite/article8VLW2-1.259501.

53. Serge Doubrovsky, *Le Livre Brisé* (Paris: Gallimard, 2003), 408.

54. Aurore Chestier, "*Le Livre Brisé* ou le Jeu de l'Écriture Tendue en Miroir," *Image (&) Narrative* 19 (2007), accessed 28 May 2013, http://www.imageandnarrative.be/inarchive/autofiction/chestier.htm.

55. Gene Kannenberg Jr., "'I Looked Just Like Rudolph Valentino': Identity and Representation," in *Maus, The Graphic Novel*, ed. Jan Baetens (Leuven: Leuven University Press, 2001), 79–91, 79.

56. "[T]hose people growing up in the late twentieth century didn't want goals so much as

they wanted roles! And that's what visual iconography is all about" (McCloud, *Understanding Comics*, 59).

57. See, for instance, Charles Hatfield, *Hand of Fire: The Comics Art of Jack Kirby* (Jackson: University Press of Mississippi, 2011), 113.

58. Brian McHale, *Postmodernist Fiction* (London: Routledge, 1987), 121.

59. Linda Hutcheon, *Narcissistic Narrative: The Metafictional Paradox* (London: Methuen, 1984), xii.

60. Eco, *Open Work*, 12.

61. Atkinson, "Why Pause?: The Fine Line between Reading and Contemplation," 69.

62. Miller, *Illustration*, 66.

63. Cf. Umberto Eco, *Semiotics and the Philosophy of Language* (Bloomington: University of Indiana Press, 1986), 85.

64. McHale, *Postmodernist Fiction*, 134. Using *Watchmen* as an example, Karin Kukkonen also emphasizes the power of metonymies, metaphors, and tropes in comics ("Beyond Language: Metaphor and Metonymy in Comics Storytelling," *English Language Notes* 46.2 [2008]: 89–98).

65. Eco, *Open Work*, 9.

66. Werner Wolf, "Metafiction and Metamusic: Exploring the Limits of Self-Reference," *Self-Reference in the Media*, ed. Winfried Nöth and Nina Bishara (Berlin: Walter de Gruyter, 2007), 303–324, 316.

67. Ann Miller, *Reading Bande Dessinée: Critical Approaches to French-Language Comic Strips* (Bristol: Intellect, 2007), 130.

68. See Gaudreault and Marion's above-cited "Transécriture and Narrative Mediatics," in which illustrated books have been used to exemplify the transposition of material from one medium into another.

69. Wagner, *Iconotexts*, 17.

70. Aron Kibédi Varga, "Criteria for Describing Word and Image Relations," *Poetics Today* 10 (1989): 31–53, 37.

71. McCloud, *Understanding Comics*, 54.

72. Varga, "Criteria," 42–43.

73. For the interdisciplinary significance of montage, see Lev Manovich's *Language of New Media* (Cambridge: MIT Press, 2002). While Foucault also affirms the hierarchical order subordinating images to words, he considers Paul Klee's works as eliminating that order through the merging of signs in indefinite space, which in turn is comparable to the full-page spreads or splashes in many comics. See Michel Foucault, "This Is Not a Pipe," *Aesthetics, Method, and Epistemology: Essential Works of Foucault, 1954–1984, vol. 2*, ed. James D. Fabion (New York: New Press, 1999), 187–205, 195.

74. This is frequently pointed out in comics theory, as with Fresnault-Deruelle's declaration regarding the influence of cinematography and camerawork on comics: "[I]l n'est que trop évident que la B.D. a été influencée par la technique de la prise de vue cinématographique" (it

is only too obvious that comics has been influenced by the technique of cinematic shooting), *La Bande Dessinée*, 118, note 1. Affirming the comparative potential between two- and three-dimensional scenarios, Marion points out that both *bande dessinée* and film are media hybrids and face a "confrontation transsémiotique," namely, the need to appropriately divide and convert the content for the new media (see Philippe Marion, "Scénario de Bande Dessinée. La Différence par le Média," *Études littéraires* 26.2 [1993]: 77–89).

75. The proximity between films and sequential narratives like comics and graphic novels is also evident in the many collaborations across the two media, ranging from Milo Manara and Federico Fellini's *Voyaggio* volumes to cinematic versions of graphic novels and comics.

76. Henri Van Lier, "La Bande Dessinée, Une Cosmogonie Dure," *Bande Dessinée. Récit et Modernité*, ed. Thierry Groensteen (Paris: Futuropolis, 1988), 5–24. Notably, Windsor McCay, whose *Little Nemo in Slumberland* is characterized by its radical panel compositions, was also a pioneer in the field of animation.

77. Ibid., 8. By concretizing instants of perception, photography revolutionized the concept of vision. For the implications of how this has been affected by the shift from analogue to digital photography, see W. J. Mitchell, *The Reconfigured Eye: Visual Truth in the Post-Photographic Era* (Cambridge: MIT Press, 2001).

78. Such comics in turn interact with older practices, such as the narration of stories through photographs and word balloons in the Italian *fotoromanzi*, or the use of photographs as backgrounds in the comics by, among others, Jack Kirby and Will Eisner.

79. Cf. Gilles Deleuze, *Cinéma, t.1: L'Image-Mouvement* (Paris: Éditions de Minuit, 1983) and *Cinéma, t.2: L'Image-Temps* (Paris: Éditions de Minuit, 1985).

80. Gilles Deleuze, "Cours, Image Mouvement Image Temps, sur Pierce," *Web Deleuze*, accessed 20 June 2014, http://www.webdeleuze.com/php/texte.php?cle=73&groupe=Image%20Mouvement%20Image%20Temps&langue=1.

81. See, for instance, Peter Paul Schnierer "Graphic 'Novels,' Cyber 'Fiction,' Multiform 'Stories'—Virtual Theatre and the Limits of Genre," *Anglistentag 1999 Mainz: Proceedings*, ed. Bernhard Reitz and Sigrid Rieuwerts (Trier: Wissenschaftlicher Verlag Trier, 2000), 533–47.

82. Miriam Rivett, "Technology into the Digital Realm," *Below Critical Radar: Fanzines and Alternative Comics From 1976 to Now*, ed. Roger Sabin and Teal Triggs (Hove: Slab-O-Concrete, 2000), 65–80, 65.

83. Gérard Genette includes other forms of intertextuality besides quotations, namely, parody, allusions, and calques. See Gérard Genette, *Palimpsests: Literature in the Second Degree*, trans. Channa Newman and Claude Doubinsky (Lincoln: University of Nebraska Press, 1997).

84. Julia Kristeva, "'Nous Deux' or a [Hi]story of Intertextuality," *Romanic Review* 93 (2002): 7–13.

85. Eco, *Semiotics and Philosophy*, 162–63. Emphasis in original.

86. Murray, "Holy Hypertexts!"

87. Jan Baetens, "M Comme Main. Une Lecture de Château de Kafka Adapté par Olivier

Deprez," *Image (&) Narrative* 8 (2004), accessed 15 January 2013, http://www.imageandnarrative.be/inarchive/issue08/janbaetens_deprez.htm.

88. For a summary and evaluation of his theory, see Jan Baetens's "Revealing Traces: A New Theory of Graphic Enunciation," *Language of Comics*, ed. Robin Varnum and Christina T. Gibbons (Jackson: University Press of Mississippi 2001), 145–55.

89. "Depuis quelques années, des voix s'élèvent pour déplorer que la bande dessinée soit en train de perdre son assise populaire pour devenir un genre élitaire, un art de musée [. . .] La couleur directe comporte et implique ce risque [. . .] le danger serait alors qu'en se rapprochant de la peinture, la bande dessinée gagnera peut-être un public d'esthètes mais perdra une partie importante de son lectorat, celle pour qui la BD est synonyme de fiction, d'évasion et de lecture facile" (For some years, it is being said that comics are losing their popular standing and turning into an elitist genre, an art for the museum [. . .] Direct color carries and implies that risk [. . .] the danger would then be that in nearing painting, comics would gain a public of aesthetes but lose a large part of its readership, those for whom comics is synonymous with fiction, escapism and easy reading). Thierry Groensteen, *Couleur Directe* (Thurn: Kunst der Comics, 1993). See also Bart Beaty's *Comics Versus Art* (Toronto: University of Toronto Press, 2012).

90. Examples of visual abstraction include the abstraction in backgrounds to convey mental, intangible states, or the iconic abstraction of emotions in the interests of brevity and simplicity. Similarly, photographic realism lies at the very extreme of the figuration axis.

91. Fresnault-Deruelle, *La Bande Dessinée*, 112.

92. Ibid. Without using the same word, McCloud also discusses verisimilitude of different drawing styles. He points out that realism is inversely proportional to the level of iconic content and provides a pyramid placing the various stylistic possibilities relative to each other. For him, this pyramid with the three vertices of reality, language, and the picture plane "represents the total *pictorial vocabulary* of comics or of *any* visual arts" (McCloud, *Understanding Comics*, 51). The zenith of the triangle is abstract art, which via its object-picture plane unity merges representation and meaning. The left vertex is that of reality, which is occupied by photography (and related genres such as realistic painting or the *fotoromanzo*). Since they are purely conceptual, words occupy the right vertex (ibid., 51–53). By contrast, and due to his focus on comics, Kunzle's categorization of styles is more simplified and unfolds along the axes of "humorous-caricatural and 'straight' (characteristic of sentimental fiction and adventure story)," David Kunzle, *The History of the Comic Strip, vol. II* (Berkeley: University of California Press, 1973), 426.

93. W. J. T. Mitchell, *Picture Theory: Essays on Verbal and Visual Representation* (Chicago: University of Chicago Press, 1994), 35.

94. Cf. McCloud's *Understanding Comics*, 63. In addition, Fresnault-Deruelle's above-mentioned cinematic parallel based on the hiatus in comics also provides an explanation for the reader's ability to link the various hiatus in a manner comparable to McCloud's description of closure in comics.

95. The division of a page into three long panels was already a medieval tradition recurrent in illuminated manuscripts and linked with the typological, triple-layered pictorial biblical ex-

egesis (divided into *ante legem, sub lege, sub gratia*), as exemplified by Nicolas Verdun's *Klosterneuburger Altar* (ca. 1181).

96. Benoît Peeters, "Four Conceptions of the Page," trans. Jesse Cohn, *ImageTexT* 3 (3) 2007, accessed 17 June 2014, http://www.english.ufl.edu/imagetext/archives/v3_3/peeters/. This translated version has been deliberately employed here because it is a meeting point for two of the main linguistic discourses for this project. While listing some inaccuracies in Benoît Peeters's tabularization of possible page layouts, Jesse Cohn admits to the greater void at the anglophone end where "*some* coherent and systematic account of the meaning-making properties of the page as designed space needs to be introduced." See Jesse Cohn, "Translator's Comments on 'Four Conceptions of the Page,'" *ImageTexT* 3.3 (2007), accessed 5 January 2008, http://www.english.ufl.edu/imagetext/archives/v3_3/cohn/.

97. For Thierry Groensteen, like Jesse Cohn, most of the layouts also appear rhetorical and he consequently finds Peeters's scheme helpful but inadequate because the categories are not mutually exclusive. Groensteen in turn proposes the somewhat disparate poles of regular and irregular, discrete and ostentatious (Groensteen, *Système de la Bande Dessinée*, 110).

98. Peeters, "Four Conceptions."

99. Martin Schüwer proposes another alternative to Peeters's system in *Wie Comics erzählen. Grundriss einer intermedialen Erzähltheorie der graphischen Literatur* (Trier: Wissenschaftlicher Verlag, 2008). While Schüwer's in-depth analysis of the workings of comics already does raise some of the points mentioned here (such as the inadequacy of Peeters's system or the mutual inexclusiveness of McCloud's transitions), his approach, in spite of the extensive delineation of technical aspects, is essentially narratological and thus does not fully account for the effects of the aesthetic appeal and workings of images.

100. The productive layout can also be seen as a self-aware, self-reflexive layout where the images take over the layout to the extent of controlling the sequence, as in "La Déviation" (Moebius, *Arzach: L'Album Mythique* [Paris: Les Humanoïdes Associés, 2006], 7–13, 8–9). This is the way in which the notion of the productive layout is applied here.

101. See Fresnault-Deruelle, *La Bande Dessinée*, 44–45.

102. Kai Mikkonen, "Presenting Minds in Graphic Narratives," *Partial Answers* 6.2 (2008): 301–328, 306. While Mikkonen suggests that free indirect discourse may be the most appropriate description of what usually occurs in panels—namely, a combination of the narrator's and character's viewpoints—this also shows the shortcomings of using literary narratology for categorizing pictorial narration: it is often impossible to describe a panel as using internal or external focalization or determining whether it is a direct or indirect mode of narration.

103. McCloud, *Understanding Comics*, 70–71.

104. McCloud declares that this also holds true for comics by Jack Kirby and Hergé, as well as Eisner's *Contract with God* and Spiegelman's *Maus*. The only difference lies in Eisner's use of some aspect-to-aspect transitions and Spiegelman's application of more scene-to-scene instead of subject-to-subject switches (McCloud, *Understanding Comics*, 71).

105. Ibid., 76. From McCloud's set of graphs, the one for Jacques Tardi is particularly unusual

due to the almost equal amount of switches between scenes, subjects, and aspects (with actions remaining, as always, the most dominant).

106. Scott McCloud, *Making Comics: Storytelling Secrets of Comics, Manga and Graphic Novels* (New York: Harper, 2006), 17. Aspect-to-aspect and subject-to-subject transitions, however, render scene-to-scene transitions superfluous; the latter are thus not considered in the close readings here. Non sequitur transitions have also been left out in the analyses. Referring to situations where there is no connection between the panels, such transitions are contested. See Mario Saraceni, "Relatedness: Aspects of Textual Connectivity in Comics," *The Graphic Novel*, ed. Jan Baetens (Leuven: Leuven University Press, 2001), 167–81. While McCloud views non sequitur transition as the "occasional nonsense gag in otherwise rational stories" that usually appears in experimental comics (McCloud, *Making Comics*, 17), such a disconnected transition still provokes the reader into linking the panels, in which case the transition is no longer non sequitur.

107. Hence, comics that have already been extensively analyzed, such as Art Spiegelman's *Maus*, Alan Moore and Dave Gibbons's *Watchmen*, Marjane Satrapi's *Persepolis*, or Chris Ware's *Jimmy Corrigan*, have been left out.

108. Tellingly, Bart Beaty and Stephen Weiner's *Critical Survey of Graphic Novels: History, Theme and Technique* (Ipswich: Salem Press, 2012) groups its discussion of genres under the "themes" subsection. Although all of the genres listed in that section are not included, such as funny animal and Westerns (which nonetheless appears on an abstracted scale in Moebius's *Arzach*), the other main genres are, to varying extents, covered by the four categories used in this book.

109. John M. Trushell, "American Dreams of Mutants: The X-Men and 'Pulp' Fiction, Science Fiction and Superheroes," *Journal of Popular Culture* 38.1 (2004): 149–68, 150.

110. Paul L. Thomas, "Adventures in Genre! Rethinking Genre through Comics/Graphic Novels," *Journal of Comics and Graphic Novels* 2.2 (2011): 187–201, 194.

111. Murray, "Holy Hypertexts!"

112. See Saige Wilson, "Baroque Mutants in the 21st Century? Rethinking Genre through Superheroes," *Contemporary Comic Book Superheroes*, ed. Angela Ndalianis (London: Routledge, 2009), 86–104. For the extent of absorption in certain comics, see Julia Round's *Gothic in Comics and Graphic Novels*.

113. See, for instance, one of the many European articles published on Eisner's death: Yves-Marie Labé, "Will Eisner, le Père de la BD Moderne," *Le Monde*, 7 January 2005. See also N. C. Christopher Couch and Stephen Weiner's *The Will Eisner Companion: The Pioneering Spirit of the Father of the Graphic Novel* (New York: DC Comics, 2004).

114. Michael Hein, "What Haunts a Soldier's Mind: Monsters, Demons and the Lost Trenches of Memory: Representations of Combat Trauma in the Works of Jacques Tardi," *The Graphic Novel*, ed. Jan Baetens, 101–113, 102.

CHAPTER ONE

1. See also Philippe Marion's *Traces en Cases: Travail Graphique, Figuration Narrative et Participation du Lecteur* (Louvain-la-Neuve: Academia, 1993).

2. Jan Baetens, "Graphic Novels: Literature without Text," *English Language Notes* 46.2 (2008): 77–88, 85. See also his article in *Belphégor* ("Autobiographies et Bandes Dessinées," IV.1, 2004), in which he describes the proliferation of autobiographical *bandes dessinées* as the outcome of an era haunted by the "refus de l'inauthenticité" (rejection of inauthenticity), as well as the medium itself.

3. See, for instance, Christophe Dony, "The Re-Writing Ethos of the Vertigo Imprint: Critical Perspectives on Memory-Making and Canon Formation in the American Comics Field," *Comicalités, La Bande Dessinée: Un Art Sans «Mémoire»?* April 2014, accessed 25 February 2015, http://comicalites.revues.org/1918.

4. Ibid., xiv. Cf. also Will Eisner, *Graphic Storytelling and Visual Narrative* (Tamarac: Poorhouse Press, 1996), 1. Eisner uses the following phrases to describe their works: "novels without words" for Frans Masereel's works; "a novel in pictures" for Otto Nückel's *Destiny*; and "satirical graphic novel" for Milton Gross's *He Done Her Wrong*.

5. Will Eisner, *The Contract with God Trilogy* (New York: W. W. Norton, 2006), ix.

6. Martin Lund, *Rethinking the Jewish-Comics Connection* (PhD dissertation, University of Lund, 2013), 222.

7. Eisner, *Contract*, 55–61.

8. Ibid., 63, 93.

9. Ibid., 451.

10. Ibid., 28, 43.

11. Ibid., 240.

12. Peeters, "Four conceptions of the page."

13. Eisner, *Contract*.

14. Ibid., 98, 190.

15. Ibid., 107.

16. Ibid.

17. Ibid., xviii.

18. Cf. Pierre Nora, ed., *Les Lieux de Mémoire* (Paris: Gallimard, 1997).

19. Eisner, *Contract with God*, 218.

20. Eco, *Open Work*, 59.

21. A minor exception is the beginning and ending of *Life Force*, with the opening lines from Mitchell Parish's 1938 song "Deep Purple," since the song's yearning and the role of dreaming as an escape route from reality makes it an apt musical theme for Joseph.

22. Though active today in the fine arts, Masse's distinctive strips have also appeared in *Pilote* and *Métal Hurlant*. In contrast to Tardi's works, however, Masse uses elaborate dialogues to narrate the story, which lead Fresnault-Deruelle to draw parallels between his works and the

nineteenth-century illustrated album. See Pierre Fresnault-Deruelle, *Images à Mi-Mots. Bande Dessinées. Dessins d'Humour* (Brussels: Les Impressions Nouvelles), 60.

23. Jacques Samson, "Stratégies Modernes d'Énonciation Picturale," *Bande Dessinée, Récit et Modernité*, ed. Thierry Groensteen (Paris: Futuropolis, 1988), 117–38, 122–23. Samson explains further: "les œuvres modernes gagnent à être lus suivant une problématique de la signification et du sens (une herméneutique) davantage que selon une problématique du signe (une sémiotique ou sémiologie au sens large)" (modern works deserve to be read in the light of the problematic of signification and meaning [hermeneutics] rather than the problematic of the sign [a semiotics or semiology in the broad sense of the word]). While this is corroborated by several artists going as far back as Winsor McCay, the extent to which artists consciously create such theoretical layers of significance is debatable.

24. Jacques Tardi, *C'était la Guerre des Tranchées: 1914–1918* (Brussels: Casterman, 1993), 7.

25. Ibid., 30.

26. Samson, "Stratégies Modernes d'Énonciation Picturale," 127.

27. Ibid., 127.

28. Ibid., 128–31. Pointing out that Tardi's narration follows a disruptive logic based on gaps, ellipses, and pauses, Samson likens these panel variations to the cinematic tools of varying shots for narrative effects and for homogenizing the content of the image with its frame.

29. Tardi, *Guerre*, 9.

30. Ibid., 19, 28.

31. Ibid., 12.

32. Ibid., 14.

33. A good example of this is the dogfight watched by Binet and the village boy that leaves both planes damaged. The page is divided into dynamically shaped panels that mirror each other, with the narrative captions conforming to the shape of the curved frames. The action is arranged equally decoratively, with the planes flying off at the left end on the left-hand side of the page and vice versa with the central panel showing a plane advancing as the other retreats in the background (ibid., 19).

34. Ibid., 31.

35. Matthew Screech, *Masters of the Ninth Art: Bandes Dessinées and Franco-Belgian Identity* (Liverpool: Liverpool University Press, 2005), 131. See also the analysis of *Adèle Blanc-Sec* below.

36. Screech, "Visions of the Past," 134.

37. Tardi, *Guerre*, 31.

38. Ibid., 40.

39. Ibid., 47.

40. Ibid., 125.

41. Ibid., 93.

42. Ibid., 94.

43. Ibid., 112–24.

44. See, for instance, the sequence on Mazure where the time rewinds to 1914 (ibid., 72).

45. Ibid., 89. This image also recalls a motif in the 1931 Russian film *Одна (Alone)* directed by Leonid Trauberg and Grigori Konzintsev.

46. Tardi, *Guerre*, 95.

47. Ibid., 49.

48. Ibid., 69.

49. Serge Tisseron, *Psychanalyse de la Bande Dessinée* (Paris: Flammarion, 2000), 111.

50. Pratt's pertinence for this book comes from his international liaisons, particularly his success in French journals. Amongst the main comics analyzed here, Pratt's works are the only ones where translations have been employed in lieu of the originals. These French translations were, however, among the first to be published and that too after close collaboration with Pratt.

51. Breccia also later illustrated Borges's *Historia Universal de la Infamia*.

52. Hugo Pratt, *Saint-Exupéry: Le Dernier Vol* (Brussels: Casterman, 1995). The *grand format* bande dessinées have hardbacks and measure around 30 x 22.5 centimeters.

53. Pratt, *Saint-Exupéry*, 80.

54. Consider, for instance, the view through the Egyptian's binoculars, Augustin's deterrence of Moroccan firing and the panel showing Felicia's death (ibid., 43, 75–76, 78).

55. For instance, Saint-Exupéry's reunion with Mermoz—who had disappeared on a transatlantic flight in 1936—is recounted in panels full of black clouds with the word balloons emerging from them. Though the page comprises of six panels, with black clouds in all of them except the last one, the contrasting size of the panels in the middle row brings in dynamism to the pages while highlighting the unreality of the conversation (Pratt, *Saint-Exupéry*, 60).

56. The main intertextual reference to the arts is Saint-Exupéry's unwilling excursion through a Dada exhibition, which covers one page and showcases the movement's major works such as Raoul Hausmann's *Dada siegt!* (1920) and Duchamp's *Roue de Bicyclette* (1913–1964). Indicating his disdain for modern art, the last long panel shows Saint-Exupéry turning his back to a poster by Kurt Schwitters and walking away on the clouds holding his diary (ibid., 56).

57. Ibid., 24.

58. Ibid., 60.

59. Ibid., 9.

60. Ibid., 22–23.

61. Ibid., 78.

62. Indeed, technology is useless; even the phone booth is unable to connect him to the people he longs for, and the radio warnings are unable to save him from enemy planes.

63. Ibid., 30.

64. First in Mermoz's summarization and later during an older flashback with the two friends, where Saint-Exupéry is shown writing the book (ibid., 30, 38).

65. Even the advice Saint-Exupéry's "other" gives to himself is identical to what Corto tells Slütter in *La Ballade*: "Ne prend pas la direction des souvenirs [. . .] c'est comme si tu visitais un

cimetière" (Pratt, *Saint-Exupéry*, 80) echoes Corto's words, "[s]'arrêter ainsi dans le passé [. . .] c'est comme garder un cimitière" (Pratt, *Ballade*, 135).

66. *Schreibheft* 51: Sprechende Bilder—Blickstörung. Vom Eigensinn der Comics, September 1998, ed. Norbert Wehr (Essen: Rigodon Verlag).

67. Jens Balzer and Martin tom Dieck, "Nicht versöhnt. Bilder und Texte im Comic," *Schreibheft* 51 (1998): 47–50, 50.

68. See Ole Frahm's *Die Sprache des Comics* (Hamburg: Philo Verlag, 2010) for an analysis emphasizing the book's deconstructivist side.

69. Jens Balzer and Martin tom Dieck, *Salut, Deleuze!* (Zürich: Arrache Cœur, 1998), 6.

70. Umberto Eco, "Le Mythe de Superman," *Communications* 24 (1976): 24–40, 40.

71. As an aside, the ferryman's bandana and simple boat recall Thomas Eakin's painting, *John Biglin in a Single Scull* (1873), an iconic work of American realism.

72. Carrying quotation marks, they function as formal citations with the sources listed at the end. The works cited include: Gilles Deleuze, *Differenz und Wiederholung* (München, 1992); Michel Foucault, *Die Ordnung der Dinge* (Frankfurt, 1974); Friedrich Nietzsche, *Also Sprach Zarathustra* (München, 1998).

73. Balzer and Tom Dieck, *Deleuze*, 15.

74. Ibid., 10.

75. Ibid., 38.

76. Ibid.

77. Ibid., 6 (the first instance, repeated in each sequence). Moreover, the comic's front cover bears a cutoff portrait of Deleuze, whereas the back cover shows the ferryman from a similar angle.

78. See the analysis of *Le Château* below.

79. Balzer and Tom Dieck, *Deleuze*, 10.

80. Ibid., 48.

81. Mikhail Bakhtin, *The Dialogic Imagination: Four Essays by Mikhail Bakhtin*, trans. Carl Emerson and Michael Holquist, ed. Michael Holquist (Austin: University of Texas, 1991), 84. That the merging of space and time is an integral aspect of art is also reflected in Benjamin's description of the aura as "[a] strange weave of space and time: the unique appearance of semblance or distance, no matter how close the object may be," in "A Small History of Photography," *One-Way Street and Other Writings*, trans. Edmund Jephcott and Kingsley Shorter (London: Verso, 1979), 240–57, 249–50.

82. Sue Vice, "'It's About Time': The Chronotope of the Holocaust in Art Spiegelman's *Maus*," *Graphic Novel*, ed. Jan Baetens, 47–60, 47. She adds that Bakhtin's chronotopes are "the combination of space and time markers which appears in any text: chronotopes consist of images of historical and biographical time, in particular locations [. . .] spatial and temporal indicators are fused into one carefully thought-out, concrete whole" (ibid.). See also Rikke Platz Cortsen's PhD thesis, *Comics as Assemblage: How Spatio-Temporality in Comics is Constructed* (University of Copenhagen, 2012), for a detailed discussion of the chronotope's relevance for comics. In her

doctoral dissertation, *Storytelling Beyond Postmodernism: Fables and the Fairy Tale* (University of Tampere, 2010), Karin Kukkonen also mentions the significance of Bakhtin's chronotope for comics.

83. Cf. the online recordings and transcriptions of his courses from the early 1980s: *La Voix de Gilles Deleuze en Ligne*, accessed 20 June 2014, http://www.univ-paris8.fr/deleuze/article.php3?id_article=1; *Web Deleuze*, accessed 20 June 2014, http://www.webdeleuze.com/php/sommaire.html.

84. Balzer and Tom Dieck, *Deleuze*, 28.

85. Ibid., 31.

86. Ibid., 40.

87. Ibid., 49.

88. Gilles Deleuze, *Difference and Repetition*, trans. Paul Patton (New York: Columbia University Press, 1994), 297.

89. Ibid., 299.

90. Ibid., 293. At the same place, he elucidates further: "Art does not imitate, above all because it repeats; it repeats all the repetitions by virtue of an internal power (an imitation is a copy, but art is simulation, it reverses copies into simulacra). Even the most mechanical, the most banal, the most habitual and the most stereotyped repetition finds a place in works of art, it is always displaced in relation to other repetitions, and it is subject to the condition that a difference may be extracted from it for these other repetitions."

91. Pierre Masson, *Lire la Bande Dessinée* (Lyon: Presses Universitaires de Lyon, 1985), 72.

92. Groensteen, *Système de la Bande Dessinée*, 131. Moreover, Groensteen transposed Deleuze's simultaneous movement-image and time-image to the spatiality of comics (see *spatiotopia*, ibid., 25–26).

93. Balzer and Tom Dieck, *Deleuze*, 46.

94. Ibid., 47.

95. E.g., *Dorian* (Hamburg: Feest/Ehapa 1996), *Elvis* (Hamburg: Ehapa, 2007), *Cash—I See a Darkness* (Wuppertal: Edition 52, 2007).

96. Reinhard Kleist and Roland Hueve, *Lovecraft* (Stuttgart: Feest Comics, 1996). Indicating Kleist's continuing interest in H. P. Lovecraft, a more recent comic, "Das Grauen im Gemäuer" (Wuppertal: Edition 52, 2002), also visualizes four short stories by Lovecraft.

97. See, for instance, *Arkham Asylum* and *Sandman* discussed below.

98. "Unhappy is he to whom the memories of childhood bring only fear and sadness. Wretched is he who looks back upon lone hours in vast dismal chambers with brown hangings and maddening rows of antique books, or upon awed watches in twilight groves [...] Such a lot the gods gave to me—to me, the dazed, the disappointed; the barren, the broken. And yet I am strangely content and cling desperately to those sere memories where my mind momentarily threatens to reach beyond to the other" (H. P. Lovecraft, "The Outsider," *The Call of Cthulhu and Other Weird Stories*, ed. S. T. Joshi [London: Penguin, 1999], 43–49, 43. *Lovecraft* uses a German translation).

99. Kleist and Hueve, *Lovecraft*, unpaginated.

100. Ibid.

101. Ibid.

102. Ibid.

103. "Louder and louder, wilder and wilder, mounted the shrieking and whining of that desperate viol. The player was dripping with an uncanny perspiration and twisted like a monkey, always looking frantically at the curtained window. In his frenzied strains I could almost see shadowy satyrs and Bacchanals dancing and whirling insanely through seething abysses of clouds and smoke and lightning" (H. P. Lovecraft, "Erich Zann," *The Thing on the Doorstep and Other Weird Stories* [London: Penguin Books, 2001], 45–52, 50).

104. Kleist and Hueve, *Lovecraft*.

105. Much of the material in this section was used in the following article, albeit with a different focus: Maaheen Ahmed, "Reading (and Looking at) *Mariko Parade*: A Methodological Suggestion for Understanding Contemporary Graphic Narratives," *Intercultural Crossovers, Transcultural Flows: Manga/Comics*, ed. Jaqueline Berndt (Kyoto: Kyoto Seika University, 2011), 119–32.

106. Titles in the series include: Ari Folman and David Polonksy's *Valse avec Bachir* (2009), José-Louis Bouquet and Catel Muller's *Kiki de Montparnasse* (2007), Ben Katchor's *Histoires Urbaines de Julius Knipl, Photographe* (2005), Jiro Taniguchi's *Le Journal de Mon Père* (2004), and Craig Thompson's *Blankets. Manteau de Neige* (2004).

107. Frédéric Boilet and Kan Takahama, *Mariko Parade* (Brussels: Casterman 2003), 3.

108. Frédéric Boilet, "La Nouvelle Manga en 2007," accessed 10 May 2013, http://www.boilet.net/fr/nouvellemanga_2006.html.

109. Julien Bastide, "Le Bilan de L'Événement Manga," accessed 10 August 2009, http://www.boilet.net/fr/nouvellemanga_bilan_1.html.

110. "Les Douze Chimères du Zodiaque," "Hohoemidô, la Cérémonie du Sourire," "Histoire Presque Sans Paroles," "Les Petites Vestes de Boilet," "Juin 2049, Eirin a 100 ans!" and "Les Ampoules de Mariko."

111. Boilet and Takahama, *Mariko*, 13.

112. Ibid., 56–59.

113. Ibid., 107.

114. Ibid., 68.

115. Ibid., 29.

116. Ibid., 58.

117. Ibid., 34, 35, 62.

118. Ibid., 109.

119. However by being in color, the book's cover undermines the contrast between Boilet's three-dimensional figure and Mariko's outline, since both appear equally three-dimensional.

120. Ibid., 158.

121. Ibid., 7.

122. Michel Foucault, *"Des Espaces Autres, Hétérotopies" Architecture, Mouvement, Continuité*, 5 (October 1984): 46–49, 47.

123. Ibid., 48.

124. Boilet and Takahama, *Mariko*, 69.

125. Ibid., 132–33.

126. Ibid., 172–77. However, some of the inserted episodes, such as "Les Ampoules," were originally published in color (albeit limited to pale washes of skin and blue).

127. Groensteen, *Système de la Bande Dessinée*, 42. For Groensteen, white gutters, by virtue of no longer being a natural support for the page, acquire greater significance through the contrast with black gutters.

128. Boilet and Takahama, *Mariko*, 112.

129. Ibid., 130–33. Nonetheless, the focus is essentially on Mariko throughout the book.

130. Ibid., 143, 171.

131. See, for instance, ibid., 147–48.

132. Alain Robbe-Grillet, *For a New Novel: Essays on Fiction*, trans. Richard Howard (Evanston: Northwestern University Press, 1989), 134.

133. Boilet and Takahama, *Mariko*, 174–75.

CHAPTER TWO

1. Umberto Eco, "È Scomparso Hugo Pratt. Ma Ci Rimane Corto Maltese," *L'Espresso*, 4 September 1995.

2. Eco, "Mythe de Superman," 25–27.

3. Hugo Pratt, *La Ballade de la Mer Salée* (Brussels: Casterman, 1975).

4. Fresnault-Deruelle, *Images à Mi-Mots*, 19.

5. The island's name alludes to *a escondida* or by stealth, strength, and *las escondidas* or hide-and-seek.

6. This is the case with the increasingly childlike portrayal of Pandora (moving away from the earlier, more seductive depictions) after her recuperation on Escondida, which emphasizes the impossibility of her developing a relationship with Slütter or Corto.

7. Regarded by Paul Gravett as an outcome of Milton Caniff's influence: "Hugo Pratt. The Call of the Sea," 29 October 2006, accessed 24 June 2013, http://www.paulgravett.com/index.php/articles/article/hugo_pratt/.

8. As is the case with the obscure setting in which Corto and the children find themselves after their second shipwreck (Pratt, *Ballade*, 32).

9. Samson, "Stratégies Modernes d'Énonciation Picturale," 134.

10. Other than the opening and closing panels of the book, narrative captions are limited to indicating the time and place but long conversations, monologues, and letter-readings do occur. On such occasions, which enable characters to recount past events or provide explanations, the narrative weight of words is at its greatest. Correspondingly, the narrative weight of pictures is at its highest in action sequences where words are rare.

11. Ibid., 124.

12. Foucault, "Des Espaces Autres," 46–49.

13. Cranio: "il n'a pas de patrie et c'est un homme libre [...]" (he does not have a country and he's a free man). Pratt, *Ballade*, 103.

14. Ibid., 60.

15. The gulls' peaceful, unobtrusive flight during Cranio and Pandora's conversation on the beach contrasts strongly with their agitation during Rasputin's frustrated attempts at attacking a scarecrow imitating the Monk (ibid., 102, 112–15).

16. Ibid., 148.

17. Ibid., 140.

18. McHale, *Postmodernist Fiction*, 57. I would not, however, go as far as McHale to call it the most effective way of embedding intertextual space since intertextual references that are in themselves layered or embedded in multiple relationships with the text seem to go further, as suggested by the other references in *La Ballade*, such as the quotes from "The Rime of the Ancient Mariner."

19. Eco, *Open Work*, 33.

20. Pratt, *Ballade*, 8. The visual inventory of Slütter's books begins with four volumes by Melville, *Typee, Mardi, Omoo*, and *Benito Cereno*, from which the first three unfold in the South Pacific (ibid., 161). Slütter's letter for Corto lies between Shelly's *To a Cloud* and *Adonais* which, combined with Rilke's poetry, are indicative of Slütter's characterization as a romantic figure, especially since he ends up choosing death instead of betrayal. Earlier, when telling Slütter to bear the impending pain like a hero, Corto had mentioned the *Nibelungenlied* (ibid., 146). In addition, Caïn calls the young Maori Tarao "Friday" upon seeing him for the first time and Tarao corrects him by pointing out the difference and the colonial bias. Caïn then tells Tarao about *Moby Dick* and quotes its lines on Jonas and the whale when a German submarine surfaces. The quote thus becomes an instance of interactive and even self-reflexive intertextuality (ibid., 55).

21. Ibid., 60.

22. Samuel Taylor Coleridge, "The Rime of the Ancient Mariner," *The Complete Poetical Works. Vol. 1: Poems*, ed. Ernest Hartley Coleridge (Oxford: Clarendon Press, 1912), 196–97.

23. Pratt, *Ballade*, 166. He adds that Euripides's *Medea* contained a passage on that episode.

24. Philip Larkin, "Church Going," *Collected Poems*, ed. Anthony Thwaite (London: Faber and Faber, 2003), 59.

25. Dave McKean and Grant Morrison, *Arkham Asylum: A Serious House on Serious Earth* (New York: DC Comics, 2004), unpaginated. This notion persists in the Joker's farewell words to Batman: "Enjoy yourself out there. In the asylum."

26. See the extract of a Carl Barks's interview from 1973 in Donald Ault's "Preludium: Crumb, Barks and Noomin. Re-Considering the Aesthetics of Underground Comics," *ImageText* 1.2 (2004), accessed 16 November 2009, http://www.english.ufl.edu/imagetext/archives/v1_2/intro.shtml.

27. Nonetheless, the asylum itself made its first appearance in *Batman* #258 (1974), with the

Joker and Two-Face as its first inmates. Arkham itself is the well-known city in Massachusetts invented by Lovecraft and based on Salem, appearing for the first time in *The Picture in the House* (1920).

28. McKean and Morrison, *Arkham*.

29. Ibid. This is complemented by a sketch of the cross-section of a human head, surrounded by psychedelic colors floating above the Mad Hatter's profile.

30. Ibid. Suggesting a certain fluidity of identities, both Arkham and Batman associate pearls with their mothers' deaths, since Batman's mother was wearing a string of pearls when she was killed and Arkham's mother committed suicide with a pearl-handled knife. Later, it is Arkham's words that simultaneously narrate his own hallucinatory, shamanistic attempt to cure himself and Batman's struggle with the last villain, Killer Croc, which is the longest battle in the book and extends over eight pages. Realistically depicted as a giant reptile, Croc makes his first appearance as Arkham mentions entering the Dark Tower of his fear to "face the *Dragon* within." The fight with Croc is consequently linked to other dragon fights from myth and literature, such as the one from St. George's legend.

31. Ibid.

32. Ibid.

33. Ibid.

34. This particular intertextual reference is popular, cropping up in several other comics discussed here as well as those that have not been included, such as Bryan Talbot's *Alice in Sunderland*.

35. McKean and Morrison, *Arkham*. Anointed by several footnotes in red, this appended script provides metafictional insight and also contains some autofictional instances, such as Morrison's claim that Arkham's horrific childhood Fun House experience was close to Morrison's own childhood experience.

36. Their employment of visual motifs that are often crossovers between film and animation, as well as their unsettling eeriness (e.g., Jan Švankmajer's 1988 *Alice*), is comparable to both the visual and literary content of *Arkham*.

37. These range from references to rock songs to Anthony Perkins's lines from *WUSA* (or *Hall of Mirrors*, 1970) to the play *Marat/Sade* (1963), by Peter Weiss, which are interspersed with random words said by Morrison and McKean. A little later, as the villains decide to hunt down Batman before the given time, Perkins appears in a distorted close-up from *Psycho* in a panel representing a TV screen.

38. Standing over Rorschach cards, Ruth muses whether the Joker's multiple, constantly changing personalities manifest a kind of "super-sanity," "[a] brilliant new modification of human perception. More suited to urban life at the end of the twentieth century" (ibid.).

39. Ibid.

40. In his commentary, Morrison acknowledges that "[m]uch of this subtextual reference was lost on the casual reader but that didn't seem to stop us from shifting mega-amounts of copies. I do believe that people respond emotionally to deep mythical patterns whether or not they

actually recognize or 'understand' them as such, but the fact that our book launched at the time of the outrageously successful *Batman* film by Tim Burton probably helped more than anything else" (ibid.).

41. Likewise, the confident tone of superhero comics is echoed by the moral lesson from Batman at the book's end: "Arkham was right; sometimes it's only madness that makes us what we are. Or destiny perhaps" (ibid.).

42. An example is Dr. Destiny, whose name is frequently shortened to D. An enemy of Batman and the Justice League of America, Dr. D. is also the most important villain in the first *Sandman* volume. Likewise, the hero Dr. Fate was part of the All-Star Squadron and was later incorporated in the series, *Infinity, Inc.*

43. This was in compliance with the requirements of the editor, Karen Berger, who sought to revive the series and wanted a new Sandman. See Neil Gaiman's afterword in: Neil Gaiman, Sam Kieth, Mike Dringenberg, and Malcolm Jones III, *The Sandman: Preludes and Nocturnes* (New York: DC Comics, 1991).

44. Gaiman et al., *Preludes*, 18.

45. Ibid., 9–10.

46. Ibid., 7–8.

47. Even in *Der Sandmann*, two versions of the same name appear: a real-life character and a fantastic one, the threatening, regular visitor to the children's father, who the mother avoids mentioning and the evil figure in the nurse's tale. Nathanael relates both versions at the beginning of his letter to Lothar. "Einmal war mir jenes dumpfe Treten und Poltern besonders graulich; ich frug die Mutter, indem sie uns fortführte: Ei Mama! wer ist denn der böse Sandmann, der uns immer von Papa forttreibt? [...]—Es gibt keinen Sandmann, mein liebes Kind, erwiderte die Mutter: wenn ich sage, der Sandmann kommt, so will das nur heißen, ihr seid schläfrig und könnt die Augen nicht offen behalten, als hätte man euch Sand hineingestreut." The nurse's account, by contrast, describes a gory, murderous being: "Das ist ein böser Mann, der kommt zu den Kindern, wenn sie nicht zu Bett gehen wollen und wirft ihnen Händevoll Sand in die Augen, daß sie blutig zum Kopf herausspringen, die wirft er dann in den Sack und trägt sie in den Halbmond zur Atzung für seine Kinderchen; die sitzen dort im Nest und haben krumme Schnäbel, wie die Eulen, damit picken sie der unartigen Menschenkindlein Augen auf." E. T. A. Hoffmann, *Nachtstücke*, accessed 12 February 2009, http://www.gutenberg.org/cache/epub/6341/pg6341.html.

48. "[A] man, young, pale and naked, imprisoned in a tiny cell, waiting until his captors passed away, willing to wait until the room he was in crumbled to dust; deathly thin, with long dark hair, and strange eyes: *Dream*. That was what he was. That was who he was" (Gaiman, *Preludes*, 238).

49. Gaiman et al., *Preludes*, 238.

50. Ibid., 78.

51. Cf. Karen Berger's introduction in *Preludes*.

52. Gaiman, *Preludes*, 239. Gaiman adds that "The Sound of Her Wings" was "the story in the sequence I felt was truly mine, and in which I knew I was beginning to find my own voice."

53. This literary connection also ties up with the rhymes used by Squatterbloat and Etrigan at the beginning. Yet, as on several other occasions, the self-belittling proclivity of comics, their refusal to uphold the standards of traditional literature and art, becomes apparent when Dream interprets the tendency to speak in rhymes as an indicator of importance in hell's hierarchy (ibid., 112).

54. Characteristically, Dream uses the Old Testament's more ambivalent names for him, such as Lucifer or the Morning Star (Book of Isaiah, 14:12).

55. Papyrus Berlin 3024, recto (Egyptian Museum and Papyrus Collection, Berlin).

56. These range from older hits such as the title song and Pat Ballad's "Mr. Sandman" to Sting's "Spread a Little Happiness."

57. Gaiman et al., *Preludes*, 88.

58. Edmond Baudoin, *Le Voyage* (Paris: L'Association, 2005), unpaginated.

59. A homeless person, whom Simon met after preventing Marc's suicide attempt in the ocean and getting into a drunken bar fight, had told him about her (ibid.).

60. Bruno Canard, "Edmond Baudoin, l'Émotion du Geste," *du9*, September 1999, accessed 20 June 2014, http://www.du9.org/entretien/edmond-baudoin-l-emotion-du-geste/.

61. The stars also refer to Olivier's reason for becoming a puppeteer that is mentioned twice in the book, the first time as: "J'adore voir briller les yeux des enfants" (I love seeing the children's eyes light up). Baudoin, *Voyage*.

62. Canard, "Edmond Baudoin, l'Émotion du Geste."

63. Ibid. As Baudoin points out: "[l]'enfant a très peur de cette ouverture qui ne lui semble pas naturelle et par laquelle 's'en va la vie.' Il faut fermer le trait comme le faisait Hergé" (The child is very afraid of this opening which to him does not seem natural and through which "life goes away." One must close the line, like Hergé did). Baudoin himself, however, had refused to close the heads of his figures as a child, which was seen by a family friend as a sign of schizophrenia.

64. Baudoin, *Voyage*.

65. Charles Baudelaire, *The Flowers of Evil*, trans. James McGowan (Oxford: Oxford University Press, 1993), 282–93.

66. Gaiman et al., *Preludes*, 234.

CHAPTER THREE

1. Hollywood film noir was termed as such by French journalists who had noticed a connection with French films of the 1930s. R. Barton Palmer also discerns a link to dark, naturalist fiction like Émile Zola's *La Bête Humaine* and points out that the film noir had its literary parallel in the roman noir. Film noir is interpreted as an outcome of a widespread cultural change, namely, the onslaught of modernism and an awareness of its negative consequences. Noir imbued the popular genre of crime and detective stories with themes such as alienation and fatal-

ism. Due to its chiaroscuro effects, tilted perspectives, and point-of-view shots, as well as the horrific distortion of reality, it also comes across as a transliteration of German Expressionism into film. R. Barton Palmer, "The Sociological Turn of Adaptation Studies: The Example of Film Noir, *Film Theory: An Introduction*, ed. Robert Stam (Malden: Blackwell, 2000), 266–77.

2. Mark C. Rogers, "Crime Pays: The Crime and Mystery Genre," *Critical Survey of Graphic Novels*, ed. Bart Beaty and Stephen Weiner (Ipswich: Salem Press, 2013), 169–72, 169.

3. Trushell, "American Dreams of Mutants: The X-Men—'Pulp' Fiction, Science Fiction and Superheroes," 150.

4. The term was applied to comics by Bruno Lecigne and Jean-Pierre Tamine in *Fac-Similé. Essai Paratactique sur le Nouveau Réalisme de la Bande Dessinée* (Paris: Futuropolis, 1963).

5. Screech, *Masters of the Ninth Art*, 131.

6. Ibid., 144.

7. The title of the newspaper that Tardi has created for this purpose, *L'Étrangleur* (*The Strangler*), references his first use of the newspaper format for *Le Secret de l'Étrangleur*, an adaptation of Pierre Siniac's crime thriller, *Monsieur Cauchemar*.

8. M. Pralong, "Propos de Tardi," *Le Matin*, 21 December 1996, accessed 29 April 2009, http://www.http://blancsecadele.free.fr/aventures.html/.

9. Eco, *Role of the Reader*, 8.

10. Notably, it was during the *fin de siècle* that horror and fantasy fiction proliferated, the cultural implications of which have been pointed out in works such as Nicholas Daly's *Modernism, Romance, and the* Fin de Siècle: *Popular Fiction and British Culture, 1880–1914* (Cambridge: Cambridge University Press, 1999).

11. Tardi, *Adèle et la Bête*, 23–25.

12. Ibid., 44.

13. Fresnault-Deruelle, *Images à Mi-Mots*, 48.

14. Ibid., 47.

15. Tardi, *Adèle et la Bête*, 7–9.

16. Hence, vertical panels are dominant when the action occurs in a high place, such as an attic or a roof (Tardi, *Adèle et la Bête*, 16). While complementing the action, the juxtaposition of extreme horizontal and vertical panels in Antoine's dream also highlights the absurd intensity of the situation (ibid., 21–22). Similarly, a regular layout, with uniform panel sizes, implies a regularity of action, free of major twists, as with the phone conversations regarding the pterodactyl, which are shown descending through the public officers' ranks (ibid., 10–11).

17. See ibid., 3 (first two panels), 13 (last panel with the bulging clock tower of the Gare de Lyon).

18. Ibid., 3, 11.

19. Thus, Adèle's real name is only mentioned halfway into the story by a threatening, anonymous caller later revealed as Lobel (ibid., 30). Initially, she tells Antoine that she is Edith Rabatjoie.

20. Benoît Mouchart, "Entretien avec Jacques Tardi," *Auracan* 10, May–June 1995, accessed 20 March 2013, http://www.auracan.com/Interviews/Tardi/.

21. Jacques Tardi, *Adèle Blanc-Sec, Le Labyrinthe Infernal, L'Étrangleur* no. 1–3 (Brussels: Casterman, 2007).

22. Tardi, *Labyrinthe*, no. 2, 6.

23. Ibid., 13–14.

24. As pointed out in Part One, openness can only unfold within a form or structure that is in itself complete. See Eco, *Open Work*, 4.

25. Tardi, *Labyrinthe*, no. 1 (Brussels: Casterman, 2007), 1.

26. Tardi, *Labyrinthe*, no. 2, 4.

27. Edgar P. Jacobs's famous characters, Blake and Mortimer, make an appearance in another Adèle volume, *Le Noyé À Deux Têtes*.

28. Tardi, *Labyrinthe*, no. 3, 1, 14.

29. Ibid., 11.

30. Screech contrasts this mélange of fantasy and the real—monsters running through an everyday Paris, for instance—with American comics, where monsters are often inserted in more unrealistic settings (Screech, *Masters of the Ninth Art*, 152).

31. Alan Moore and Eddie Campbell, *From Hell* (London: Knockabout Comics, 2007).

32. Thus, the page preceding the prologue contains the "salutation to Ganesa" symbol (the unrotated swastika) referring to the Hindu elephant god, Ganesa, patron of the arts and sciences as well as the lord of beginnings, obstacles, and success.

33. The original publication of *From Hell* in serial form, like many comics miniseries or graphic novels, is comparable to the publication of novels in newspapers during the nineteenth century. However, the chapters in *From Hell* are self-contained and do not break off at a tantalizing point, as in many serialized works of popular fiction.

34. Moore and Campbell, *From Hell*, Appendix 1, 14.

35. In contrast to the factual claims of historical fiction, history is revealed as an evident "poetic construct" in historiographic fiction. Cf. Linda Hutcheon, *Narcissistic Narrative: The Metafictional Paradox* (London: Methuen, 1984), xiv. See also Hutcheon's *A Poetics of Postmodernism: History, Theory, Fiction* (London: Routledge, 1988).

36. Most of the information regarding the actual Ripper case utilized here has been retrieved from the database, *Casebook: Jack the Ripper*, accessed 20 June 2014, http://www.casebook.org/intro.html.

37. The continuing popularity of the Ripper case amongst bestselling crime novelists is evident in the fact that already in 1978, Stephen King published *Jack the Ripper: The Final Solution*. More recently, Patricia Cornwell published the pseudo-historical *Portrait of a Killer: Jack the Ripper—Case Closed* (2002). Moore's reliance upon King's book is confirmed in the appendix. The other bibliographic sources are then chronologically listed, including Iain Sinclair's *White Chapell, Scarlet Tracings* (1987), which explores the connection between the murders and Hawksmoor's churches.

38. Moore and Campbell, *From Hell*, Appendix 1, 23.

39. Ibid., 29.

40. Ibid., Chapter 9, 2.

41. Ibid., Appendix 1, 30. The legend that in the sixteenth century a woman was killed by an insane monk on Mitre Square was indeed revived in the wake of Katie's and Elizabeth's murders through souvenirs like the walking sticks capped by the monk's head. These in turn are evoked by a similar stick carried by Abberline in the epilogue, this time with a woman's head on it. Similarly, in the second appendix, complemented by a panel with a picture-less poster of *From Hell*, Moore describes the Ripper products as making up "the theme park," adding, "[t]ruth is, this has never been about the murders, nor the killer nor his victims. It is about us. About our minds and how they dance" (ibid., Appendix 2, 22).

42. Cf. Giambattista Vico, *The New Science: Principles of the New Science Concerning the Common Nature of Peoples, Book III: Discovery of the True Homer* (London: Penguin, 1999), 310–13.

43. Cf. Erich Auerbach, *Mimesis. Dargestellte Wirklichkeit in der abendländlischen Literatur* (Tübingen: Francke Verlag, 2001).

44. It is especially regarding the details of the Freemasons that Moore is unable to draw a clear line between fact and fiction and admits to the impossibility of confirming the truth for "an obscuring Victorian fog starts to engulf the facts of our narrative. Given that the tortuous story of the Whitechapel murders is filled with liars, tricksters, and unreliable witnesses, it is a fog we shall encounter often" (Moore and Campbell, *From Hell*, Appendix 1, 3). And he even encourages corrections from the readers regarding the depiction of Masonic rituals (ibid., 4).

45. Ibid., 8.

46. Ibid., 10.

47. Ibid., Appendix 2, 15.

48. Ibid., 1.

49. Ibid., 3.

50. Ibid., 7.

51. Ibid., 16.

52. Ibid., Chapter 9, 15.

53. Blake's official comment on the tempera painting was that the monster was created in the process of sketching a flea that had explained to him that fleas were the souls of bloodthirsty men who had been confined to minute bodies in order to control their insatiable thirst. "William Blake—The Ghost of a Flea," *Tate*, accessed 20 June 2014, http://www.tate.org.uk/art/artworks/blake-the-ghost-of-a-flea-n05889.

54. Moore and Campbell, *From Hell*, Chapter 14, 16–17.

55. Ibid., Chapter 11, 33.

56. Ibid., Chapter 2, 14.

57. Ibid., 1. By comprising exclusively of word balloons against a black background, this

opening page exemplifies the wordless comics narrative that Campbell often employs, where the narration is carried out through a dialogue between several speech balloons.

58. Ibid., Chapter 14, 24.

59. *Jahaa! Autorencomics aus den nordischen Ländern*, Nordische Botschaften Gemeinschaftshaus (Berlin: Felleshus, 2009). See also "Comic durchbricht in vieler Hinsicht die Grenzen," *Botschaft von Finnland*, Berlin, 16 November 2009, accessed 20 June 2014, http://www.finnland.de/Public/default.aspx?contentid=179252&culture=de-DE.

60. Annemari Hietanen and Marko Turunen, *Kuolema Kulkee Kintereillä* (Helsinki: Daada, 2004).

61. Ibid., 79.

62. Ibid., 20, 41.

63. Jeanne Floreani, "Marko Turunen, du9, l'autre bande dessinée, accessed 20 June 2014, http://www.du9.org/entretien/marko_turunen/.

64. Hietanen and Turunen, *Kuolema*, 85–86.

65. Ibid., 53–54.

66. This is evident early in the book when R-Rautanainen wonders whether her money will last (ibid., 35).

67. Ibid., 28–30.

68. Ibid., 6, 38.

69. In this respect, *Kuolema* is similar to *Taxi van Gohin Korvaan*. Nonetheless, the visualization and the main narrative support their classification under noir and fantasy, respectively.

70. Ibid., 92.

71. Ibid., 41.

72. Ibid., 83.

73. Ibid., 74–80.

74. Ibid., 61–62.

75. Jyrki Heikkinen, *Tohtori Futuro* (Oulu: Asema, 2007), unpaginated.

76. Eco, "Le Mythe de Superman," 25.

77. Heikkinen, *Futuro*.

78. Such as the act of showering which is suggested through the depiction of the shampoo bottle's different states and the trickling shower (Hietanen and Turunen, *Kuolema*, 17–19).

CHAPTER FOUR

1. Pascal Lefèvre, "Le Fantastique, un Genre Indéfinissable?" *Image (&) Narrative* 2 (2001), 17 June 2014, http://www.imageandnarrative.be/inarchive/fantastiquebd/pascallefevre.htm.

2. William Coyle, "Introduction: The Nature of Fantasy," *Aspects of Fantasy, Selected Essays from the Second International Conference on the Fantastic in Literature and Film*, ed. William Coyle (London: Greenwood Press, 1981), 2.

3. Ibid., 1.

4. Fantasy in American comics usually unfolds in the superhero and adventure genres. See

Jean-Paul Gabilliet, "Fantastique Bande Dessinée," *Image (&) Narrative* 2 (2001), accessed 17 June 2014, http://www.imageandnarrative.be/inarchive/fantastiquebd/jeanpaulgabilliet.htm.

5. Ibid.

6. Ibid.

7. Lefèvre, "Le Fantastique."

8. Jan Baetens, "Choses Vues. Du Regard en Fantastique," *Image (&) Narrative* 2 (2001), accessed 17 June 2014, http://www.imageandnarrative.be/inarchive/fantastiquebd/janbaetens.htm.

9. Trushell, "American Dreams of Mutants," 149.

10. Paul L. Thomas, "Science Fiction," *Critical Survey of Graphic Novels*, 207.

11. Thierry Smolderen, *Naissances de la Bande Dessinée: De William Hogarth à Winsor McCay* (Brussels: Les Impressions Nouvelles, 2009), 16.

12. Peter Mikelbank, "Twists of Fate," *France Magazine* 64 (2002–2003), accessed 20 April 2013, http://www.francemagazine.org/articles/issue64/article51.asp?issue_id=64&article_id=51.

13. Ibid.

14. Screech, *Masters of the Ninth Art*, 118.

15. Moebius *Arzach. L'Album Mythique* (Paris: Les Humanoïdes Associés, 2006), 5.

16. Patrice van Eersel, "Moebius. Une Matinée avec une Aventurier de l'Esprit," *CLES*, accessed 20 June 2014, http://www.cles.com/debats-entretiens/article/une-matinee-avec-un-aventurier-de-l-esprit.

17. Screech, *Masters of the Ninth Art*, 98.

18. Moebius, *Arzach*, 7–13. First published in 1973 and signed by Gir. Although the strip bears its own page numbers, as with the other comics, the numbers in the footnotes refer to those in the album.

19. Ibid., 49–53.

20. Likening Moebius's visual precision to that of the Classicists, Fresnault-Deruelle declares: "L'enchaînement des cases conduit à un effect d'accumulation qui est l'origine d'un veritable monde" (the sequence of panels leads to a cumulative effect that is the origin of a real world). Fresnault-Deruelle, *Images à Mi-Mots*, 120. Yet these worlds are vague, based on random glimpses, and the key concern is clearly visualization instead of narration.

21. Ibid., 119.

22. Ibid., 3. As an aside, a 1988 *Silver Surfer* volume illustrated by Moebius was also subtitled "Parable."

23. Ibid., 7.

24. Ibid., 8.

25. Ibid., 9.

26. Ibid., 10.

27. The fourth page is a good example of the combination of a variety of visual styles—with a different one for almost each panel—to form an aesthetically cohesive whole (ibid., 11).

28. Ibid., 8.

29. Ibid., 9.

30. Ibid., back cover.

31. Ibid.

32. Ibid., 42.

33. Screech, *Masters of the Ninth Art*, 96.

34. As was already the case in his later *Blueberry* comics (see Screech, *Masters of the Ninth Art*, 98).

35. For instance, Arzach's second voyeuristic escapade (the fifth episode in the book) unfolds across a page with four uneven, dynamic panels. The nude's glowing yellow is dominant and buttressed by its compound colors, including green for the walls and orange for Arzach's skin (Moebius, *Arzach*, 41).

36. Ibid., 48–53.

37. The V appears on the third page as well—albeit in a more curved form—with depictions of Char-Limpota's happy and doomed selves, as well as the face of the evil sorcerer Sarukin forming a vertical line cutting through the ductile V (ibid., 50).

38. Ibid., 51. Although speech balloons are still absent, short lines link the words with their speaker.

39. Ibid., 53. The first is a wide shot illustrating the mixed army led by Arzach before Sarukin's citadel, a structure in intense blue that is more beautiful than frightening.

40. Ibid., 52.

41. Ibid., 50.

42. Ibid., 3.

43. Ibid.

44. Fresnault-Deruelle, *Images à Mi-Mots*, 119.

45. Jasmina Sopova, "Enki Bilal: A Journey to the End of Time," *UNESCO Courrier*, accessed 21 August 2009, http://www.unesco.org/courier/2000_04/uk/dires.htm.

46. "Enki Bilal—Der Schlaf des Monsters. Ein Interview (January 1999)," *Parnass. Die Kulturzeitschrift im Internet*, accessed 20 June 2014, http://www.parnass.scram.de/comicdetail.php?nr=51.

47. Sopova, "Enki Bilal."

48. Keeping up the tradition of name puns in *bandes dessinées*, Choublanc comes from the expression *faire choux blanc* or to fail at doing something.

49. Bilal, Enki, *La Foire aux Immortels* (Paris: Dargaud, 1980), 34.

50. Ibid., 23.

51. Sopova, "Enki Bilal," 49.

52. Ibid.

53. Kai Mikkonen, "The Paradox of Intersemiotic Translation and the Comic Book: Examples from Enki Bilal's *Nikopol* Trilogy," *Word & Image* 22.2 (2006): 101–117, 103.

54. Bilal, *La Foire*, 47.

55. Baudelaire, *Flowers of Evil*, 59.

56. Bilal, *La Foire*, 48: "Les jambes en l'air, comme une femme lubrique/Brûlante et suant les poisons/Ouvrait d'une façon nonchalante et cynique/Son ventre plein d'exhalaisons" (Baudelaire, *Flowers of evil*, 59: Her legs spread out like a lecherous whore/Sweating out poisonous fumes/Who opened in slick invitational style/Her stinking and festering womb).

57. Bilal, *La Foire*, 49, Baudelaire, *Flowers of Evil*, 59.

58. Bilal, *La Foire*, 49.

59. Baudelaire, *Flowers of Evil*, 61.

60. Bilal, *La Foire*, 60: "Comme les anges à l'œil fauve/Je reviendrai dans ton alcôve/Et vers toi glisserai sans bruit/Avec les ombres de la nuit [. . .]" (Baudelaire, *Flowers of Evil*, 131: Like angels who have bestial eyes/I'll come again to your alcove/And glide in silence to your side/In shadows of the night).

61. Bilal, *La Foire*, 61, Baudelaire, *Flowers of Evil*, 131.

62. Bilal, *La Foire*, 61.

63. Ibid., 62.

64. Ibid., 64.

65. Baudelaire, *Flowers of Evil*, 249

66. Ibid., 248.

67. Ibid., 249.

68. Ibid., 132–33.

69. Ibid., 67.

70. Ibid., 68. Baudelaire, *Flowers of Evil*, 269.

71. Mikkonen, "Paradox of Intersemiotic Translation," 103.

72. Ibid., 115. Correspondingly, when Horus makes Nikopol unconscious to take complete control over his body—as during the match and meeting with Choublanc—the events are not depicted directly, but shown from a distance.

73. Bilal, *Froid Équateur*, 55.

74. Ibid.

75. Baudelaire, *Fleurs du Mal*, 157.

76. See, for instance, William Olmsted, "Immortal Rot: A reading of 'Une Charogne,'" *Understanding Fleurs du Mal: Critical Readings*, ed. William Thompson (Tennessee: Vanderbilt University Press, 1997), 60–71.

77. Sopova, "Enki Bilal."

78. Bilal, *Froid Équateur*, 56.

79. Ibid.

80. Sopova, "Enki Bilal."

81. Bilal, *Froid Équateur*, 53.

82. Ault, "Preludium: Crumb, Barks and Noomin."

83. Fresnault-Deruelle, *Images à Mi-Mots*, 91; Charles Hatfield, *Alternative Comics: An Emerging Literature* (Jackson: University Press of Mississippi, 2005), ix.

84. Material in this section was used for the following article: Maaheen Ahmed, "Fallen An-

gels and Shattered Skies: Rejected Conventions in Yslaire's Cloud 99 (*XXe Ciel*)," *International Journal of Comic Art* 12.1 (2010): 61–75.

85. Incompletely published in English as the *Cloud 99* miniseries.

86. "Expo Yslaire XXe ciel.com," *Librairie La Main Blanche*, accessed 20 June 2014, http://www.lamainblanche.com/Public/Event_View.aspx?e=6.

87. Ibid.

88. Yslaire, *Introduction au XXe ciel. http://www.yslaire.be* (Paris: Delcourt, 1997), 58.

89. Moreover, *mémoires19<00>* contains an extremely large bibliography of roughly fifty books which is accompanied by the nonchalant remark: "J'en oublie certainement" (I am definitely forgetting some of them). See Yslaire, *XXe ciel.com. http://www.xxeciel.com/mémoires<19>00* (Paris: Les Humanoïdes Associés, 2004).

90. Yslaire, *Introduction*, 3.

91. These pages also evoke the repeated promise that God shall wipe away the believers' tears, along with the appearance of a blood red moon in the Apocalypse of John (8:9).

92. *Yslaire*, accessed 23 August 2009, http://www.yslaire.be/fr/pages/introduction-au-xxe-ciel.cfm.

93. Notably, one of the few *bande dessinée* traditions preserved in the book is the continuous play on names: Ysler's homonymy with Hislaire and Yslaire (both of which are pseudonyms used by the book's artist) is underscored in Ysler's biography. The other names are metaphorical since Farouge's full name contains "Dyeu" in it (which is a homophone for *dieu* or god), and Frank Stern's family name echoes the star-shaped wound on his forehead.

94. Though not explicitly mentioned as a possible reference to Walter Benjamin's "Angel of History," the link is difficult to ignore.

95. Yslaire, *mémoires19<00>*, 1–9.

96. See W. J. Mitchell's *Visual Truth in the Photographic Era* (Cambridge: MIT Press, 2001) on the implications of the shift from analogue to digital technology.

97. Yslaire, *Introduction*, 11.

98. Starting out with comics and experimenting with a variety of styles, Vaughn-James switched to paintings in the 1980s, creating ambivalent pieces hovering between photography, painting, and drawing.

99. Ibid., 29.

100. Ibid., 61.

101. This echoes the titles of Yslaire's later albums, *Ciel Au-Dessus de Bruxelles* (2006), as well as the "Krieg im Himmel" episode in John's Apocalypse when Michael and his angels fight against the seven-headed beast.

102. Yslaire, *mémoires19<00>*, 19.

103. Ibid., 13.

104. Lacking the exact dates or information about his disappearance, Ysler's biography mentions several likely places of his birth and education. The uncertainty whether Frank continued to live through the century with a star-shaped bomb scar on his forehead, instead of dying dur-

ing the seventh battle at Isonzo in 1916, is heightened by his photograph from 1976—taken by an anonymous photographer at an unspecified place—where his extended shadow has the shape of wings. In *mémoires19<00>*, Frank has several youthful versions.

105. Yslaire, *Introduction*, 36.
106. Ibid., 58.
107. Ibid.
108. Ibid., 63.
109. Philippe Sohet, "Quand Lire C'est Écrire. À Propos d'*Iphigénie* de Xavier Löwenthal, *Image (&) Narrative* 8 (2004), accessed 17 June 2014, http://www.imageandnarrative.be/inarchive/issue08/philippesohet.htm.
110. Yslaire, *mémoires19<00>*, 28.
111. Yslaire, *Introduction*, 62.
112. Ibid.
113. Ibid., 32.
114. Yslaire, *Introduction*, 63.
115. Ibid., 62.
116. Ibid., 32.
117. Ibid., 27.
118. See Eco, *Open Work*, 12, already cited above.
119. Pierre Christin and Jean-Claude Mézières, *Lady Polaris* (Paris: Autrement, 1987).
120. One intermedial reference involves two panels from a pornographic comic (Christin and Mézières, *Lady Polaris*, 20).
121. This also occurs in Pratt's *Saint-Exupèry*, where the sky embodies the uncertainty of the protagonist's disappearance.
122. Sopova, "Enki Bilal."
123. Material in this section was used for the following article, focusing on the autofictional aspect:
Maaheen Ahmed, "The Art of Splicing: Autofiction in Words and Images," *International Journal of Comic Art* 16.1 (2014): 322–38.
124. Even though Mäkilä has already held several individual exhibitions for his comics at, among others, Helsinki's Amos Anderson Art Museum, he is not mentioned in comics catalogues such as *Jahaa!* (Berlin: Felleshus, 2009) and *Sarjakuva* (Helsinki: Sarjakuvatekijät, 2008).
125. He also has a tendency to incorporate references to Renaissance, Baroque, Mannerist, and Romantic art. See Kimmo Sarje, "Stimulating Chaos, Supporting Cosmos: Jarmo Mäkilä as Artist and Observer," *Jarmo Mäkilä. The Picture of Dorian Gray*, Amos Anderson Art Museum, August–November 2002 (Helsinki: University of Helsinki Press, 2002), 15.
126. See Mika Hannula, "The Past of the Future: Jarmo Mäkilä's Gesamtkunstwerk," *Jarmo Mäkilä* (Helsinki: Helsinki City Art Museum, 2008), 7–9.
127. Jarmo Mäkilä, *Taxi van Goghin Korvaan* (Helsinki: Itikka Kustannus, 2008), 6.
128. Ibid., 11.

129. Ibid., 10.
130. Ibid., 26.
131. Ibid., 43–44.
132. *Jarmo Mäkilä*, Galerie Kaj Försblom (April–May 1990) Helsinki: Naantali 1990, not paginated.
133. Mäkilä, *Taxi*, 31–33.
134. Ibid., 9, 26, 35, 43.
135. While Sarje was referring to Mäkilä's paintings, her observation is also applicable to the splashes on pages 9 and 35 in *Taxi*.
136. Sarje, "Stimulating Chaos," 15.
137. Mäkilä, *Taxi*, 10
138. Ibid., 22.
139. Ibid., 21.
140. Ibid., 17.
141. Ibid., 40.
142. Such a figure recalls Tiresias in T. S. Eliot's *The Waste Land*. Since both take up the modern condition of disjunction and self-alienation, the comic does have additional (but probably unintentional) parallels with the poem.

CHAPTER FIVE

1. Baetens calls such adaptations of literary novels "visual literature" (Baetens, "Graphic Novels: Literature without Text," 77–88).

2. For an analysis of *City of Glass*' metafictional aspects, see Paul Atkinson's "The Graphic Novel as Metafiction," *Studies in Comics* 1.1 (2010): 107–125. For its interaction with crime and detective fiction, as well as the parallels between Stillman's search for a new language and the comic's innovative visualization, see David Coughlan's "Paul Auster: The City of Glass," *Modern Fiction Studies* 52.4 (2006): 832–54. Like Atkinson, Coughlan also finds that Karasik and Mazzucchelli "match Auster's textualization with their visualization" (ibid., 843).

3. Paul Auster, Paul Karasik, and David Mazzucchelli, *City of Glass: The Graphic Novel* (New York: Picador, 2004), ii.

4. Bill Kartalopoulos, "Coffee with Paul Karasik," *Indy Magazine*, Spring 2004, accessed 4 April 2013, http://www.indyworld.com/indy/spring_2004/karasik_interview/.

5. Auster et al., *City of Glass*, ii.

6. Ibid., i. While the original *Classics Illustrated* series has been revived, newer adaptations of classics are also being issued, including publications by the recently set up British publishing house, Classical Comics (see Paul Gravett, "Classical Comics: Turning Classics into Comics," 9 November 2008, accessed 10 June 2013, http://paulgravett.com/index.php/articles/article/classical_comics).

7. This is complemented by the cover picture of the 2004 Picador edition, showing Quinn's multiple reflections spliced through the windows of a passing train.

8. Auster et al., *City of Glass*, 2.

9. Ibid., 107.

10. See McHale, *Postmodernist Fiction*.

11. Auster et al., *City of Glass*, 137

12. As the narrator's remark during Quinn's desperate attempt to decide which of the Stillman look-alikes to follow proves: "There was no way to know: not this, not anything" (ibid., 54).

13. While the narrator's words are typewritten at the top of the last page, they conclude in Quinn's handwriting against the background of a fire burning pages from his notebook and other objects established as symbols in the comic, such as the marionette representing the younger Peter Stillman (ibid., 138).

14. Ibid., 2.

15. McCloud, *Understanding Comics*, 59.

16. Ibid., 42.

17. Ibid., 39, 41, 43.

18. Kartalopoulos, "Breakfast with Paul Karasik."

19. Auster et al., *City of Glass*, 15–23.

20. See, in particular, *Grandes Heures de Rohan* from ca. 1430 (MS 9471, Bibliothèque nationale de France), "The Dying Man and His Judge" (f. 159), where a similar word balloon floats from the dying man's lips.

21. Auster et al., *City of Glass*, 26–29.

22. Ibid., 4. The panels on most of the pages form a rigid 3 x 3 grid. Though the number and size of the panels frequently vary, they always adhere to the grid's outline. Disruptions of the grid occur during key moments in the comic, such as Quinn's conversation with Virginia, his reading of Stillman's book, later pursual of the man, and his own disappearance.

23. These objects include the windows in Quinn's room (ibid., 6) the jail bars from which Peter's words snake through (ibid., 22), and the background for the silhouettes of Henry Dark and his mother (ibid., 42).

24. Ibid., 27, 45.

25. Ibid., 37.

26. Ibid., 127–38.

27. Groensteen, *Système de la Bande Dessinée*, 61. The grid is used in a comparable, figurative manner in *Salut, Deleuze!* and *From Hell*.

28. Auster et al., *City of Glass*, 8.

29. Ibid., 23, 138.

30. The closest could have been parallel combinations, if one could add the word "appear" in McCloud's definition as follows: "Words and pictures [appear] to follow different courses" (McCloud, *Understanding Comics*, 154).

31. Auster et al., *City of Glass*, 7, where a child's drawing of a screaming boy interrupts the sequence.

32. Ibid., 20.

33. The citing of Alice's encounter with Humpty Dumpty in *Through the Looking Glass* (which also condenses Stillman's fascination for the relationship between words and their meanings) is accompanied by an illustrated panel of his falling against a blank space, with Stillman's voiceover likening it to the fall of man (ibid., 74–75). The illustration reappears as part of a book being read by a child and his mother during Stillman and Quinn's last conversation in the park.

34. A visualization of this drifting occurs on a splash showing Quinn walking upon a map of New York (ibid., 101). True to the original text, references to New York are visually preserved, and the story frequently unfolds against a backdrop of the city's typical locales, including Central Park, Grand Central Station, and the tenements. Other places, like Stillman's hometown of Boston, are only depicted abstractly.

35. Another visual reference, which is only alluded to through the visual style, appears during Quinn's observation of the sky, where the panels focusing on the clouds resemble John Constable's cloud studies (ibid., 112).

36. Ibid., 102–104.

37. Ibid., 104.

38. Ibid., 116.

39. Ibid., 5.

40. Ibid., 104 and 119 (when Quinn learns of Stillman's death).

41. Ibid., 130–134.

42. Ibid., 91, 97.

43. Ibid., 131.

44. See Gaudreault and Marion, "Transécriture and Narrative Mediatrics," and Marion, "Scénario."

45. McCloud, *Understanding Comics*, 28.

46. Auster et al., *City of Glass*, 127.

47. This hand-drawn element has a parallel in Laurence Sterne's *Tristram Shandy*.

48. Compare Auster et al., *City of Glass*, 62–64, with Paul Auster, *The New York Trilogy* (London: Faber & Faber, 1987), 67–69

49. Auster et al., *City of Glass*, 57.

50. Several books by Mattotti were initially published—or are only available—in French.

51. For him "images avait dicté certaines lois émotionnelles" (images dictated certain emotional laws). See Lorenzo Mattotti, *Métamorphoses. Conversations avec Eddy Devolder* (Paris: Vertige Graphic, 1992), 43.

52. Lorenzo Mattotti and Jerry Kramsky, *Dr. Jekyll and Mr. Hyde* (Brussels: Casterman, 2002), 3.

53. Robert L. Stevenson, *The Strange Case of Dr. Jekyll and Mr. Hyde* (London: Penguin, 1979), 37–38.

54. Ibid., 37.

55. Mattotti and Kramsky, *Jekyll & Hyde*, 6.

56. Ibid., 9.

57. Cf. Stevenson, *Jekyll & Hyde*, 81–97.

58. Mattotti, *Métamorphoses*, 21.

59. Stevenson, *Jekyll & Hyde*, 48.

60. Ibid., 53.

61. Ibid., 79.

62. Mattotti and Kramsky, *Jekyll & Hyde*, 29.

63. Ibid., 55.

64. Stevenson, *Jekyll & Hyde*, 95.

65. Mattotti and Kramsky, *Jekyll & Hyde*, 56. The parade of skeletons, monsters, and deformed humans also contains a female figure whose deathly pale skin, heavy under-eye circles, and bare breasts recall Edvard Munch's *Madonna* pictures, with the main difference lying in the curling red tongue which links her with the women depicted earlier in the comic.

66. Ibid., 59–63.

67. Ibid., 16–17.

68. Stevenson, *Jekyll & Hyde*, 83.

69. Cf. Mattotti, *Métamorphoses*.

70. See, for instance, Mattotti and Kramsky, *Jekyll & Hyde*, 9, 25.

71. Ibid., 13, 19.

72. Mattotti, *Métamorphoses*, 38.

73. "He's an extraordinary looking man, and yet I really can name nothing out of the way," says Enfield, and Utterson confirms this by declaring that "he gave an impression of deformity without any nameable malformation" (Stevenson, *Jekyll & Hyde*, 34, 40).

74. Ibid., 82.

75. Ibid., 83.

76. Mattotti and Kramsky, *Jekyll & Hyde*, 26–27.

77. Stevenson, *Jekyll & Hyde*, 82.

78. See Robert Crumb and David Zane Mairowitz, *Introducing Kafka* (New York: Totem Books, 1993), 8–9, 20–21, 100–102, etc. The illustrations often contain word balloons (ibid., 25, 27).

79. Eisner calls these "texts reading as images." See *Comics and Sequential Art: Principles and Practice of the World's Most Popular Art Form* (Tamarac: Poorhouse Press, 1995), 10–11.

80. From the other two instances, only the former incorporates Kafka's words into the illustration; the latter shows him manically writing as his convoluted words wind across an abstract background (Crumb and Mairowitz, *Kafka*, 67, 103).

81. Ibid., 72–73.

82. Ibid., 6–7.

83. Ibid., 7–22, whereby Kafka's relationship to this Jewish heritage is only discussed on pages 18, 20, and 25.

84. Ibid., 128.

85. Ibid., 140–41.

86. Ibid., 166–73.
87. Ibid., 168, 171–73.
88. Ibid., 97.
89. Ibid., 102.
90. Ibid., 73.
91. Ibid., 59.
92. Ibid., 134.
93. Ibid., 10–11.
94. Ibid., 39.
95. Ibid., 71.
96. Ibid., 166.
97. Groensteen, *Système de la Bande Dessinée*, 18.

98. Amongst the renowned artists of wordless stories, Otto Nückel was German, whereas the Italian Giacomo Patri immigrated to America and published most of his works there. Their publications not only inspired similar works by, among others, Lynd Ward, but also comics, such as those by Eisner, as mentioned in George A. Walker's introduction to *Graphic Witnesses: Four Wordless Graphic Novels by Frans Masereel, Lynd Ward, Giacomo Patri, and Laurence Hyde* (Ontario: Firefly Books, 2007).

99. Frans Masereel, *Mein Stundenbuch. Ein Leben in Bildern* (München: Paul List Bücher, 1957), originally published as *Mon Livre d'Heures*. Highlighting the difference in the status of woodcut novels and comics, the German edition carries a very positive preface by Thomas Mann, who had a professed dislike for comics (see Jeet Heer and Kent Worchester's *Arguing Comics: Literary Masters on a Popular Medium* [Jackson: University Press of Mississippi, 2004]).

100. Seth refuses to call these works graphic novels (or less anachronistically, "comics novels") because of the fact that the woodcut artists wanted to distinguish themselves from the makers of comics and stress their affiliation to the fine arts instead (Walker, *Graphic Witnesses*, 415).

101. Mentioning Robert Wiener's *The Cabinet of Dr. Caligari* (1920) and F. W. Murnau's *The Last Laugh* (1924), Beronä holds that the combination of realism and fantasy was easily transposable to printed images. See David A, Beronä, *Wordless Books: The Original Graphic Novels* (New York: Abrams, 2008), 12.

102. Groensteen, *Système de la Bande Dessinée*, 157.
103. Ibid., 18.

104. Maria Nikolajeva and Carole Scott, *How Picturebooks Work* (London: Garland Publishing, 2001). The notion itself was adopted from music by Joseph Schwarcz (Joseph Schwarcz, *Ways of the Illustrator: Visual Communication in Children's Literature* [Chicago: American Library Association, 1982]).

105. See Vincent Fortemps's remarks in Bruno Canard's "Fréon, les Agitateurs Culturels,"

du9, September 1999, accessed 20 June 2014, http://www.du9.org/entretien/freon-les-agitateurs-culturels/.

106. Robey, "Introduction," *Open Work*, xi.

107. Olivier Deprez, *Le Château* (Montreuil: Fréon, 2003), 20–21.

108. Baetens, "M Comme Main."

109. Franz Kafka, *The Castle*, trans. Anthea Bell (Oxford: Oxford University Press, 2009), 5.

110. A particularly long instance of this is when K. looks for Barnabé in the snowy night which Deprez stretches across five pages (Deprez, *Château*, 64–68).

111. Deprez also makes use of this occasion to make a significant ellipsis, bringing in a much later moment in *The Castle* when K. waits in vain for Klamm before visiting Barnabé's house. Nevertheless, in altering the sequence of episodes, Deprez exchanges similar incidents, with ambiguous panels of K. swallowed in chaotic, amorphous surroundings serving as transitions (e.g., Deprez, *Château*, 68–77). Thus, the episode of K's fruitless wait for Klamm and his talk with the coachman in the eighth and ninth chapters of the original novel flows into his meeting with the schoolmaster in the first chapter, before returning to K. shouting after Barnabé in a flurry of snow (ibid., 84).

112. Eco, *Role of the Reader*, 10.

113. Deprez, *Château*, 59.

114. Ibid., 198.

115. As during K's conversation with the sledge owner (ibid., 40–41).

116. Ibid., 35–37. A changing, framed picture hanging in the background of these three pages conveys the sense of surveillance haunting the entire novel, while underscoring the theme of fluctuating, uncertain identities and echoing the obscurity haunting the story. Another living portrait personifies the concept of perpetual surveillance by appearing in a scene with K., Frieda, and the two assistants on the bed (ibid., 121).

117. Ibid., 7.

118. Ibid., 97.

119. Ibid., 141.

120. Ibid., 156.

121. Ibid., 162–63, Kafka, *Castle*, 113–14.

122. Deprez, *Château*, 195–97. These images adhere closely to Kafka's text, beginning with an introduction to the inn and continuing through two chapters: "The servant extinguished his lantern, for there was bright electric light here, where everything was built on a small scale [...] The best possible use was made of the space. You could only just walk upright along the corridor; door after door opened off the sides of it, all the doors close to each other" (Kafka, *Castle*, 213).

123. Deprez, *Château*, 52–53.

124. Ibid., 54.

125. Ibid., 34–35.

126. Kafka, *Castle*, 49.

127. Deprez, *Château*, 118.

128. Ibid., 177.

129. Ibid., 221–22.

130. Ibid. 3.

131. Mark Harman, "'Digging the Pit of Babel': Retranslating Franz Kafka's *Castle*," *New Literary History* 27.2 (1996): 291–311.

132. See Guy Schraenen, *Hommage an Stéphane Mallarmés Würfelentwurf* (Bremen: Institut Francais Bremen amd Neues Museum Weserburg Bremen, 1997).

133. Miller, *Illustration*, 75.

134. Ibid., 69.

135. Eco, *Open Work*, 13.

136. See Stéphane Mallarmé, "Sur le Livre Illustré," *Œuvres Complètes*, ed. G. Jean-Aubry and Henri Mondor (Paris: Pléaide, 1945), 878. See, in addition, Mallarmé's essays "Quant au Livre" and "Le Livre, Instrument Spirituel," originally published in *Divagations* (1897).

137. Riva Castleman, *A Century of Artists Books* (New York: MoMA, 1994), 7.

138. Ibid., 23.

139. Ibid., 24.

140. Drucker, *Artists' Books*, 206.

141. Ibid., 3.

142. Ibid., 4.

143. Ibid., 11.

144. Mitchell regards Blake's self-illustrated books—which are often referred to as illuminated works to strengthen their proximity to medieval manuscripts—as early relatives of artists' books which "tend to exhibit flexible, experimental, and 'high-tension' relations between words and images. The 'normal' relations of image and word (in the illustrated newspaper or even in the cartoon page) follow more traditional formulas involving clear subordination and suturing of one medium to the other" (Mitchell, *Picture Theory*, 91). This tension can be said to be playing on the conflict-ridden relationship between words and images highlighted by J. Hillis Miller (*Illustration*, 75).

145. Castleman, *Century of Artists Books*, 42.

CONCLUSION

1. Mentioned in the context of a conference with Eco on the open work in the Louvre on November 14, 2009.

2. Eco, *Open Work*, 15.

3. McCloud, *Understanding Comics*, 63.

4. Fresnault-Deruelle, *Images à Mi-Mots*, 33. The examples he mentions include *Arzach*.

5. Lefèvre, "Le Fantastique."

6. Mikkonen, "Presenting Minds in Graphic Narratives," 303.

7. Fresnault-Deruelle, *Images à Mi-Mots*, 12.

8. Varga, "Criteria," 37.

9. Montages can also be seen as intermedial references to film. See Johanna Drucker, "What is Graphic about Graphic Novels?" *English Language Notes* 46.2 (2008): 39–56.

10. Fresnault-Deruelle, *Images à Mi-Mots*, 49.

11. Eco, *Role of the Reader*, 39.

12. Foucault, "This Is Not a Pipe," 195.

13. Fresnault-Deruelle, *Images à Mi-Mots*, 185.

14. In Cambier's words, "en étant soumise au processus de la reproduction-duplication, l'image ne devient plus qu'une caricature d'elle même. Avec la démultiplication des images mimétiques, la nature même de l'image est galvaudée" (in being subjected to the process of reproduction-duplication, the image is nothing more than a caricature of itself. With the proliferation of mimetic images, the very nature of the image becomes hackneyed). Alain Cambier, "Introduction, L'Image, la Visibilité et l'Invisibilité, *Les Dons de l'Image*, ed. Alain Cambier (Lille: L'Harmattan, 2003), 17–38, 22.

15. As Samson points out, the reactionary, transgressive practice of the post-1960s comics emphasized artistic expression in order to efface the medium's affiliation to mass culture (Samson, "Stratégies Modernes d'Énonciation Picturale," 120).

16. Martin Heidegger, "Der Ursprung des Kunstwerkes, *Holzwege* (Frankfurt am Main: Vittorio Klostermann, 2003), 1–24.

17. McCloud, *Making Comics*, 28.

18. Miller, *Illustration*, 150.

19. Cambrier, "Introduction," 26 (referring to Fresnault-Deruelle's article in the same volume, "Le Dessin Hors-Sujet," 163–77).

20. David Mack, another artist fond of using collages and mixed media in his comics sees such intermedial references as an intrinsic feature of comics: "I realized that the medium of comic books is a format I could integrate all other mediums into [. . .] it had no limitations and encompassed aspects of every other medium." See his interview "The Whole Brained Approach: David Mack," *The Education of a Comics Artist*, Michael Dooley and Steven Heller (New York: Allworth Press, 2005), 86–90, 89. Mack mentions earlier that it was the graphic design courses that taught him "the synthesis of type and image" (ibid., 86).

21. Samson, "Stratégies Modernes d'Énonciation Picturale," 133.

22. Including, for instance, the use of alternating panels concentrating on the changing speakers during a conversation, or the wide, establishing shots introducing a setting at the beginning of a new scene.

23. Reacting against the early, inconspicuous, and smooth filming and clear storylines, the *nouvelle vague* cineastes favored unusual narratives and drew the viewer's attention to the technique of filmmaking through the unnatural editing and perspectives, thus fuctioning as *autoréflexion sur le medium*. Despite being in part inspired by hardboiled American detective fiction, many of the New Wave films also mocked established American genres such as thrillers and romance.

24. Baetens, "Graphic Novels," 1146.

25. Screech, *Masters of the Ninth Art*, 131.

26. Robey, "Introduction," *Open Work*, xi.

27. Roger Sabin, "Ally Sloper: The First Comics Superstar?" *Image (&) Narrative* 7 (2003), accessed 2 May 2013, http://www.imageandnarrative.be/inarchive/graphicnovel/rogersabin.htm.

28. Consider, for instance, the separator immediately following Léa's first appearance in the comic, where Léa and Simon's grotesquely conflated forms are shown amongst the waves and where her serenity contrasts with his horror (Baudoin, *Voyage*).

29. Hutcheon, *Narcissistic Narrative*, 154. The subversiveness of many experimental comics is one of the reasons why Hatfield prefers the term "alternative comics" (see Hatfield, *Alternative Comics*).

30. Christopher Murray, "Superman vs Imago: Superheroes, Lacan and Mediated Identity," *International Journal of Comic Art* 4.2 (2002): 186–208, 188.

31. Antonio Altarriba, "Propositions pour une Analyse Spécifique du Récit en Bande Dessinée," *Bande Dessinée, Récit et Modernité*, 25–44, 35.

32. Mikkonen, "Paradox of Intersemiotic Translation," 113.

33. For Altarriba, metamorphosis is a characteristic motif of the comic strip due to its visual essence, which makes comics concentrate on external transformations instead of internal development (Altarriba, "Propositions pour une Analyse Spécifique," 35–36).

34. Fresnault-Deruelle, *Images à Mi-Mots*, 107.

35. Foucault, "Introduction à Binswanger, *Le Rêve et l'Existence*," *Dits et écrits* (Paris: Gallimard, 1994), 65–119, 114.

36. Foucault, "The Thought of the Outside," *Essential Works of Foucault*, 147–71, 153.

37. Cambier, "Introduction," 17. In the same volume and along similar lines, Védrine declares "pas d'imagination sans être–dans–le monde, mais pas non plus de conscience sans cette possibilité de nier le monde" (no imagination without being–in–the world and no consciousness without this possiblity of denying the world). Hélène Védrine, "Déclin du Sujet et Retour de l'Imaginaire," *Les Dons de l'Image*, 71–84, 74.

38. Ernst Gombrich, *Art and Illusion: A Study in the Psychology of Pictorial Representation* (Princeton: Princeton University Press, 2000), 345.

39. Lefèvre, "Le Fantastique."

40. Kunzle, *History of the Comic Strip II*, 426.

41. See, for instance, Cambier, "L'image," 17: "L'image [. . .] semble se situer entre la réalité et l'imaginaire ou osciller entre perception et imagination" (The image [. . .] seems to situate itself between reality and the imaginary or oscillate between perception and imagination).

42. The additional reciprocal uneasiness between reality and representation becomes even more apparent in Magritte's *Les Deux Mystères*, which appeared four decades later and incorporated an easel with the painting, *Ceci n'est pas une pipe*, and a larger pipe on the wall. Foucault called this work a calligram, a form that "aspires playfully to efface the oldest oppositions of our alphabetical civilization: to show and to name; to shape and to say; to reproduce and to articulate; to imitate and to signify; to look and to read" (Foucault, "This Is Not a Pipe," 190).

43. Fresnault-Deruelle, *Images à Mi-Mots*, 48.

44. Van Lier, "Cosmogénie Dure," 23.

45. Védrine, "Déclin du Sujet," 83–84.

46. Eco, "È scomparso Hugo Pratt."

47. See Patricia Waugh, *Metafiction: The Theory and Practice of Self-Conscious Fiction* (London: Routledge, 1984).

48. See W. J. T. Mitchell, *What do Pictures Want? The Lives and Loves of Images* (Chicago: University of Chicago Press, 2005).

49. Eco, *Open Work*, 13.

50. Bondanella, *Umberto Eco and the Open Text*, 29–30.

51. Nabil El Haggar, "Avant-Propos," *Les Dons de l'Image*, 13–14, 13. Becoming a growing area of research in the humanities as well as the sciences (cf. Heinrich Dilly, "Bildgeschichten und Bildkritik der traditionellen Kunstgeschichte," *H-Soz-u-Kult*, 20 January 2004, accessed 20 June 2014, http://hsozkult.geschichte.hu-berlin.de/forum/id=390&type=diskussionen), the visual obsession of the present age led Mitchell to speak of a "pictorial turn," which is "a phrase [. . .] attempting to isolate a perennial anxiety about images and representation that has become part of both mass consciousness and disciplined intellectual reflection in our time." Brad Bucknell and Christine Wiesenthal, "Essays into the Imagetext: Interview with W. J. T. Mitchell, *Mosaic: A Journal for the Interdisciplinary Study of Literature* 33.2 (2004): 1–23, digital version. Mitchell distinguishes this from Gottfried Böhm's notion of the "iconic turn" by referring to the concrete everyday image rather than the icon underlying the image and its cognitive value.

52. Raymond Bellour, "The Double Helix," trans. James Eddy, *Electronic Culture: Technology and Visual Representation*, ed. Timothy Druckery (New York: Aperture, 1996), 173–99, 199.

53. In 2008, for instance, the British government sanctioned the adaptation of classics into graphic novels. Cf. Paul Gravett, "Classical Comics."

54. Miller, *Illustration*, 73.

55. Alan Moore, for instance, calls for stories with relevance, namely, "stories that actually have some sort of meaning in relation to the world about us [. . .] that are *useful* in some way" (Jacen Burrows and Alan Moore, *Writing for Comics* [Rantoul: Avatar Press 2003], 2). Notably, Moore devotes a considerable portion of the book on ways of reaching the reader.

56. Kunzle, *History of the Comic Strip II*, 9. Likewise, Tisseron accorded the change in the contemporary reception of the bande dessinée to the massive transformation of the image in an era of information technology (Tisseron, *Psychanalyse de la Bande Dessinée*, 12).

57. See, for instance, Frahm's *Die Sprache des Comics* for an analysis of the self-reflexivity in *Krazy Kat*.

58. In the obituary for *Time.Comix* (2002–2007), Andrew D. Arnold points out that "graphic novels have gone from a publishing backwater to being the only book category displaying any growth at all." See "The End," *Time.Comix*, 18 March 2007, accessed 25 January 2010, http://www.time.com/time/columnist/arnold/article/0,9565,1600432,00.html.

59. This has been pointed out by, among others, Gravett in his comments to Tara Mulholland

in "More than Words: Britain Embraces the Graphic Novel," *New York Times*, 22 August 2007, accessed 20 August 2009, http://www.nytimes.com/2007/08/21/arts/21iht-gnovel.1.7197081.html. According to Lev Manovich, it was in the 1990s (and consequently close to the graphic novel boom) that "moving-image culture went through a fundamental transformation"—namely, the incorporation of several kinds of media to the extent that "hybrid media became the norm" (Lev Manovich, "Understanding Hybrid Media," accessed 19 February 2010, http://www.manovich.net/DOCS/ae_with_artists.doc).

60. See, for instance, Eco, *Open Work*, 90–93. Eco used the term in relation to *art informel*.

BIBLIOGRAPHY

PRIMARY SOURCES

Auster, Paul, *The New York Trilogy* (London: Faber & Faber, 1987).

Auster, Paul, Paul Karasik, and David Mazzucchelli, *City of Glass: The Graphic Novel* (New York: Picador, 2004).

Balzer, Jens, and Martin tom Dieck, *Salut, Deleuze!* (Zürich: Arrache Cœur, 1998).

Baudelaire, Charles, *Les Fleurs du Mal*, trans. James McGowan (Oxford: Oxford University Press, 1993).

Baudoin, Edmond, *Le Voyage* (Paris: L'Association, 2005).

Bilal, Enki, *La Femme Piège* (Paris: Les Humanoïdes Associés 2003).

——, *La Foire aux Immortels* (Paris: Dargaud, 1980).

——, *Froid Équateur* (Paris: Les Humanoïdes Associés, 2001).

Boilet, Frédéric, and Kan Takahama, *Mariko Parade* (Brussels: Casterman, 2003).

Christin, Pierre, and Jean-Claude Mézières, *Lady Polaris* (Paris: Autrement, 1987).

Coleridge, Samuel Taylor, "The Rime of the Ancient Mariner," *The Complete Poetical Works. Vol. 1: Poems*, ed. Ernest Hartley Coleridge (Oxford: Clarendon Press, 1912), 196–97.

Crumb, Robert, and David Zane Mairowitz, *Introducing Kafka* (New York: Totem Books, 1993).

Deprez, Olivier, *Le Château* (Montreuil: Fréon, 2003).

Doubrovsky, Serge, *Le Livre Brisé* (Paris: Gallimard, 2003).

Eisner, Will, *The Contract with God Trilogy* (New York: W. W. Norton, 2006).

Gaiman, Neil, Sam Kieth, Mike Dringenberg, and Malcolm Jones III, *The Sandman: Preludes and Nocturnes* (New York: DC Comics, 1991).

Heikkinen, Jyrki, *Tohtori Futuro* (Oulu: Asema, 2007).

Hietanen, Annemari, and Marko Turunen, *Kuolema Kulkee Kintereillä* (Helsinki: Daada, 2004).

Kafka, Franz, *The Castle*, trans. Anthea Bell (Oxford: Oxford University Press, 2009).

——, *Das Schloß* (Frankfurt: Fischer Taschenbuch Verlag, 1977).

Kleist, Reinhard, and Roland Hueve, *Lovecraft* (Stuttgart: Feest Comics, 1996).

Lovecraft, H. P., "Erich Zann," *The Thing on the Doorstep and Other Weird Stories* (London: Penguin Books, 2001), 45–52.

——, "The Outsider," *The Call of Cthulhu and Other Weird Stories*, ed. S. T. Joshi (London: Penguin, 1999), 43–49.

Mäkilä, Jarmo, *Taxi van Goghin Korvaan* (Helsinki: Itikka Kustannus, 2008).

Masereel, Frans, *Mein Stundenbuch. Ein Leben in Bildern* (München: Paul List Bücher, 1957).

Mattotti, Lorenzo, *Metamorphoses. Conversations avec Eddy Devolder* (Paris: Vertige Graphic, 1992).

Mattotti, Lorenzo, and Jerry Kramsky, *Dr. Jekyll and Mr. Hyde* (Brussels: Casterman, 2002).
McKean, Dave, and Grant Morrison, *Arkham Asylum: A Serious House on Serious Earth*, fifteenth anniversary edition (New York: DC Comics, 2004).
Moebius, *Arzach, L'Album Mythique* (Paris: Les Humanoïdes Associés, 2006).
Moore, Alan, and Eddie Campbell, *From Hell* (London: Knockabout Comics, 2007).
Pratt, Hugo, *La Ballade de la Mer Salée* (Brussels: Casterman, 1975).
———, *Saint-Exupéry: Le Dernier Vol* (Brussels: Casterman, 1995).
Stevenson, Robert Louis, *The Strange Case of Dr. Jekyll and Mr. Hyde* (London: Penguin, 1979).
Tardi, Jacques, *Adèle Blanc-Sec, Le Labyrinthe Infernal, L'Étrangleur* no. 1–3 (Brussels: Casterman, 2007).
———, *Les Aventures Extraordinaires d'Adèle Blanc-Sec, t.1, Adèle et la Bête* (Brussels: Casterman, 1976).
———, *C'était la Guerre des Tranchées. 1914–1918* (Brussels: Casterman 1993).
Walker, George A., *Graphic Witnesses: Four Wordless Graphic Novels by Frans Masereel, Lynd Ward, Giacomo Patri, and Laurence Hyde* (Ontario: Firefly Books, 2007).
Yslaire, *Introduction au XXe ciel. http://www.yslaire.be* (Paris: Delcourt, 1997).
———, *XXe ciel.com. http://www.xxeciel.com/mémoires<19>00* (Paris: Les Humanoïdes Associés, 2004).

SECONDARY SOURCES

Abell, Catharine, "Comics and Genre," *The Art of Comics: A Philosophical Approach*, ed. Aaron Meskin and Roy T. Cook (Hoboken: WileyBlackwell, 2014), 68–84.
Adams, Jeff, "A Critical Study of Comics," *Journal of Art and Design Education* 20.2 (2001): 133–43.
Arnold, Andrew D., "The End," *Time.Comix*, 18 March 2007, accessed 25 January 2010, http://www.time.com/time/columnist/arnold/article/0,9565,1600432,00.html.
Atkinson, Paul, "The Graphic Novel as Metafiction," *Studies in Comics* 1.1 (2010): 107–125.
———, "Why Pause?: The Fine Line between Reading and Contemplation," *Studies in Comics* 3.1 (2012): 63–81.
Auerbach, Erich, *Mimesis. Dargestellte Wirklichkeit in der abendländischen Literatur* (Tübingen: Francke Verlag, 2001).
Ault, Donald, "Preludium: Crumb, Barks and Noomin. Re-Considering the Aesthetics of Underground Comics," *ImageText* 1.2 (2004), accessed 16 November 2009, http://www.english.ufl.edu/imagetext/archives/v1_2/intro.shtml.
Baetens, Jan, "Autobiographies et Bandes Dessinées," *Belphégor* IV.1 (2004), accessed 17 June 2014, https://dalspace.library.dal.ca/bitstream/handle/10222/47689/04_01_Baeten_autobd_fr_cont.pdf?sequence=1.
———, "Choses Vues. Du Regard en Fantastique," *Image (&) Narrative* 2 (2001), accessed 17 June 2014, http://www.imageandnarrative.be/inarchive/fantastiquebd/janbaetens.htm.

———, "Graphic Novels," *The Cambridge History of the American Novel* (Cambridge: Cambridge University Press, 2011), 1137–53.

———, "Graphic Novels: Literature without Text," *English Language Notes* 46.2 (2008): 77–88.

———, "Of Graphic Novels and Minor Cultures: The Fréon Collective," *Yale French Studies* 114 (2008): 95–114.

———, "M Comme Main. Une Lecture de Château de Kafka Adapté par Olivier Deprez," *Image (&) Narrative* 8 (2004), accessed 15 January 2013, http://www.imageandnarrative.be/inarchive/issue08/janbaetens_deprez.htm.

Baetens Jan, ed., *The Graphic Novel* (Leuven: University of Leuven, Press, 2001).

Bakhtin, Mikail, *The Dialogic Imagination: Four Essays by Mikhail Bakhtin*, trans. Carl Emerson and Michael Holquist, ed. Michael Holquist (Austin: University of Texas, 1991).

Balzer, Jens, and Martin tom Dieck, "Nicht versöhnt. Bilder und Texte im Comic," *Schreibheft* 51 (1998): 47–50.

Bastide, Julien, "Le Bilan de L'Événement Manga," accessed 10 August 2009, http://www.boilet.net/fr/nouvellemanga_bilan_1.html.

Baudelaire, Charles, *The Flowers of Evil*, trans. James McGowan (Oxford: Oxford University Press, 1993).

Beaty, Bart, *Comics Versus Art* (Toronto: University of Toronto Press, 2012).

Beaty, Bart, and Stephen Weiner, eds., *Critical Survey of Graphic Novels: History, Theme and Technique* (Ipswich: Salem Press, 2012).

Bellour, Raymond, "The Double Helix," trans. James Eddy, *Electronic Culture: Technology and Visual Representation*, ed. Timothy Druckery (New York: Aperture, 1996), 173–99.

Benjamin, Walter, "A Small History of Photography," *One-Way Street and Other Writings*, trans. Edmund Jephcott and Kingsley Shorter (London: Verso, 1979), 240–57.

Beronä, David A., *Wordless Books: The Original Graphic Novels* (New York: Abrams, 2008).

Boilet, Frédéric, "La Nouvelle Manga en 2007," accessed 10 May 2013, http://www.boilet.net/fr/nouvellemanga_2006.html.

Bonash, David, "From Advertising to the Avant-Garde: Rethinking the Invention of Collage," *Postmodern Culture* 14.2 (2004): 1–38.

Bondanella, Peter, *Umberto Eco and the Open Text: Semiotics, Fiction and Popular Culture* (Cambridge: Cambridge University Press, 1997).

Bucknell, Brad, and Christine Wiesenthal, "Essays into the Imagetext: Interview with W. J. T. Mitchell," *Mosaic: A Journal for the Interdisciplinary Study of Literature* 33.2 (2004): 1–23, digital version.

Burrows, Jacen, and Alan Moore, *Writing for Comics* (Rantoul: Avatar Press 2003).

Cambier, Alain, *Les Dons de l'Image* (Paris: L'Harmattan, 2003).

Canard, Bruno, "Edmond Baudoin, l'Émotion du Geste," *du9*, September 1999, accessed 20 June 2014, http://www.du9.org/entretien/edmond-baudoin-l-emotion-du-geste/.

———, "Fréon, les Agitateurs Culturels," *du9*, September 1999, accessed 20 June 2014, http://www.du9.org/entretien/freon-les-agitateurs-culturels/.

Casebook: Jack the Ripper, accessed 20 June 2014, http://www.casebook.org/intro.html.

Castleman, Riva, *A Century of Artists Books* (New York: MoMA, 1994).

Chestier, Aurore, "*Le Livre Brisé* ou le Jeu de l'Écriture Tendue en Miroir," *Image (&) Narrative* 19 (2007), http://www.imageandnarrative.be/inarchive/autofiction/chestier.htm, accessed May 28, 2013.

Christiansen, Hans-Christian, and Anne Magnussen, "Introduction," *Comics Culture: Analytical and Theoretical Approaches to Comics* (Copenhagen: Museum Tusulanum Press, 2000), 7–27.

Chute, Hillary, and Patrick Jagoda, "Special Issue: Comics & Media," *Critical Inquiry* 40.3 (2014): 1–10.

Cohn, Jesse, "Translator's Comments on 'Four Conceptions of the Page,'" *ImageTexT* 3.3 (2007), accessed 5 January 2008, http://www.english.ufl.edu/imagetext/archives/v3_3/cohn/.

Cohn, Neil, "The Architecture of Visual Narrative Comprehension: The Interaction of Narrative Structure and Page Layout in Understanding Comics," *Frontiers in Psychology* 5 (2014), accessed 13 February 2015, http://journal.frontiersin.org/Journal/10.3389/fpsyg.2014.00680/full.

———, "The Limits of Time and Transitions: Challenges to the Theories of Sequential Image Comprehension," *Studies in Comics*, 1.1 (2010): 127–47.

Coleridge, Samuel Taylor, "The Rime of the Ancient Mariner," *The Complete Poetical Works. Vol. 1: Poems,* ed. Ernest Hartley Coleridge (Oxford: Clarendon Press, 1912), 196–97.

Collins, Billy, "Introduction to Poetry," *The Apple that Astonished Paris* (Fayetteville: University of Arkansas Press, 1988), 58.

"Comic durchbricht in vieler Hinsicht die Grenzen," *Botschaft von Finnland*, Berlin, 16 November 2009, accessed 20 June 2014, http://www.finnland.de/Public/default.aspx?contentid=179252&culture=de-DE.

Cortsen, Rikke Platz, *Comics as Assemblage: How Spatio-Temporality in Comics is Constructed* (PhD dissertation, University of Copenhagen, 2012).

Couch, Christopher N. C., and Stephen Weiner, *The Will Eisner Companion: The Pioneering Spirit of the Father of the Graphic Novel* (New York: DC Comics, 2004).

Coughlan, David, "Paul Auster: The City of Glass," *Modern Fiction Studies* 52.4 (2006): 832–54.

Couleur Directe (Thurn: Kunst der Comics, 1993).

Coyle, William, ed., *Aspects of Fantasy: Selected Essays from the Second International Conference on the Fantastic in Literature and Film* (London: Greenwood Press, 1981).

Daly, Nicholas, *Modernism, Romance, and the* Fin de Siècle: *Popular Fiction and British Culture, 1880–1914* (Cambridge: Cambridge University Press, 1999).

Deleuze, Gilles, *Cinéma, t.1: L'image-mouvement* (Paris: Éditions de Minuit, 1983).

———, *Cinéma, t.2: L'image-temps* (Paris: Éditions de Minuit, 1985).

———, "Cours, Image Mouvement Image Temps, sur Pierce," *Web Deleuze*, accessed 20 June 2014, http://www.webdeleuze.com/php/texte.php?cle=73&groupe=Image%20Mouvement%20Image%20Temps&langue=1.

———, *Difference and Repetition*, trans. Paul Patton (New York: Columbia University Press, 1994).

———, *La Voix de Gilles Deleuze en ligne*, accessed 20 June 2014, http://www.univ-paris8.fr/deleuze/article.php3?id_article=1.

Dilly, Heinrich, "Bildgeschichten und Bildkritik der traditionellen Kunstgeschichte," *H-Soz-u-Kult*, 20 January 2004, accessed 20 June 2014, http://hsozkult.geschichte.hu-berlin.de/forum/id=390&type=diskussionen.

Dony, Christophe, "The Re-Writing Ethos of the Vertigo Imprint: Critical Perspectives on Memory-Making and Canon Formation in the American Comics Field," *Comicalités, La Bande Dessinée: Un Art Sans «Mémoire»?* April 2014, accessed 25 February 2015, http://comicalites.revues.org/1918.

Dooley, Michael, and Steven Heller, *The Education of a Comics Artist* (New York: Allworth, 2005).

Drucker, Johanna, *The Century of Artists' Books* (New York: Granary Books 1995).

———, "What is Graphic about Graphic novels?" *English Language Notes* 46.2 (2008): 39–56.

Eco, Umberto, "Le Mythe de Superman, *Communications* 24 (1976): 24–40.

———, *The Open Work*, trans. Anna Cancogni (Cambridge: Harvard University Press, 1989).

———, *The Role of the Reader: Explorations in the Semiotics of Texts* (Bloomington: University of Indiana Press, 1984).

———, *Semiotics and the Philosophy of Language* (Bloomington: University of Indiana Press, 1986).

———, "È Scomparso Hugo Pratt. Ma Ci Rimane Corto Maltese, *L'Espresso*, 4 September 1995.

Eisner, Will, *Comics and Sequential Art: Principles and Practice of the World's Most Popular Art Form* (Tamarac: Poorhouse Press, 1995).

———, *Graphic Storytelling and Visual Narrative* (Tamarac: Poorhouse Press, 1996).

"Enki Bilal—Der Schlaf des Monsters. Ein Interview (January 1999)," *Parnass. Die Kulturzeitschrift im Internet*, accessed 20 June 2014, http://www.parnass.scram.de/comicdetail.php?nr=51.

"Expo Yslaire 'XXe ciel.com," *Librairie La Main Blanche*, accessed 20 June 2014, http://www.lamainblanche.com/Public/Event_View.aspx?e=6.

Farron, Ivan, "Die Fallen der Vorstellungskraft. Autofiktion—ein Begriff und seine Zweideutigkeit(en)," trans. Barbara Villiger Heilig, *Neue Zürcher Zeitung*, 31 May 2003, accessed 20 June 2014, http://www.nzz.ch/aktuell/startseite/article8VLW2-1.259501.

Floreani, Jeanne, "Marko Turunen, *du9, l'autre bande dessinée*, accessed 20 June 2014, http://www.du9.org/entretien/marko_turunen/.

Foucault, Michel, *Aesthetics, Method, and Epistemology: Essential Works of Foucault, 1954–1984*, vol. 2, ed. James D. Fabion (New York: New Press, 1999).

———, "Des Espaces Autres," *AMC. Architecture-Mouvement-Continuité* 5 (1984): 46–49.

———, "Introduction à *Binswanger, Le Rêve et l'Existence*," *Dits et écrits* (Paris: Gallimard, 1994), 65–119.

Frahm, Ole, *Die Sprache des Comics* (Hamburg: Philo Verlag, 2010).
Fresnault-Deruelle, Pierre, *La Bande Dessinée, Essai d'Analyse Sémiotique* (Paris: Hachette 1972).
———, *Images à Mi-Mots. Bande Dessinées. Dessins d'Humour* (Brussels: Les Impressions Nouvelles, 2008).
Gabilliet, Jean-Paul, "Fantastique Bande Dessinée," *Image (&) Narrative* 2 (2001), accessed 17 June 2014, http://www.imageandnarrative.be/inarchive/fantastiquebd/jeanpaulgabilliet.htm.
Gaudreault, André, and Philippe Marion, "Transécriture and Narrative Mediatics," *Companion to Literature and Film*, ed. Robert Stam and Alessandra Raengo (Hoboken: Wiley-Blackwell, 2004), 58–70.
Genette, Gérard, *Palimpsests: Literature in the Second Degree*, trans. Channa Newman and Claude Doubinsky (Lincoln: University of Nebraska Press, 1997).
Gombrich, Ernst, *Art and Illusion: A Study in the Psychology of Pictorial Representation* (Princeton: Princeton University Press, 2000).
Gravett, Paul, "Classical Comics: Turning Classics into Comics," 9 November 2008, accessed 10 June 2013, http://paulgravett.com/index.php/articles/article/classical_comics.
———, "Hugo Pratt: The Call of the Sea," 29 October 2006, accessed 24 June 2013, http://www.paulgravett.com/index.php/articles/article/hugo_pratt/.
Groensteen, Thierry, ed., *Bande Dessinée, Récit et Modernité* (Paris: Futuropolis 1988).
———, *Système de la Bande Dessinée* (Paris: PUF, 2011).
Harman, Mark, "'Digging the Pit of Babel': Retranslating Franz Kafka's *Castle*," *New Literary History* 27.2 (1996): 291-311.
Hatfield, Charles, *Alternative Comics: An Emerging Literature* (Jackson: University Press of Mississippi, 2005).
———, *Hand of Fire: The Comics Art of Jack Kirby* (Jackson: University Press of Mississippi, 2011).
Heer, Jeet, and Kent Worchester, eds., *Arguing Comics: Literary Masters on a Popular Medium* (Jackson: University Press of Mississippi, 2004).
Heidegger, Martin, "Der Ursprung des Kunstwerkes," *Holzwege* (Frankfurt am Main: Vittorio Klostermann, 2003), 1–24.
Hoffmann, E. T. A., *Nachtstücke*, accessed 12 February 2009, http://www.gutenberg.org/cache/epub/6341/pg6341.html.
Hutcheon, Linda, *Narcissistic Narrative: The Metafictional Paradox* (London: Methuen, 1984).
———, *A Poetics of Postmodernism: History, Theory, Fiction* (London: Routledge, 1988).
Iser, Wolfgang, *The Fictive and the Imaginary: Charting Literary Anthropology* (Baltimore: Johns Hopkins University Press, 1993).
Jahaa! Autorencomics aus den nordischen Ländern, Nordische Botschaften Gemeinschaftshaus (Berlin: Felleshus, 2009).
Jarmo Mäkilä, Helsinki City Art Museum (Helsinki: Helsinki City Art Museum, 2008).
Jarmo Mäkilä. The Picture of Dorian Gray, Amos Anderson Art Museum, August-November 2002 (Helsinki: University of Helsinki Press, 2002).

Jarmo Mäkilä, Galerie Kaj Forsblom, April–May 1990 (Helsinki: Naantali, 1990).

Kartalopoulos, Bill, "Coffee with Paul Karasik," *Indy Magazine*, Spring 2004, accessed 4 April 2013, http://www.indyworld.com/indy/spring_2004/karasik_interview/.

Kristeva, Julia, "'Nous Deux' or a [Hi]story of Intertextuality," *Romanic Review* 93 (2002): 7–13.

Kukkonen, Karin, "Beyond Language: Metaphor and Metonymy in Comics Storytelling," *English Language Notes* 46.2 (2008): 89–98.

———, *Contemporary Comics Storytelling* (Lincoln: University of Nebraska Press, 2013).

———, *Storytelling Beyond Postmodernism:* Fables *and the Fairy Tale* (PhD dissertation, University of Tampere, 2010).

Kunzle, David, *The History of the Comic Strip, vol. II* (Berkeley: University of California Press, 1973).

Labé, Yves-Marie, "Will Eisner, le Père de la BD Moderne," *Le Monde*, 7 January 2005.

Larkin, Philip, "Church Going," *Philip Larkin: Collected Poems*, ed. Anthony Thwaite (London: Faber and Faber, 2003), 58–59.

Lefèvre, Pascal, "Le Fantastique, un Genre Indéfinissable?" *Image (&) Narrative* 2 (2001), 17 June 2014, http://www.imageandnarrative.be/inarchive/fantastiquebd/pascallefevre.htm.

Lewis, Alan David, "The Shape of Comic Book Reading," *Studies in Comics* 1.1 (2010): 71–81.

Lund, Martin, *Rethinking the Jewish-Comics Connection* (PhD dissertation, University of Lund, 2013).

Mallarmé, Stéphane, *Œuvres Complètes*, ed. G. Jean-Aubry and Henri Mondor (Paris: Pléaide, 1945).

Manovich, Lev, *The Language of New Media* (Cambridge: MIT Press, 2002).

———, "Understanding Hybrid Media," accessed 19 February 2010, http://www.manovich.net/DOCS/ae_with_artists.doc.

Marion, Philippe, "Scénario de Bande Dessinée. La Différence par le Média," *Études littéraires* 26.2 (1993): 77–89.

———, *Traces en Cases: Travail Graphique, Figuration Narrative et Participation du Lecteur* (Louvain-la-Neuve: Academia, 1993).

Masson, Pierre, *Lire la Bande Dessinée* (Lyon: Presses Universitaires de Lyon, 1985).

Mattotti, Lorenzo, *Métamorphoses. Conversations avec Eddy Devolder* (Paris: Vertige Graphic, 1992).

McCloud, Scott, *Making Comics: Storytelling Secrets of Comics, Manga and Graphic Novels* (New York: Harper, 2006).

———, *Understanding Comics: The Invisible Art* (New York: Harper, 1994).

McHale, Brian, *Postmodernist Fiction* (London: Routledge, 1987).

Mikelbank, Peter, "Twists of Fate," *France Magazine* 64 (2002–2003), accessed 20 April 2013, http://www.francemagazine.org/articles/issue64/article51.asp?issue_id=64&article_id=51.

Mikkonen, Kai, "The Paradox of Intersemiotic Translation and the Comic Book: Examples from Enki Bilal's *Nikopol* Trilogy," *Word & Image* 22.2 (2006): 101–117.

———, "Presenting Minds in Graphic Narratives," *Partial Answers* 6.2 (2008): 301–328.

Miller, Ann, *Reading Bande Dessinée: Critical Approaches to French-Language Comic Strips* (Bristol: Intellect, 2007).

Miller, J. Hillis, *Illustration* (London: Reaktion, 1992).

Mitchell, W. J. T., *Picture Theory: Essays on Verbal and Visual Representation* (Chicago: University of Chicago Press, 1994).

———, *The Reconfigured Eye: Visual Truth in the Post-Photographic Era* (Cambridge: MIT Press, 2001).

———, *What do Pictures Want? The Lives and Loves of Images* (Chicago: University of Chicago Press, 2005).

Mouchart, Benoît, "Entretien avec Jacques Tardi," *Auracan* 10, May–June 1995, accessed 20 March 2013, http://www.auracan.com/Interviews/Tardi/.

Mulholland, Tara, "More than Words: Britain Embraces the Graphic Novel," *New York Times*, 22 August 2007, accessed 20 August 2009, http://www.nytimes.com/2007/08/21/arts/21iht-gnovel.1.7197081.html.

Murray, Christopher, "Holy Hypertexts!—The Pose of Post-modernity in Comics and Graphic Novels of the 1980s," *Reflections on Creativity*, ed. Hamid van Koten (Dundee: Duncan of Jordanstone College of Art and Design, 2007), accessed 13 February 2009, http://artanddesign.dundee.ac.uk/reflections/pdfs/ChrisMurray.pdf.

———, "Superman vs Imago: Superheroes, Lacan and Mediated Identity," *International Journal of Comic Art* 4.2 (2002): 186–208.

Nikolajeva, Maria, and Carole Scott, *How Picturebooks Work* (London: Garland Publishing, 2001).

Nora, Pierre, ed., *Les Lieux de Mémoire* (Paris: Gallimard, 1997).

Olmstead, William, "Immortal Rot: A Reading of 'Une Charogne,'" *Understanding Fleurs du Mal: Critical Readings*, ed. William Thompson (Tennessee: Vanderbilt University Press, 1997), 60–71.

Palmer, R. Barton, "The Sociological Turn of Adaptation Studies: The Example of Film Noir," *Film Theory: An Introduction*, ed. Robert Stam (Malden: Blackwell, 2000), 266–77

Peeters, Benoît, "Four conceptions of the page," trans. Jesse Cohn, *ImageTexT* 3 (3) 2007, accessed 17 June 2014, http://www.english.ufl.edu/imagetext/archives/v3_3/peeters/.

Pralong, M., "Propos de Tardi," *Le Matin*, 21 December 1996, accessed 29 April 2009, http://www.http://blancsecadele.free.fr/aventures.html/.

Reynolds, Richard, *Super Heroes: A Modern Mythology* (Jackson: University Press of Mississippi, 1994).

Robbe-Grillet, Alain, *For a New Novel: Essays on Fiction*, trans. Richard Howard (Evanston: Northwestern University Press, 1989).

Round, Julia, *Gothic in Comics and Graphic Novels* (Jefferson: McFarland, 2014).

Sabin, Roger, "Ally Sloper: The First Comics Superstar?" *Image (&) Narrative* 7 (2003), accessed 2 May 2013, http://www.imageandnarrative.be/inarchive/graphicnovel/rogersabin.htm.

Sabin, Roger, and Teal Triggs, *Below Critical Radar: Fanzines and Alternative Comics from 1976 to Now* (Hove: Slab-O-Concrete, 2000).

Schnierer, Peter Paul, "Graphic 'Novels,' Cyber 'Fiction,' Multiform 'Stories'—Virtual Theatre and the Limits of Genre," *Anglistentag 1999 Mainz. Proceedings*, ed. Bernhard Reitz and Sigrid Rieuwerts (Trier: Wissenschaftlicher Verlag Trier, 2000): 533–47.

Schraenen, Guy, *Hommage an Stéphane Mallarmés Würfelentwurf* (Bremen: Institut Francais Bremen and Neues Museum Weserburg Bremen, 1997).

Schüwer, Martin, *Wie Comics erzählen. Grundriss einer intermedialen Erzähltheorie der graphischen Literatur* (Trier: Wissenschaftlicher Verlag, 2008).

Screech, Matthew, *Masters of the Ninth Art: Bandes Dessinées and Franco-Belgian Identity* (Liverpool: Liverpool University Press, 2005).

Smolderen, Thierry, *Naissances de la Bande Dessinée: De William Hogarth à Winsor McCay* (Brussels: Les Impressions Nouvelles, 2009).

Sohet, Philippe, "Quand Lire C'est Écrire. À Propos d'*Iphigénie* de Xavier Löwenthal, *Image (&) Narrative* 8 (2004), accessed 17 June 2014, http://www.imageandnarrative.be/inarchive/issue08/philippesohet.htm.

Sopova, Jasmina, "Enki Bilal: A Journey to the End of Time," *UNESCO Courrier*, accessed 21 August 2009, http://www.unesco.org/courier/2000_04/uk/dires.htm.

Thomas, Paul L., "Adventures in Genre! Rethinking Genre through Comics/Graphic Novels," *Journal of Graphic Novels and Comics* 2.2 (2011): 187–201.

Tisseron, Serge, *Psychanalyse de la Bande Dessinée* (Paris: Flammarion, 2000).

Trushell, John M., "American Dreams of Mutants: The X-Men—'Pulp' Fiction, Science Fiction, and Superheroes," *Journal of Popular Culture* 38.1 (2004): 149–68.

Van Eersel, Patrice, "Moebius. Une Matinée avec une Aventurier de l'Esprit," *CLES*, accessed 20 June 2014, http://www.cles.com/debats-entretiens/article/une-matinee-avec-un-aventurier-de-l-esprit.

Varga, Aron Kibédi, "Criteria for Describing Word and Image Relations," *Poetics Today* 10 (1989): 31–53.

Varnum, Robin, *The Language of Comics: Word and Image* (Mississippi: University Press of Mississippi, 2002).

Vico, Giambattista, *The New Science: Principles of the New Science Concerning the Common Nature of Peoples, Book III: Discovery of the True Homer* (London: Penguin, 1999).

Wagner, Peter, ed., *Icons—Texts—Iconotexts: Essays on Ekphrasis and Intermediality* (Berlin: Walter de Gruyter, 1996).

Waugh, Patricia, *Metafiction: The Theory and Practice of Self-Conscious Fiction* (London: Routledge, 1984).

Whitlock, Gillian, "Autographics: The seeing 'I' of comics," *Modern Fiction Studies* 52.4 (2006): 965–79.

"William Blake—The Ghost of a Flea," *Tate*, accessed 20 June 2014, http://www.tate.org.uk/art/artworks/blake-the-ghost-of-a-flea-n05889.

Wilson, Saige, "Baroque Mutants in the 21st Century? Rethinking Genre through Superheroes," *Contemporary Comic Book Superheroes*, ed. Angela Ndalianis (London: Routledge, 2009), 86–104.

Wolf, Werner, "Metafiction and Metamusic: Exploring the Limits of Self-Reference," *Self-Reference in the Media*, ed. Winfried Nöth and Nina Bishara (Berlin: Walter de Gruyter, 2007), 303–324.

Yslaire, accessed 23 August 2009, http://www.yslaire.be/fr/pages/introduction-au-xxe-ciel.cfm.

INDEX

Adèle et la Bête (Tardi), 76–80, 157, 188
Alice in Wonderland (Carroll), 64, 97–98
ambiguity, 6–8, 17, 52, 55, 64, 92, 138, 150, 156, 159–60
Arkham Asylum (Morrison and McKean), 12, 54–55, 60–68, 73, 152, 154, 158–63
artists' books, 146–49
Arzach (Moebius), 15, 20, 22, 93–96, 98–101, 108, 150, 153, 175
Atkinson, Paul, 13, 169, 197
Auster, Paul, 124–25, 130, 197
autobiography, 11, 23, 25, 36, 43–44, 46, 52–53, 150, 165
autofiction, 11, 46, 53, 94–95, 101, 122, 161, 164–65

Bacchus (Campbell), 81
Baetens, Jan, 10, 16, 94, 158, 174, 176–77, 180, 197
Bakhtin, Mikhail, 40, 180–81
Balzer, Jens, 5, 37
Barthes, Roland, 38
Batman: The Dark Knight Returns (Miller), 61
Baudelaire, Charles, 33, 73, 101–3, 106–7, 158
Baudoin, Edmond, 13, 21, 45, 69–72, 155, 164, 187, 205
Berger, Karen, 60, 186
Berio, Luciano, 4
Bidouille et Violette (Yslaire), 109
Bilal, Enki, 11, 22, 94, 101–3, 107–8, 118, 122, 139
Binky Brown meets the Holy Virgin Mary (Green), 53

Blake, William, 23, 83–85, 148
Blood Song: A Silent Ballad (Drooker), 141
Blueberry (Moebius and Charlier), 95, 97
Boilet, Frédéric, 21, 46–52, 158, 182
Borges, Jorge Luis, 34, 179
Breccia, Alberto, 28, 33–34, 57, 179

Calder, Alexander, 5
Cambier, Alain, 155, 163, 204–5
Campbell, Eddie, 16, 21, 81–82, 92, 164, 190–91
Caniff, Milton, 56–57, 170, 183
Casey, Michael, 121
Castleman, Riva, 147
Castle, The (Kafka), 22, 123, 137, 202. See also *Das Schloss* (Kafka)
Céline, Louis-Ferdinand, 29, 33
C'était la Guerre des Tranchées (Tardi), 21, 23–24, 28–33, 52, 76, 156, 158, 161–62, 164
"Changing the Face of Comics" (Berger), 60
Charlier, Jean-Michel, 95
Chevallier, Gabriel, 29
chiaroscuro, 34–35, 45, 57, 60, 75, 86, 92, 141, 188
Christin, Pierre, 117
"Church Going" (Larkin), 60
Chute, Hillary, 21
Cités Obscures (Schuiten and Peeters), 15
City of Glass: The Graphic Novel (Auster, Karasik, and Mazzucchelli), 22, 123–30, 136, 149, 156, 160, 162, 164–65, 197
Civilisation (Baudoin), 69
closed text, 3–4, 6, 10, 77, 92, 101, 117, 136, 138
Cohn, Neil, 9, 18

Coleridge, S. T., 58–59, 158
Colombo, Gianni, 150
comics theory, 7, 19, 37, 172
Contract with God, A (Eisner), 21, 24–25, 27, 52, 136, 150, 153, 157, 175
Contract with God Trilogy, The (Eisner), 23–28, 157
Corto Maltese (Pratt), 35
Courrier Sud (Saint-Exupéry), 36
Coyle, William, 93
Crowley, Aleister, 64, 84
Crumb, Robert, 22, 136–38, 153, 200

Das Schloss (Kafka), 142. See also *Castle, The* (Kafka)
Deleuze, Gilles, 15, 21, 33, 37–42, 153, 180–81
Deprez, Olivier, 5, 14, 16, 22, 138, 142–47, 202
Die Verwandlung (Kafka), 138
Différence et Répétition (Deleuze), 38–39, 42
disjointedness, 16, 117, 151–56, 162, 166
Divina Commedia (Dante), 7, 69
Doubrovsky, Serge, 11
Drifting Life, A (Tatsumi), 23
Dr. Jekyll & Mr. Hyde (Mattotti and Kramsky), 22, 123, 130–36, 149, 152, 155, 200
Dr. Jekyll & Mr. Hyde (Stevenson), 131
Drooker, Eric, 141
Dropsie Avenue (Eisner), 21, 25
Drucker, Johanna, 147–48, 204
Duchamp, Marcel, 148, 179

Eco, Umberto, 3–7, 13, 28, 38, 55, 59, 146, 167, 170
Eidrigevičius, Stasys, 64
Eisner, Will, 21, 24–28, 52, 60, 75, 124, 153, 158, 177
Erlich, Laurence, 110–11, 114–15
Ernst, Max, 8

Fantastic Four, The (Morrison), 60

fantasy, 20, 22, 31, 43, 54, 76, 88, 92–122
Fate of the Artist, The (Campbell), 81
figuration, 13–16, 30, 55, 64, 76, 81, 123, 136, 141, 150, 165
Finnegans Wake (Joyce), 4–5, 7
Flood! A Novel in Pictures (Drooker), 141
Foucault, Michel, 38, 49, 58, 154, 172, 205
Fresnault-Deruelle, Pierre, 8–10, 78, 100, 108, 151–52, 154, 156, 162–63
Froid Équateur (Bilal), 101, 103, 106–7, 157
From Hell (Moore and Campbell), 16, 22, 75–76, 81–85, 153, 156, 158, 161, 163–65

Gabilliet, Jean-Paul, 93, 192
Gaiman, Neil, 13, 21, 65–68, 186–87
Gaudreault, André, 14, 172
Genette, Gérard, 16, 173
Ghost of a Flea, The (Blake), 84, 190
Gibbons, Dave, 81
Gillain, Joseph. See Jijé
Giraud, Jean, 95–96, 100. See also Moebius
Good Omens (Gaiman and Pratchett), 65
graphic novels, 21, 25, 82, 139, 155, 158
Graphic Witnesses: Four Wordless Graphic Novels (Masereel, Ward, and Walker), 139–40, 201
Graphic Women: Life Narratives and Contemporary Comics (Chute), 21
Green, Justin, 53
Green Box, The (Duchamp), 148
Groensteen, Thierry, 7, 17–18, 42, 127, 141–42, 198

Heidegger, Martin, 41, 155
Heikkinen, Jyrki, 22, 89–90
Hietanen, Annemari, 22, 86–87, 191
Hogarth, William, 85, 95, 139
Hueve, Roland, 43, 181
Hutcheon, Linda, 12, 82, 160, 189, 205
Hyde, Laurence, 139–41, 201

hypertext, 8, 15, 111, 117

identity, 125, 160–62
intermediality (intermedial references), 10, 24, 55, 76, 89, 101, 118, 122, 141, 165
intertexuality (intertexual references), 9, 16, 24, 42, 59, 122
Introducing Kafka (Mairowitz and Crumb), 22, 123, 136–38, 150, 153, 200
Introduction au XXe ciel (Yslaire), 109–12, 114–18, 153, 155, 165
Invisibles, The (Morrison), 60
Iser, Wolfgang, 9–10, 169

Jijé, 57, 95, 98
Jodorowsky, Alexandro, 95
Joyce, James, 4, 7, 128
Jung, C. G., 64, 113, 115–16
Justice League of America, The (Morrison), 60, 186

Kafka, Franz, 6, 22, 123, 136–38, 142–46, 149, 200, 202
Karasik, Paul, 22, 123–24, 126, 197
Kinderbook (Takahama), 50
Kirby, Jack, 66, 68, 173, 175
Klee, Paul, 145, 154, 172
Kleist, Reinhard, 43–45, 162, 181
Kramsky, Jerry, 22, 130–33, 161, 200
Kristeva, Julia, 16
Kukkonen, Karin, 9, 170, 172, 181
Kunzle, David, 163, 174
Kuolema Kulkee Kintereillä (Turunen and Hietanen), 22, 75–76, 86–90, 92, 159–60, 164, 191
Kuper, Peter, 141

La Ballade de la Mer Salée (Pratt), 21, 34, 54–60, 73, 150, 158–61, 179, 184. See also *Una Ballata Del Mare Salato* (Pratt)

"La Ballade d'Enoshima" (Boilet and Takahama), 47–50
Lacan, Jacques, 38
"La Déviation" (Moebius), 22, 96, 98–100, 162, 175
Lady Polaris (Mézières and Christin), 117, 196
La Femme Piège (Bilal), 101, 107, 160
La Foire aux Immortels (Bilal), 22, 101, 103–5, 107–8, 157, 165
L'Album Mythique (Moebius), 22, 94–101, 175
La Passion d'un Homme (Masereel), 140
La Peur (Chevallier), 29
Larkin, Philip, 60–61
La Trilogie Nikopol (Bilal), 11, 22, 33, 93–94, 101–8, 118, 155, 157–59, 161, 163
layouts, 18, 45, 100, 150, 152–54, 165, 170, 175
L'Eau Amère (Takahama), 50
Le Château (Kafka and Deprez), 5, 14, 16, 22, 138, 142–46, 148–49, 155–56, 159–63
Lefèvre, Pascal, 93–94, 151, 163
Le Labyrinthe Infernal (Tardi), 76, 79–80
Le Monde diplomatique, 37, 154
Le Petit Prince (Saint-Exupéry), 36, 72
L'Épinard de Yukiko (Boilet), 47, 49
Le Rayon Vert (Boilet), 46, 51
"Le Revenant" (Baudelaire), 104–5
Les Aventures Extraordinaires d'Adèle Blanc-Sec (Tardi), 21, 29, 75–81, 91–92, 97, 150
"Les Douze Chimères du Zodiaque" (Boilet), 47
Les Fleurs du Mal (Baudelaire), 103, 105, 107, 158
"Les Petites Vestes de Boilet" (Boilet), 47, 51–52
Le Voyage (Baudoin), 21, 53–55, 69–74, 92, 152, 156, 160, 163
Le Voyage d'Urien (Gide), 147
LeWitt, Sol, 148
Life Force, A (Eisner), 21, 25–27, 177
L'Incal (Jodorowsky and Moebius), 95

Lovecraft, Howard Philips, 21, 33, 42–45, 160, 162, 181–82, 185
Lovecraft (Kleist), 24, 43–46, 52, 148, 152–54, 156, 162, 164–65

Mairowitz, David, 22, 136–37, 200
Mäkilä, Jarmo, 22, 94, 119–22, 139, 196–97
Mallarmé, Stéphane, 5, 123, 146–47
manga, 19, 21, 23, 46–48, 51, 68, 176, 182
Mariko Parade (Boilet), 15, 17, 20–21, 24, 45–52, 58, 156, 160, 164–65
Marion, Philippe, 14, 17, 172–73
Maserel, Frans, 22, 25, 53, 113, 139–41, 177, 201
Masse, Francis, 28, 177
Masson, Pierre, 42
Mattotti, Lorenzo, 22, 130–35, 139, 155, 161, 199–200
Maus (Spiegelman), 53, 175
Mazzucchelli, David, 22, 123–24, 197
McCloud, Scott, 8, 10, 12, 14, 19, 126, 128, 152, 174–76
McHale, Brian, 12, 59, 172, 184
McKean, Dave, 14, 21, 44, 60, 63–64, 66, 68, 164, 184–85
mediatization, 109, 118, 157, 163
Mémoires du XXe Ciel 98 (Yslaire), 109–11, 157
metafiction, 11–12, 14, 24, 42–45, 51, 72–73, 76, 158, 160, 164–65
Métal Hurlant, 28, 95–96, 153, 177
Mézières, Jean-Claude, 117, 196
Mikkonen, Kai, 19, 103, 106, 161, 175
Miller, Ann, 14, 167
Miller, Frank, 61, 124
Miller, Joseph Hillis, 9, 13, 146, 156, 203
minimalism, 39, 41, 71, 73, 95, 124, 126, 130
Mobiles (Calder), 5
Moebius, 22, 28, 30, 76, 78–79, 95–101, 118, 122, 139, 154, 161. See also Giraud, Jean

Mon Livre d'Heures (Masereel), 22, 53, 139–40, 201
Moore, Alan, 13, 16, 21, 81–85, 189–90, 206
Morgan (Pratt), 34
Morrison, Grant, 12, 21, 60–66, 81, 184–85
Murray, Christopher, 20, 161
"Music of Erich Zann, The" (Lovecraft), 43–45, 182

narrative structure, 77, 118, 135, 170, 191
Neue Abenteuer des Unglaublichen Orpheus [Die Rückkehr von Deleuze] (Balzer and tom Dieck), 37
New X-Men, The (Morrison), 60
Nietzsche, Friedrich, 38, 41
Nikolajeva, Maria, 142, 201
Nückel, Otto, 25, 139, 177, 201

open text, 3, 6, 9, 77
"Outsider, The" (Lovecraft), 43, 181

Patri, Giacomo, 139–41, 201
Peanuts (Schulz), 38, 90
Peeters, Benoît, 13, 15, 18, 26, 35, 97, 175
Perloff, Marjorie, 10, 171
Perramus (Breccia and Sasturain), 34
Persepolis (Satrapi), 53
Pilote, 28, 101, 177
Pratt, Hugo, 21, 33–36, 55–57, 60, 75, 160, 165, 184
Putain de Guerre (Tardi), 29

Rebillot, Joseph (General), 30–31, 33, 158
Reynolds, Richard, 11
"Rime of the Ancient Mariner, The" (Coleridge), 59, 158, 184
Rivett, Miriam, 15
Robbe-Grillet, Alain, 52
Role of the Reader, The (Eco), 6, 169
Roth, Dieter, 148

Round, Julia, 9, 169, 176

Saint-Exupéry, Antoine de, 21, 33–36, 52, 72, 152, 160
Saint-Exupéry: Le Dernier Vol (Pratt), 24, 33–37, 44, 52, 152, 156, 164
Salut, Deleuze! (Balzer and tom Dieck), 5, 24, 36–42, 52–53, 148, 153, 155–56, 167
Samson, Jacques, 28–29, 57, 157, 178, 204
Sandman (Gaiman), 12, 21, 25, 54–55, 65–69, 73, 158, 160–61, 163
Sarje, Kimmo, 121, 196–97
Sasturain, Juan, 34
Satrapi, Marjane, 21, 53
Schraenen, Guy, 146
Schreibheft, 37
Schuiten, François, 15
Scott, Carole, 142, 201
Screech, Matthew, 31, 76, 189
self-reflexivity, 7, 11, 13, 51–52, 95, 101, 118, 156–58, 160–61, 164–65
semiotics, 9, 15, 28, 152, 155, 171, 178
Sertillanges, Abbé, 31, 158
Seth, 139, 141, 201
Southern Cross, A Novel of the South Seas (Hyde), 140–41
Spiegelman, Art, 53, 124, 175
Spirit, The (Eisner), 24
Sprague de Camp, Lyon, 43
Starowieyski, Franciszek, 64
"Statement of Randolph Carter, The" (Lovecraft), 43
Stevenson, Robert Louis, 56, 131–35
Stockhausen, Karlheinz, 4
Strutturazione Fluida (Colombo), 150
subversion, 7, 75, 79, 89, 108, 150, 160–61, 166
suggestiveness, 7, 16–20, 52, 62, 94, 118, 130, 150, 165
Superman (Morrison), 60, 77
surrealism, 64, 72, 93–95, 115, 121

Švankmajer, Jan, 64
System, The (Kuper), 141

Takahama, Kan, 21, 46–48, 50–51
Tardi, Jacques, 21, 28–30, 34, 76–80, 175, 177–78, 188
Tatsumi, Yoshihiro, 23
Taxi van Goghin Korvaan (Mäkilä), 22, 93–94, 101, 119–22, 156, 162–63
Terry and the Pirates (Caniff), 56
Thomas, Paul L., 20, 94
Thus Spake Zarathustra (Nietzsche), 41
Tisseron, Serge, 33, 206
Todorov, Tzvetan, 10
Tohtori Futuro (Heikkinen), 22, 75, 89–92, 156
tom Dieck, Martin, 5, 37
Transmetropolitan (Morrison), 60
Treasure Island (Stevenson), 56, 131
Trial, The (Kafka), 6
Trou d'Obus (Tardi), 29
Turunen, Marko, 22, 86, 191

Una Ballata Del Mare Salato (Pratt), 21, 56. See also *La Ballade de la Mer Salée* (Pratt)
Un Coup de Dés Jamais N'Abolira le Hazard (Mallarmé), 123, 146
Une Semaine de Bonté (Ernst), 8

Varga, A. Kibédi, 14, 152, 154
Verne, Jules, 94
Verney, Jean-Pierre, 29
Vertigo, 60, 65, 177
visual arts, 95, 119, 122, 174
visual poetry, 14
visual style (technique), 55, 76, 89, 118, 123, 149, 156, 165–66
Voyage au Bout de la Nuit (Céline), 29

Walton, Saige, 20
Ward, Lynd, 139–41, 201

Watchmen (Moore and Gibbons), 11, 81, 92, 102, 172
Wells, H. G., 94
White Collar (Patri), 140
Wild Pilgrimage (Ward), 140–41
Wolf, Werner, 14
woodcut novels, 22, 53, 86, 123, 138–47, 149, 155, 201
word-image narration, 7–8, 14, 18–19, 22, 76, 118, 136, 152–53, 165
wordless novels, 138–42, 191, 201

XXe Ciel (Yslaire), 8, 11, 15, 22, 93–94, 101, 109–18, 155, 157–60, 162–64

Yslaire, 109–11, 113–18, 122, 139, 157, 165

www.ingramcontent.com/pod-product-compliance
Lightning Source LLC
Chambersburg PA
CBHW030620230426
43661CB00053B/2086